IN THE WAKE OF JUNG

IN THE WAKE OF JUNG

A Selection from *Harvest*

EDITED BY
Molly Tuby

COVENTURE LTD
London

IKON

T

First published as a collection in 1983.
Reprinted 1986.

The editor gratefully makes acknowledgement for the use of copyright material, as specified in the notes to each chapter, and in particular to Routledge & Kegan Paul Ltd. and Princeton University Press for permission to quote from the Collected Works of C.G. Jung, and to the Guild of Pastoral Psychology.

Cover illustration: *Alignment Four: Flight Path, Littlington, Sussex* by Clifford Bayly ARWS, reproduced by permission of the artist.
Cover typography: Jutta Laing.

ISBN 0 904575 23 3

Printed and bound in Great Britain by Whitstable Litho Ltd., Whitstable, Kent.

Contents

PREFACE *Molly Tuby*

INTRODUCTION *Gerhard Adler*

1. A session with Jung *Vera von der Heydt*
2. Jung and Society *Marie-Louise von Franz*
3. Transformations of the persona *Fay Pye*
4. Healing the child within *Culver Barker*
5. Woman as mediator *Irene Claremont de Castillejo*
6. The Medusa archetype today *Andrea Dykes*
7. Opposites and the healing power of symbols *Molly Tuby*
8. The Beyond (Death and renewal in East and West) *Barbara Hannah*
9. Reflections on Jung's concept of synchronicity *Rosemary Gordon*
10. Physics and psyche *Claude Curling*
11. Gnosis and the single vision *Ean Begg*
12. Jung and Marx: alchemy, Christianity and the work against nature *David Holt*
13. The inner journey of the poet *Kathleen Raine*

Preface

This book is a selection from articles first appearing in *Harvest**
Whether these articles originated in talks addressed to the club, or
in papers written specifically for *Harvest,* they all represent vital
aspects of Jung's approach. Moreover, some of the authors were
among the very first Jungians in England and the founders of the
London Analytical Psychology Club.

It its early days, this club gathered together those people who
wanted to share the unusual experience of analysis. Thirty years
later, the picture has changed considerably, but for many the
teaching of Jung's work remains the fountainhead of inspiration,
not only for clinical work with patients, but, most important, for
the inner journey of countless men and women struggling to find
their individual way in these times of turmoil and social
disintegration.

It seemed important to include two authors who are not directly
involved in Jungian psychology, but who feel that they have been
touched in some deep way by the *Collected Works,* and by their
contact with Jungian ideas. One is an eminent physicist and the
other a much loved scholar and poet.

It is hoped that this modest collection of writings will find a
special niche amid the proliferation of analytical psychology
publications.

*The journal published since 1954 by the Analytical Psychology Club,
London.

Introduction

by Gerhard Adler

*GERHARD ADLER, PhD., is past honorary president of the Association
of Jungian Analysts and past president of the International Association for
Analytical Psychology, and of the Analytical Psychology Club, London. He
is co-editor of C.G. Jung's* Collected Works *and* Letters *and author of*
Dynamics of the Self, The Living Symbol *and other books and articles.
He practises in London.*

It has often been remarked that Jung himself was the best
advertisement of his ideas, that he represented the most convincing
example of an integrated and individuated personality. It is indeed
not easy to grasp the full message of Jung without having met him
in the flesh. His maturity and serenity, his earthiness and sense of
humour, the almost unbelievable range of his knowledge, came so
vividly across and formed such a colourful illustration of what he
was teaching and aiming at, that a dimension of his theories seems
to be missing without the embodiment of their practical fulfilment
in his person. But, of course, it has to be accepted that to more and
more people Jung's ideas are familiar only from his books, or, may
be, from analysis with one of his direct or indirect pupils.

Perhaps it will help if I introduce my theoretical exposition with
the narration of a personal experience right towards the end of
Jung's life. It was the last time I saw Jung, a few months before his
death. It was a Sunday morning and I had gone out to his Tower at
Bollingen. His housekeeper told me to go upstairs to the study. I
knocked at the door and went in. There the old man sat in his
highly informal country clothes at his writing desk, with a writing-
pad in front of him and a fountain-pen in his hand. He had not
heard me come in, and I stood, deeply moved, and almost
embarrassed about my intrusion, for there, looking out over the
lake of Zürich but clearly looking out very much further and
deeper, he sat, completely unaware of my presence, intensely still
and absolutely concentrated, utterly alone with himself and

engrossed in his inner images — the picture of a
sage completely absorbed in a world of his own, which yet is the
infinite universe. This lasted only a few moments; then he noticed
me; one could feel how he returned from far away, and the spell
was broken. No doubt I had interrupted him, but he showed no
trace of it, no sign of disturbance: there he was, at once deeply
related to the other person and open to his presence.

I shall never forget the image of the sage contained in his inner
universe, or the immediate return to the reality of the actual
human situation. Both were the same man, and the interplay
reveals a great deal about the nature of his genius.

It was indeed a long way which he had travelled to achieve such
exceptional level of integration and it is this way which I shall now
trace in its barest outlines and main stations. It started very early on
in Jung's career with his doctoral dissertation *On the Psychology and
Pathology of So-Called Occult Phenomena*. There already he had
pointed out the *prospective nature of the unconscious* and what he
called then "a highly developed intellectual activity of the
unconscious."[1] His *Studies in Word Association* (1904-1907)[2] are
generally well-known and thus I want to remind you here only of
his discovery in that period of the *feeling-toned complexes*.

Since the word "complex" has entered common language in an
often inaccurate way it may be useful to give Jung's own definition.
He describes complexes as "psychic entities which are outside the
control of the conscious mind. They have been split off from
consciousness and lead a separate existence in the dark realm of
the unconscious being at all times ready to hinder or reinforce the
conscious functioning."[3]

Jung's discovery and experimental proof of complexes was an
important step in putting the idea of the unconscious on firm
ground. Freud was the first to recognize and acknowledge the
importance of Jung's discovery and it made him eager to make
Jung's acquaintance and win his co-operation. Jung sent Freud a
copy of his *Studies in Word Association*, but Freud, who had heard of
Jung's researches, was so impatient to know the results that he
bought his own copy before Jung's had arrived.

Then there came the revolutionary publication in 1907 of *The
Psychology of Dementia Praecox*[4] — as schizophrenia was called then
— which showed the hidden or lost meaning behind the facade of
apparently senseless behaviour and words. In consequence of this
research Jung became the first psychiatrist to undertake the
psychological treatment of schizophrenia, up to then thought

unamenable to psychotherapy.

Jung's work on complexes and schizophrenia led to his collaboration with Freud. But it is worth remembering that Jung had already established himself with his writings, dealing with aspects of the unconscious before he met Freud and having made important contributions to the psychiatry of his time. In spite of various reservations, clearly expressed right from the beginning and right through the period of friendship, it was only with the publication of *Symbols of Transformation,* in 1912/13,[5] that the final break came. The correspondence between the two men, now available in print, gives a vivid picture of the vicissitudes of their relationship. Freud could not accept Jung's wider definition of the *nature of the libido* as not purely sexual and equally he could not accept Jung's idea of the *symbolic incest*. The break was felt most seriously by both men. In spite of much bitterness engendered by it, Freud, towards the end of his life, could admit that Jung's departure had been a serious loss to himself and to the psychoanalytical movement; Jung, for his part, continued to honour and respect Freud's courageous pioneering in psychodynamics.

Yet the break with Freud led to an almost total isolation, forcing Jung to a completely new assessment and approach. We have only to read the chapter on "Confrontation with the Unconscious" in Jung's *Memories* to realize what a difficult and critical — but equally creative — time it was for him. A period of intense introspection laid the ground-work for most of Jung's later work. What had been called his heresy proved to be the foundation of a new creative approach, based on hitherto unknown empirical data. The break-through came with the *Psychological Types*[6] of 1921 in which Jung defined the two attitude-types of *introversion* and *extraversion,* with the sub-division of *four functional types*. This typology has often been misunderstood as trying to give a schematic cut-and-dried system of the psyche. In fact, however, the types are not static positions but point to the dynamic interplay of opposites by which any particular type of person is impelled by the need to complement this one-sidedness by the gradual assimilation of the missing adaptation.

Here then we find already the concept which would become more and more central to Jung's approach; that of the *opposites in the psyche and their union*. This union is achieved in a process of integration which Jung termed the process of *individuation*. It can be defined as a constantly progressing assimilation of unconscious contents or as a constantly growing synthesis between the conscious mind and the unconscious. This presupposes a potentially *constructive function of the unconscious* by which it exerts a *compensatory effect* on the ego. In this way the unconscious functions are the constant regulators of the unconscious mind so that the psyche, consisting of conscious and unconscious, appears as a *self-regulating system*. Here the concept of homeostasis springs to mind. It has, however, to be understood that, in contradistinction to bodily homeostatic mechanisms, the psychic self-regulating system is progressive.[7] It is exactly these progressive acts of self-regulation which, in the ideal case, lead to the integrated and individuated personality whose centre in contradistinction to the *ego* as the centre of the conscious mind, Jung has termed the *self*.

The concept of the psyche as a self-regulating system is based on Jung's theory of *psychic energy*.[8] Jung holds that the psyche cannot be understood from a purely causal point of view, but that this approach has to be complemented by a teleologic sense, according to which "causes are understood as means to an end",[9] in other words a point of view which interprets psychic facts as symbolic expressions of psychic developments.

In talking about the psyche as a self-regulating system we have to mention Jung's use and definition of the term *symbol*. Here again, to this crucial psychological concept, Jung has made a distinctive and powerful contribution. To Freud symbols are the last irreducible translation of a dream-element into an image, e.g., stick or pistol for the male organ, or any form of container for the female organ. Jung regards this use of the term symbol as too static and points out that in Freud's instances we would do better to speak of signs. To Jung symbols express a reality so novel and complex as to transcend intellectual formulation: "When something is 'symbolic,' it means that a person divines its hidden, ungraspable nature and is trying desperately to capture in words the secret that eludes him."[10] Symbols thus represent psychic contents that cannot be expressed in any other form, and for this reason a true symbol is bound to contain a non-rational element that eludes conscious definition. This is exactly its function and explains the dynamic effect of any living symbol: by and in it unconscious contents are condensed and are forced into consciousness so that it acts as a *transformer of energy* and has a constructive integrative function. Here religious symbols spring to mind, as for instance those used in the Mass and particularly that of the Cross.

The main form in which we experience symbols is as dream images. Thus, the *dream* itself fulfils a creative function in the process of integration. Far from regarding dreams as an illusory wish fulfilment or as "a pathological product",[11] Jung considers them as the entirely normal "spontaneous self-portrayal, in symbolic form, of the actual situation in the unconscious."[12] They have a *compensatory function* by revealing trends or states of which the conscious mind is unaware "either because of repression or through mere lack of realization."[13]

To give only one example: a highly intelligent man, an academic teacher in his mid-fifties, with a rather overdeveloped intellect and corresponding feeling-problem, sees in his dream a woman of exquisite beauty. While he is still admiringly looking at her she changes suddenly into a tall slender white lit candle of quite inexpressible beauty — if possible even more beautiful than the angelic woman. This graceful serenely-burning candle is perched on a tall stool, a kind of alter inspiring reverence and awe. The woman here is an unequivocal symbol of what Jung has called *anima*, the *femme inspiratrice*, the eternal feminine. But even she, in spite of her wonderful appearance, has to be divested of all possible personal implications and transformed into a symbol of spiritual illumination beyond rational human definition. This dream shows what Jung means by a symbol, just as it shows how *archetypes*, to which I shall turn presently, manifest themselves in the here and now of space and time.

The discussion of the process of individuation and of the symbol leads on to Jung's perhaps most important discovery, that of the *collective unconscious* and the *archetypal images* through which it manifests itself. This theory has undergone considerable development and modification in the course of time, as is only natural with a man whose creative working life extended over more than six decades. But its roots lie in Jung's earliest period.

As early as 1906, Jung made a decisive observation, which, however, at the time was too isolated and novel to be sufficiently understood and evaluated by him. One day a schizophrenic patient of his made him look out of a window and "showed" him the "*sun's phallus*" explaining that "if he moved his head from side to side the sun-phallus would move too, and that was the origin of the wind."[14] It was only some years later, in 1910, that Jung came across a book dealing with certain ancient mythological material in which he found to his astonishment a vision described in terms closely akin to the hallucination of the patient; it spoke of "a tube hanging down from the disc of the sun", which was "the origin of the ministering wind."[14] Starting from this surprising parallelism Jung soon discovered that it was by no means fortuitous but that numerous mythological images turned up in dreams and fantasies of his patients who could not possibly have acquired knowledge of their existence.

These archaic *archetypal images* in their entirety form the impersonal substratum of the human psyche which Jung has termed the *collective unconscious.* This latter concept indicates that there are psychic contents in the unconscious of the individual which are not acquired during his personal life but are inherent in the specifically human psychic structure and organisation. Like anything else that enters consciousness they appear as ideas or images. Just as the *instincts* are typical *modes of action* so *archetypes* are typical *forms* of *behaviour.* Just as it is obvious that man has specific instinctive patterns, so he has also specific human patterns of behaviour. As such the archetypes act as unconscious *"regulators"* or *"dominants."* Jung has expressed this in the analogy of "the axial system of a crystal which, as it were, preforms the crystalline structure in the mother liquid, although it has no material existence of its own ... The axial system determines only the stereometric structure but not the concrete form of the individual crystal", and similarly "the archetype in itself is empty and purely formal ...,"[15] a possibility of representation which is given *a priori.* It is thus not a fixed image as such that is innate in the psyche but the potentiality for certain types of images or actions.

It is noteworthy that in his last, unfinished work, *An Outline of Psychoanalysis,* written over twenty years after Jung had first formulated the concept of the collective unconscious, Freud came virtually to express the same idea. He wrote then "Dreams bring to light material which cannot have originated either from the dreamer's adult life or from his forgotten childhood. We are obliged to regard it as part of the archaic heritage which a child brings with him into the world, before any experience of his own, influenced by the experience of his ancestors. We find the counterpart of this phylogenetic material in the earliest human legends and in surviving customs."[16]

To return to the concept of the archetypes, it has to be understood that the archetype as such is a hypothesis, and that its existence can only be deduced from the archetypal images which appear in consciousness. Thus a clear distinction has to be made between the irrepresentable archetype and the archetypal image. I should like to give two examples of such archetypal images — one in human form, the other in a relatively abstract form.

"Mother", as the earliest and most influential figure, is the most decisive encounter in everybody's life, and accordingly produces a large amount of conscious and unconscious reactions and reaction formations. There is, however, more to it than just the reaction to the personal mother: in our psyche there is preformed, as it were, our expectation of the innumerable powerful aspects of the "maternal", which can very summarily be defined as "nature" and "matter", manifesting themselves as the life-giving and nourishing force on the one hand, but as the destructive and devouring force on the other. These various aspects are activated in our experience with the actual mother. They are brought to the surface in innumerable images which are all aspects of the underlying *mother-archetype*.

The child/mother-(and the child/parent)-relationship represents, therefore, always more than just the actual experience: in it and through it there are constellated instinctual patterns transcending the merely personal relationship and adding dimensions of intensity and meaning that are not given in the actual situation. The same can be said of all interpersonal encounters, among which the most powerful, apart from the parental experience and in part based on it, are the contrasexual experiences: man of woman and woman of man, and both constellate archetypal reactions transcending the merely personal experience. Jung has termed these two archetypes *animus* and *anima,* for which latter I have given an example in the previously mentioned dream.

Another, more abstract, archetypal image is linked up directly with the process of individuation. Jung found that this innate idea of individuation or psychic *wholeness* or totality found its symbolical expression in countless variations of the basic image of the circle (or square). In studying this phenomenon he discovered that circle and square are archetypal images of wholeness appearing in virtually every phase and culture of mankind.

Jung has dealt extensively with the symbol of the circle in his writings on the *mandala*.[17] Here I want to illustrate the appearance and function of this symbol by two short dreams. A woman patient of thirty-six dreamt the following dream before the start of her analysis: "I am in a semi-circular enclosed room and want to get into the corresponding room next door. I realize that I have to go right downstairs a long way and then up another way in order to get in." Here we have the symbolical expression for wholeness — the circular room to be completed — which can only be achieved after a descent into the unconscious. About three years later and towards the end of her analysis the same patient had another dream. She found herself in a round tower with four rooms arranged inside it like a Celtic cross. It is her own house, and she is immensely pleased with it. Here the combination of circle and square is a symbolic indication of the state of relative wholeness and centredness which she had achieved in her analytical work.

This *process of individuation* has in time become the focus and point of synthesis of all Jung's work. In view of a frequent misunderstanding of the concept of "individuation" as "individualism" I want to underline the fact that the two are not only not the same but diametrically opposed. Thus the process of individuation has been misrepresented as "an esoteric process which engages only the few."[18] As a matter of fact the process of individuation is an intrinsically normal process of growth and development leading to a mature and fully adjusted personality, attuned to both external and inner reality. Far from being esoteric or turning "the development of one's own personality into a kind of religion"[19] it leads to a fully responsible personality, willing and capable to play his role in the human community. Equally important, society consists of individuals and only when there are sufficient individuals in their own right, that is integrated and mature individuals, can society grow and blossom.

Jung's preoccupation with the process of individuation was also the reason behind his *alchemical studies*[20] to which he devoted so much of his later years. Here he found the historical link between early Christian Gnosticism and the modern discovery of the unconscious. In *alchemy* he saw the symbolical expression of inner experiences, aiming at psychic wholeness. He showed that a considerable part of alchemy was concerned not so much with pseudo-or-proto-chemistry but was a projection of unconscious psychic contents and images into the chemical process which thus served only as the projection screen for the adept's meditative realizations. In their experiments, the meditative side of which corresponded as a matter of fact to the process which Jung has called *active imagination*, these alchemists found their way of redemption, and the incorruptible *lapis,* the philosphers' stone, was the symbol of the archetype of the redeemer.

Alchemy, thus considered, has a profound relationship to the symbolism of dreams and to that of *religion*. Very early on in his work Jung had become convinced that the integrative function of the psyche was closely linked with religious images, and that in the symbols of religion mankind had at its disposal the creative answer to many of its problems. To mention only two of his essays, the one on the *Trinity* and the other one on the *Mass*[21] both showed the profound symbolical content of Christian concepts and rituals. It is equally borne out be his *Answer to Job*,[22] which has aroused a great deal of controversy, but to many, including myself, is his most personal and moving book. To Jung religion was of enormous significance for the health of the individual and the community alike, giving man's life meaning and direction and containing the answer to the syndrome of modern times, to *alienation*. Needless to say, it was not so much religion in any traditional or dogmatic sense that was Jung's concern as the individual's own and immediate experience of religious contents and images. To open and show the way to such experiences was the true purpose of his writings on religious subjects.

Here we have to mention also Jung's important theory of *synchronicity*.[23] By this concept he has provided a principle of explanation which complements an exclusively causal way of explanation. To quote Jung's own definition, it is "a coincidence in time of two or more causally unrelated events which have the same or a similar meaning."[24] By this new principle of explanation so far inexplicable phenomena become understandable, such mantic methods – e.g. that of the Chinese oracle of the *I Ching* — telephathy, clairvoyance, or other manifestations of ESP; equally, other strange phenomena, so far explained — or explained away — as "chance" or "accident" gain a new meaning. Another field where this concept can provide new insights is the relationship between body and soul, in that the interdependence of psychic and physical processes in the living organism can be understood not so much as a causal relationship but as a synchronistic phenomenon.

Synchronistic phenomena, and in particular those of ESP, convinced Jung of the existence of a transcendental *"absolute knowledge"*, independent of the senses[25]. It is transcendental in that "synchronicity postulates a meaning which is a priori in relation to human consciousness and *apparently exists outside man*" (my italics).[26] It is needless to stress the importance of such conclusions for religious thought.

Researches like these or into alchemy and *religious symbolism* have led to the frequent misunderstanding of Jung as a mystic, and he has often been attacked for lack of clarity and vagueness. Jung was fully aware of this problem. He expressed it once to me when I had mentioned certain points in his *Psychological Types* which did not seem clear enough. He said: "People complain that my findings are too intuitive, but they don't understand what I have to try and do. I have to catch the reflections of the primeval fire in mirrors I put around it; and of course, the mirrors are not always a perfect fit at the corners."

From his remark we can understand that, what has been regarded as inexactitude, springs from his familiarity with irrational and *numinous processes* inaccessible to most people and evading strictly rational definition. In the same way the symbol has, as we have seen, an irrational aspect precisely because it deals with experiences beyond purely logical description. Jung's attitude has to be understood as comprising both rational and irrational facts and thus initiating a completely new scientific approach.

Jung himself has made a revealing comment on this problem of "inexactitude." In a letter of 1952 he wrote: "The language I speak must be ambiguous, must have two meanings in order to be fair to the dual aspect of our psychic nature. I strive quite consciously and deliberately for ambiguity of expression because it is superior to unequivocality and reflects the nature of life. My whole temperament inclines me to be very unequivocal indeed. That is not difficult, but it would be at the cost of truth. I purposely allow all the overtones and undertones to be heard, partly because they are there anyway, and partly because they give a fuller picture of reality. Unequivocality makes sense only in establishing facts but not in interpreting them."[27]

An interesting comment on the power and effect of Jung's concepts has often been provided to me by people remarking that although they could not really follow Jung's ideas they felt deeply moved by them; or, in one extreme case, when a woman patient said: "I hardly understood a word of what I read, but I knew I had to go to Zürich." And she did. Remarks like those make it evident that Jung's words, although they are somehow equivocal, speak to the unconscious of people, to their guts, and stir much deeper layers than those of reason.

Jung was strongly attracted to the rejected areas of the psyche. His interest in the border areas of the human psyche and their numinous contents did not spring from a mystical inclination but from insatiable curiosity and intellectual honesty. It led him to explore phenomena which other people carefully avoided as unfashionable or "unscientific." He had to study these and other subjects simply because they existed and manifested vital aspects of the psyche. His discursive, intuitive style and *open system* are the direct results of an interest much wider than in the usual fields of research. He refused to develop a closed system exactly because he was open to every human phenomenon.

This attitude has, however, the most decisive consequences. One of its most important results is the significance it lends to a deeper and wider understanding of human history, as well as of religious and artistic creativity. It is in these fields that the concept of the collective unconscious and of the archetypes shows its general significance and can lead to new creative insights. All human behaviour is lastly dependent on and directed by archetypal forces, and the archetype mediates between the unconscious foundations of the human psyche and the conscious mind. It is from this angle that Jung's later researches have to be understood. In them he considered individuation not merely from the point of view of the individual but as a process of the development of human consciousness in general. But all these researches even where they concern themselves with highly complex collective symbolism lead in the end back to the part the individual has to play in the growth of human consciousness.

In particular Jung's concepts of the *shadow* and of the mechanism of *projection* — so important for the psychology of the individual — can be most fruitfully applied to man's social and political activities. We are all only too aware of the deep split running through the world as well as through our own body politic. Jung was deeply concerned about these splits — witness his *"Undiscovered Self"* (which in German carried the much more indicative title "Present and Future"). His whole work convinced him that only the realization and withdrawal of such projections, accompanied by the growing consciousness of individuals relating to the archetypal foundations of the human psyche, could lessen the tension and lead us out of the critical situation of our time.

As far as *religious* or *artistic creativeness* is concerned they have to be understood as the ego's — successful or unsuccessful — endeavours to get in touch with the eternal images and to reformulate them through the medium of consciousness. Here the idea of the archetypes as regulators or dominants has proved itself highly relevant for the general human situation. Jung's essays on such diverse subjects as Picasso or James Joyce,[29] on the symbolism of the Trinity or the Mass, or on the political situation of our time bear witness to the importance of these findings which far transcend the narrow field of medical psychology. His researches amount to the realization that the external world cannot be understood without reference to the inner world of the eternal archetypal images, indeed, that all the elements of external knowledge rest on these psychic images.

In a more general way this means that the split between "outside" and "inside" has become reconciled and that the connection between subject and object has been reconstituted. Here true religion can play a decisive role, and that explains Jung's intense interest in religion. Religion, as has been mentioned, to him was a tremendously individual concern: all collective formulations were only preliminary, and genuine *personal experience* of the eternal images was the final aim. Thus he has been attacked by both religious and materialistic thinkers; to the first he appeared as an iconoclast, to the latter as a mystic. But his real concern was with man's psychic health and balance which could only be restored by an individually responsible connection with and commitment to the realm of eternal images. Thus Jung has restored the dignity of the individual as the creative nuclear element of human civilization and created the basis for a new ethic, based on the authenticity and commitment of the individual.

Perhaps Jung's significance is best expressed in the short words formulated by the proverbially sober Swiss in the document given to him in 1955, when they made him an honorary doctor of science of the Federal Technical University of Zürich:

To the rediscoverer of the totality and polarity of the human psyche and its striving for unity–

To the diagnostician of the crisis of man in the age of science and technique–

To the interpreter of the primeval symbolism and of the individuation process of mankind...

NOTES

1. C. G. Jung CW 1, par. 148
2. In CW 2.
3. CW par. 923.
4. In CW 3.
5. Now in revised form in CW 5.
6. CW 6.
7. Michael Fordham, *The Objective Psyche* (London, 1958), p. 82.
8. cf. CW 8.
9. Ibid., par. 4
10. CW 15, par. 185.
11. Sigmund Freud, *New Introductory Lecture on Psychoanalysis*, Stand. Ed., Vol. 22.
12. CW 8, par. 505.

13. Ibid., par. 477.
14. CW 8, par. 317f.
15. CW 9.1, par 155.
16. Freud, *An Outline of Psychoanalysis* Stand. Ed., Vol. 23.
17. cf. e.g. CW 91.
18. Anthony Storr, *Jung*, (London, 1973), p. 81
19. Ibid., p. 90
20. cf. CW 12, 13, 14.
21. In CW 11.
22. Ibid.
23. In CW 8.
24. Ibid., par 849.
25. Ibid., par 948.
26. Ibid., par 942.
27. *Letters*, Vol. 2, p. 70.
28. In CW 10.
29. Both in CW 15.

A Session with Jung[1]

by Vera von der Heydt

VERA VON DER HEYDT is a former lay therapist at the Davidson Centre in Edinburgh. She is a professional member of the Society of Analytical Psychology, Honorary Fellow of the Guild of Pastoral Psychology and president of the Analytical Psychology Club, London. She is the author of Prospects for the Soul.

A long time ago, I was walking down the Zürichberg to go to a seminar by Dr. von Franz when I suddenly became aware that I was crying. I was surprised, stood still, but there was no doubt about it, I felt the tears running down my face. I felt slightly odd and did not understand at all what was happening when I got the sensation of bleeding from the upper part of my body; my hands felt sticky, I thought that I was standing in a pool of blood and I had to look at my hands to realise that I was not.

I was distressed but at the same time very determined that I would not miss the seminar. So when I passed a chemist shop, I went in, asked for and got some sort of a tranquilliser. I managed to sit through the seminar, but then I went home as I still felt decidedly strange in myself. The next morning I thought that I was all right; but as I was walking down the hill, the same thing happened, only much more intensely; there was not only blood, but this time I knew that it came from a wound just under my heart and from small wounds all along my left arm. I got frightened and instead of going on I rang my analyst. She told me to go to bed and said that she thought I should see Jung as soon as possible and that she would arrange it. On my way home I passed a small chapel where I always went to Mass. I went in and sat down in front of one of the side altars. I thought this would help me as I felt so panicky. As I sat, I suddenly saw a priest come in, walk up the main altar, and begin to say Mass. This was so unusual for that time of day that I gazed at the figure of the priest. He turned round, and I saw that it was the Lord. In a curious way this seemed right to me. When the moment of taking Communion came, I walked up to the altar rails; He gave me the Host and then offered me the Chalice; this was too much, I drew back, but He insisted and so I drank; it was very, very bitter. And after that He was no longer there, and the chapel quite empty. I went home, but could not stop myself from crying.

In the evening I got a message that Jung was expecting me, the next morning. He did not know what had happened to me; my analyst had only said that I was disturbed. I told him the whole story; he listened very carefully and then he began to ask me questions. Had I ever had such experiences before? Was I frightened of blood? How old had I been when I had my first period? Had I minded about it? What had my sexual relationship been with my husband? Had I ever expected a baby? Had I been unhappy that I had not had children? Had I had my menopause? When had I had the hysterectomy? How long had I been ill? What about haemorrhages? What had I felt before the operation, during my stay in hospital and how long had I felt unwell or unhappy or resentful? His questioning did not stop; he took me through many of them more than once, encouraging me to remember, to associate what my feelings had been and in particular my bodily pain. After about an hour I knew that I was back in my body; I was no longer afraid, indeed I felt peaceful. We sat in silence for a bit, then Jung got up and told me that he had to leave me. He stretched out his hand, took mine, smiled and said: 'I think that is all, isn't it?' There was no need to discuss or even mention my vision, and he knew that I knew this.

For me this interview was of the profoundest importance; first of all because Jung had been able to bring me down into my body and into my senses. Sensation is my superior function, but for years I had attempted to replace it by thinking. I did not want to see or hear or taste, nor be aware of my senses in any other way, but Jung, so I felt, had accepted the language of my senses and of my body; he had taken my hurt, my wounds, seriously and helped me to dwell on them and to recognise them as belonging to my life and to my totality. And my mystical experience he had given supreme value to by not discussing it. I felt healed in the deepest sense of the word; for the first time I really understood that healing is a process that is a constant transformation when one is sufficiently awake to remember all the different parts of one's being.

NOTES

1. First published in *Harvest* in 1975.

Jung and Society[1]

by Marie-Louise von Franz

MARIE-LOUISE VON FRANZ has lived in Switzerland nearly all her life and worked with Jung from the thirties until his death. She collaborated with him in his work on alchemy and herself published Aurora Consurgens *in translation, with a commentary. She is also the author of, among other things,* Number and Time, Puer Eternus, Lectures on Jung's Typology *with James Hillman, and many published and unpublished commentaries on fairy tales which arose from her memorable seminars. With Emma Jung she wrote* The Grail Legend. *She was one of the founders of the C.G. Jung Institute in Zürich, where she has taught since 1948. She is also a practising psychotherapist.*

We live in a period of time when the problem of human contact has become more acute than it ever was before. The reasons begin to be well known: it is the development of rationalism, which in its turn brought about technology and the industrialisation of our society. The small rural communities, with their close network of human contacts, are dissolving and in the big industrial cities people live side by side as strangers; everybody feels oppressed by the idea of his or her non-entity because of the grey meaningless mass of unknown people around him. Except for small groups, which are held together by some common religious conviction or common vice, there are only groups which are united through commercial, sport or political interests and which generally have no real deeper human connection.

This crucial situation, which is spreading all over the world, has led to an increasing interest in sociology and, in its wake, also in psychology, but it is mostly concerned with our social behaviour. It mainly began in the U.S.A. with behaviouristic studies and all the different group-experiments, which have since spread also to Europe and into the field of psychiatry. In a way it has led to a belated recognition of facts which had already been partly discovered by Alfred Adler. Aggression and its inhibitions, the

pecking-order-game, and the social role we play—which Jung
called the *persona*—have come into the foreground of discussion.

However, from a Jungian point of view this is only skimming the
surface of the problem. We must probe deeper into the instinctual
human unconscious in order to find what really controls our social
behaviour and our human relatedness.

Man has always lived, as far as we know, as a *zoon politikon*, a social
animal, as Aristotle called it, i.e. in small groups or clans of about
15 to 50 individuals, and we should therefore expect to find an
instinctual basis there for our social behaviour. Now we can observe
man from outside and statistically—as behaviourism does—and
describe man's average actions and reactions; through this we can
find man's "patterns of behaviour" which are in no way basically
different from those of animals. But we can and must also try to see
the inner psychic events which occur simultaneously. If we
investigate the latter, we can see that, together with instinctual
patterns of action, man experiences, inwardly and psychologically,
the upsurge of typical fantasy-images, emotions and ideas. This
latter aspect of our unconscious human structure Jung called, as you
all know, the *archetypes*. They are inherited dispositions which
cause us to react to generally human outer or inner problems in a
typical way. Probably every instinct has its corresponding
archetypal structure. The totality of these inherited structures is
what Jung called the *collective unconscious*. To give an example: the
instinct of aggression manifests itself inwardly in people's dreams,
for instance, as the figure of a war-god, Mars, Wotan, Shiva the
destroyer etc., whereas the maternal instinct appears in the mother
figures of all religions and myths, and the instinctual urge towards
renewal and change manifests itself in the myth of a divine child
which we find in all religions and mythological systems.

Such archetypal images spontaneously come up to the surface in
the unconscious of single individuals whenever a generally human
deeper problem is constellated in his life. It is as if we then have to
reach back and down to the wisdom of our instinctual inheritance
to find a solution for our problems within the chaos of outer and
inner conditions.

Whenever we abandon the search for rational and outer
solutions of our problems and turn within to see what is wrong
there—we first discover, as Jung has shown, all sorts of unadapted,
repressed, forgotten psychological trends and representations,
which are mostly not agreeable to our conscious view of ourselves.
These trends are often personified in dreams in the figures of our

"best" enemies, for they really are a kind of enemy within—or sometimes not so much an enemy but a person we utterly despise. This aspect of ourselves Jung has called, as you probably know, the *shadow*. If we do not see the shadow in ourselves, it is projected onto outer people who then exert a fascinating power over us—we have to think about them all the time; we get emotional about them, or even pursue them. This does not mean that some people, whom we hate, are not really nasty creatures but, even so, we could handle them quite reasonably or avoid them if it were not for the projection of our own shadow, which always causes all sorts of emotional exaggerations and fascinations. As the process of individuation—as Jung called the process of becoming conscious of oneself with the help of the objective materials of the unconscious —inevitably first forces us to become conscious of our shadow, it generally changes our social relationships a great deal. It mainly silences for ever all our megalomanic idealistic wishes to "improve society" and our fellowmen, it makes us more humble and at the same time less naïve towards evil attacks from outside. The pot cannot any longer call the kettle black. And also the blackness of the pot "knows" about the blackness of the kettle, which is a great advantage for the pot. Most of our so-called "bad" qualities are not quite superfluous in life—one can legitimately use one's claws when one is unjustly attacked, one can use one's shrewdness to avert another person's plot, one can use one's brutality to subdue some dangerous inclinations in oneself, etc. It is all a question of consciously knowing one's shadow and integrating it reasonably and moderately into one's life. The shadow is generally, at least in our countries, the more animal, more primitive person in ourselves, who is not evil if consciousness keeps an eye on it, and only gets really wicked and perverted if we repress it.

That this phase of individuation, the becoming conscious of one's shadow and the withdrawing of one's shadow projections from others, has a beneficial social effect needs not to be proven—it is evident. One often hears against Jungian analysis—because it is individual and from outside looks like an individualistic, even solipsistic, occupation with oneself—the reproach that it is not socially useful. But you can see already that this is not so: for instance if a teacher integrates his own power shadow and replaces it by the more mature attitude of a conscious person, innumerable children will profit from it. All neurotic unconscious people create hell in their surroundings, so that any improvement in one person helps many others as well. Countless quarrels, both useless and time and energy consuming, are due to the fact that we are far too unconscious of our shadow, and project it accordingly onto others. All the great political dissensions are due to this same fact.

But this is only the first step in the process of individuation. When an individual has more or less integrated his own shadow his unconscious assumes another aspect: it personifies itself in a contrasexual partner image: in man as a female figure which Jung calls the *anima* and in woman in a male figure, the *animus*. These unconscious parts of our personality are not always projected onto contrasexual partners. In the past they were often experienced as divinities which belonged to the ruling religious system, onto some goddess or in the Middle Ages onto the Virgin Mary, and in the case of women onto some god, for instance Dionysius, and in the Middle Ages onto Christ. Many accounts of dreams and visions could be brought to prove this. This projection of anima and animus onto religious figures was in some ways very useful; it protected the individual from overestimating and deifying the other sex and thus created some room for a simple reasonable human relationship. However it had also a great disadvantage: people could become conscious only of the general collective aspect of these inner factors, but they could not discover or live their individual aspects. The service of his lady in medieval knighthood was a first attempt to mend this—the knight chose the lady of his heart whom he then served like a goddess, yet she was a woman with individual qualities, a personification, not of *the* anima—but of *his* anima, and thus he had a chance to realise the special traits of his own inner feminine nature. This first attempt towards individualisation of the anima, however, was soon suppressed by the Church.

Today the religious symbols, which could serve as a vessel for projecting animus and anima, have lost their meaning for many people; animus and anima then return into the unconscious of men and women themselves, and complicate—as Jung has shown—their relationships. The enormous number of wrecked modern marriages is due to this fact.

The anima, when she shows her negative traits—and this she does mainly when the man is not conscious of her—manifests as irrational moods, ill-tempered outbursts, sudden poisonous coldness or sentimentality, hysterical fits, unreal sexual fantasies and, last but not least, by inducing the man to choose an inappropriate wife or partner. She can even cause states of complete possession

—a recent well-known example would be Hitler with his irrational hysterical outburts, which even showed in the effeminate rising of his voice when he spoke. In others the anima makes the man whiney and "depressive", babyishly jealous, like an inferior woman, or vain. All this has a very irritating effect on others, especially on women.

The animus, when unconscious, makes women argumentative, stubbornly opinionated, sometimes brutal or constantly acting and talking beside the point—all the things men dislike most in women. Under the influence of anima and animus all people lie.

One finds a lot of animus today in the women's liberation movement: the tyrannical boss of a man that they want to be freed from is not so much the outer man, but the animus tyrant within themselves, whom they have projected onto outer men. Such women even seem to attract tyrants in their surroundings or choose them as partners, not recognising that this is due to the secret worship of their own animus who thus gets them into a condition in which their true femininity is suppressed. The same is sometimes true in men: they become misogynous homosexuals, not seeing that the cold ruthlessness and tyrannical manners, which they criticise in all women, dwell in their own heart.

When men and women become more conscious of anima and animus, they can get on much better with the other sex and also redeem these figures within themselves. This means that a man can develop positive feminine qualities such as a more personal relatedness and sensitiveness, and also artistic and creative gifts, for the anima also mediates between his rational consciousness and the deeper unconscious layers. Like Beatrice in Dante's life, the anima then becomes the leader into the spiritual depths and heights of the psyche. In a woman the animus can give her courage, constancy, strength, spiritual inspiration and also creativity.

Whilst the integration of the shadow makes one get on much better with people of the same sex, the integration of animus and anima bridges the gap of understanding between the sexes and thus eliminates many unnecessary and childish tragedies. How much the next generation always suffers when brought up in wrecked or unhappy marriages does not need to be mentioned— every social worker knows about that.

What I have tried so far to show is that the process of individuation can remove many severe disturbances of our social life, though I must frankly admit that it is very hard work to make people see their shadow, and even more difficult to help them to become conscious of animus or anima. Man seems to have a great unwillingness to reflect truthfully on himself and greatly prefers to accuse outer circumstances when things in his life go wrong!

Up till now the process of individuation seems to be mostly a process of withdrawing illusionary projections on other people and abolishing the childish prejudices we like to have about them. This means becoming more reflective and reasonable. It also makes one a bit more independent of other people. However, we have not yet found any instinctual basis for a *relatedness* to mankind in any *active* way.

It is only when we go still one step further into the depths of the unconscious that we meet that archetypal factor which actively unites mankind and forms the basis of all our social instincts; it is that inner entity which Jung has called the *Self*.

Whenever a man tries to have it out consciously with his anima or a woman with her animus, this leads to some deep crucial conflict situations which often seem to be without solution. If the ego stands the suffering and does not run away, this activates the deepest layer of the psyche, the atomic nucleus of the soul, so to speak, a centre which seems to regulate the whole psychic system of each individual. In situations of great distress or disorientation, or in a conflict which seems to have no solution, Jung observed that in the dreams and spontaneous fantasies of his patients a symbol very frequently turned up, which seems to mean oneness and wholeness—a fourfold or circular structure which he called by the Sanscrit term *mandala*. The appearance of this symbol brings with it inner balance and order. It is an image which plays a central role in the eastern religions, where it denotes the cosmic-individual oneness and meaning of all being. The indologist Tucci calls it a psycho-cosmic order. In the western hemisphere we find the same symbol generally used to symbolise either the Godhead or the structure of the world, the latter being a copy-image of its Creator—as well as of the ultimate structure of the human soul. It was generally described by the sentence: "God (and the cosmos) is an infinite spiritual sphere, whose periphery is nowhere and whose centre is everywhere." In late romantic German philosophy this was also thought to describe the transcendental creative I, (but not the ordinary everyday ego!). Looked at from an empirical standpoint, this centre seems to represent the core which regulates the whole homeostatic balance of our psychic system; it is the centre from which the regulating and healing function of dreams comes forth, and which is subjectively experienced as an ultimate goal and fulfilment of life—it often even gives rise to a religious experience which in many ways resembles the satori experience in Zen-Buddhism.

However, this nuclear atom of the psyche as one might call it, the Self, does not only appear in dreams and fantasies in such an abstract mathematical form: it can also appear *personified*. In this case it manifests in the psyche of a man as a divine or semi-divine male human being, as a wise old man or leader and teacher; in the psyche of women it manifests as a kind of cosmic mother figure, or wise earth mother, or Sophia-figure. And in both cases it often shows hermaphroditic traits, because it unites all opposites, even those of male and female.

Whenever the Self constellates in the unconscious of a human being it brings with it a unique and creative solution of his or her problem. It constellates a big leap forward towards consciousness and freedom. Jung therefore saw in it the very core of each human being. To come into contact with the Self seems to be the ultimate goal of the process of individuation. Now, the fact that the Self is the source of creativity has not only great importance for the individual but also for the community. A polarisation between creative individual and collective social behaviour seems to have existed already far back on the animal level. The zoologist, Adolf Portmann, has shown that all innovations of collective animal behaviour patterns stem from the unique enterprise of one individual, which tries it out first at its own risk.

Creative individuality thus seems to be much older than man's ego-consciousness. A bird, for instance, of a species which usually migrates to South Africa, stays for one winter in our countries. If it succumbs, nothing more is heard of it, but if it survives, others begin to imitate it and this can eventually lead a whole group to change its habits. Japanese zoologists have observed that in a group of Macaque apes, who live on an island, a single younger female introduced the whole group into the new habit of washing their food in sea water before eating it. The so-called abnormal individual animal seems doomed to succumb, the creative individual on the contrary seems destined to enrich the community. Thus a problem, individual versus collectivity, existed as far back as our animal ancestors, and isolated individuals always have either threatened or enriched their tribe.

If we look closer at what happens in isolated human individuals, namely at what happens in their unconscious, we can see that those individuals who are doomed or act destructively for their tribe, are possessed one-sidedly by an autonomous complex—what was called in the past: possessed by a demon. *Such a state of complex-possession always creates fear, hatred and separation in the surroundings.*

The creative individual, on the contrary, generally has an especially close connection with that centre which Jung called the Self. In his book on *Shamanism,* Mircea Eliade has collected a great wealth of documents which show this more clearly. The Nordic shamans—and similarly the primitive medicine-men of many other countries—are generally individuals who receive what is described as a call from the ghosts or gods of their tribe. After a severe psychic crisis, which isolates them from their surroundings—sometimes this isolation is also actively sought for—they learn, generally through the guidance of older medicine-men, how to have the right kind of dialogue and contact with these powers, which we nowadays would call archetypal contents of the collective unconscious. *They do not get possessed* by them, except sometimes voluntarily in a short state of trance. They remain their normal human self but they *know* about these powers of the Beyond (the unconscious) and thus act as prophets, healers and therapists, and at the same time, in many places, also as the artists and poets of their community. On this early cultural level the symbols of the Self are frequently magic animals. In the northern countries it is most frequently the bear who is a great nature divinity and represents what we would call the Self for the shaman. He does all his healing and creative actions through the bear. In Africa it is often the lion or elephant, but it can also be some other magic animal, which represents the supreme divine power of nature and the soul. This fact that what we call the Self appears personified in the dreams and visions of medicine-men and creative individuals in an animal form, suggests that it is first experienced as a purely *unconscious* instinctual urge, greater and more powerful than man's ego, but also completely unconscious. It represents, and has the whole wisdom of, nature, but it has *not* the light of human consciousness.

There is in nature no animal drive without its specific *form* from which we can read its purpose and meaning. And further, all instinctual impulses are *not* unlimited, they have their time-rhythm, their goal, their specific inhibitions and mechanisms. For man these limiting forms of the instincts are his religious customs and taboos.

They express—if observed from within—the *meaning* of our instincts, which is expressed in symbolic fantasies. Religion thus was originally the psychological regulating system which ordered our instinctual drives. Only if religious systems freeze into a stiff formalism do they become negative and anti-instinctual. Normally spirit and instinctive drive constitute a compensatory pair of opposites which complement each other harmoniously. In innumerable cases in history, the tension of opposites between spirit and instinct has become negative—as it has also in the last centuries of our own culture. In such cases the unconscious produces new religious symbols which are meant to bridge the gap, and bring back to man the memory of his original nature. It is generally a new symbol of the Self, of psychic wholeness, which reunites the opposites that have fallen apart.

Whilst the totem-animal expresses a deeply unconscious form of such a wholeness and symbol of social coherence, we find on a somewhat higher cultural level a new symbol which takes its place: namely the symbol of a great all-encompassing *human* figure which Jung calls the *Anthropos*. Like the totem-animal, the Anthropos is regarded as the ancestor of all human beings, he unites them and in many myths he is even the raw material from which the whole cosmos was formed. He is regarded as the life-principle and meaning of all human life on earth—the totem not of a single tribe but of mankind as a whole.

According to many creation myths of different nations, the whole universe arose originally from the parts of a huge human figure. In the Germanic *Edda* it was the giant Ymir: "From Ymir's flesh the earth was formed, from his bones the mountains..." etc. In China it is the dwarf *and* giant P'an Ku, who became the cosmos. P'an means egg shell and "to make firm", and Ku means underdeveloped, unenlightened or embryonic. When P'an Ku cried the Yellow river and Yang-Tse-Kiang came into being, when he breathed the wind sprang up, when he spoke, thunder arose, when he looked around lightning flashed. When he died the four holy mountains of China (with the Sung-mountain as fifth in the middle) came from his body. His eyes became the sun and the moon—much later he reincarnated through a virgin, "the holy mother of the first cause" and became a cultural hero. The meaning of these myths which describe the Anthropos as the origin of the cosmos refers to the fact that all our experience of reality is a psychic one and pre-formed by our psychic structure.

Similar ideas exist in the old India Vedic literature. There, it was the cosmic ancestor of mankind, Yama, who later became (in the *Upanishads*) the Purusha, a name which means: Man, Person. He represents the individual Self or innermost psychic nucleus in

every individual and, at the same time, a collective and even cosmic
Self, an all pervading divine principle.

In the *Rigveda* (X.19) the four castes sprang from the body of the
thousand-eyed Purusha. And later, when the other gods sacrificed
him, the moon came from his mind, the sun from his eye, the air
from his navel, the sky from his skull. "He is," a text says, "all that
was and all that will be"..."verily he is the inner Self of all beings."[2]

In the old Iranian religion the corresponding figure is Gayômart. The word comes from *gayô,* eternal life, and *maretan,* mortal
existence. Gayômart was the semen of the good god Ohrmazd, and
the first priest-king. When he was killed by the evil god Ahriman,
the eight metals flew out of his corpse; and from the gold, his soul,
sprang a rhubarb plant, from which came the first couple, who
generated mankind.

These myths, among other things, express the idea that
originally mankind had a kind of collective soul—all men were
psychologically *one* being. This points to the fact which we can
actually still observe, that insofar as we are unconscious we are not
distinguished from other people: we act, react, think and feel
completely like them. This is the phenomenon which Jung called
archaic identity or *participation mystique,* using a term conceived by
Levy-Brühl. When we analyse the dreams of small children, we can
often see that they dream about problems which are not at all their
own, but those of their parents. In family groups, or other closely-
knit communities, individuals often dream about the problems of
people in their surroundings—it is as if in the deeper spheres of
the unconscious we cannot distinguish what belongs to whom, our
unconscious psyche merges, so to speak, with that of others. The
negative aspect of this phenomenon lies in the fact that as long as
we are unconscious we are laid wide open to psychic infections.
The complexes of other people can affect us even to the extent of
possessing us.

They can even cause states of collective possession. Another
negative aspect of this "archaic identity" is the fact that it makes us
assume that others are psychologically the same as we are. This
seems to give us the right to judge and to want to "improve" them,
even to manipulate them or force our ideas upon them.

But archaic identity has also a positive aspect—it is the basis of all
possible empathy, the archetypal foundation of all our social
instincts—even of their highest expression such as Christian love or
Buddhistic all-compassion. All human relatedness is based on the

archetype of the Anthropos—in some sense he is even the personification of Eros, *par excellence.*

In the Jewish legends Adam, the Jewish version of the Anthropos, and the first man, is often described as a cosmic giant. God assembled red, black, white and yellow dust from all four corners of the world to form him. According to the Cabbalist Isaac Lurja, the souls of all human beings were contained in Adam "like the wick of a lamp is woven from many threads". In this tradition, too, the primeval man is the Self of a whole nation, even of mankind. He is a sort of group-spirit, from which all draw their life. This aspect of being a collective soul explains why some traditions assert that the body of Adam Qadmon consisted of all the prescriptions of the Law. Viewed psychologically, this would mean that on this level of historical development the personality of man manifests only within the religious traditions. The individual is conscious of his own individual inner Self or "eternal man" only through religious traditions; *they* express the spiritual essence of his being. As Helmuth Jacobsohn has shown, in old Egypt, even during the middle Kingdom (until 2200 B.C.), man expected to meet his own non-collective individuality only after death in the form of his so-called Ba-soul—or Birdlike being which personified his own true individual inner Self. In his lifetime however he only felt real as a collective being who functioned within the laws and rules of his religion.

Only after the year 2000 did the Egyptian begin to realise his individuality more consciously and endeavoured to find it already during his lifetime. This led to the spread of the Isis-Osiris mysteries, which fused with other Mediterranean mystery cults that had a similar meaning. They all represented some aspects of the process of individuation in a projected symbolic form.

We thus come to discover a most puzzling paradox: the symbol of the Anthropos appears in individuals as their Self; i.e. as the very unique innermost core of his or her individuality and at the same time he is represented in myths and religious systems as the "Totem" of mankind, as that archetypal factor which actively creates all forms of positive human relatedness![3] The Hindu philosophers were obviously right when they described their Purusha as the innermost Self of each man and simultaneously as a kind of cosmic Self. In this symbol the opposites of the one and the many are united; it is individual and collective in one.[4]

In practical terms this means that the more we individuate, i.e. truly become our unique Self, the better related and the closer we become to our fellow men. We can, as Jung stressed, achieve inner wholeness only through the soul, and the soul of man cannot exist without relationship of one individual to another. But man cannot truly relate to another person before he has become truly himself in an intra-psychic process of unification. Jung says:

> If the inner consolidation of the individual is not conscious, it will occur spontaneously and will then take the well-known form of that incredible hard-heartedness which collective man displays towards his fellow men ... (then) ... *his soul which can live only in and from human relationships is irretrievably lost* ... without the conscious acknowledgement and acceptance of our kinship with those around us there can be no synthesis of personality ... relationship to oneself is at once relationship to our fellow man, and no one can be related to the latter until he is related to himself.[5]

This paradoxical fact is expressed in the symbol of the Anthropos who is the core of each one of us and simultaneously the Totem-symbol of mankind. The Anthropos symbol does not only unite the opposites of one and many, but also of the culturally differentiated and the common man. In dreams and fantasies he often appears as a very low class nameless common man—especially if the conscious attitude of the ego indulges in some social, intellectual or aesthetical snobbism—but he also often appears as a royal figure, especially if the individual feels crushed by its collective non-entity. The Anthropos is just man—in his lowest and highest aspects. Christ, who is the Anthropos figure of our civilisation, has therefore also been called "the king of kings" on one side and "the least amongst us" or the despised servant on the other.

Modern experimental studies of group-psychology have shown that all groups after a time of chaotic probing begin to concentrate around some centre. This can be either the group-leader, or some idea, purpose or theme of discussion, etc. This centre can be a simple purpose as it most often is in sport or in political and commercial groups, or it can be of a higher order such as the Totem in primitive societies or a God-image in higher civilisations. The more archetypal such a centre is, the more a tight and lasting coherence of the group is effected.

It is the world religions, up till now, that have produced the coherence of the largest human groups. Their centre is an Anthropos symbol: Buddha, Christ or Mohammed. By living their own inner wholeness to the utmost, these men have attracted the projection of the Self, of the cosmic man or divine cosmic mind. Both Buddha and Christ were therefore also represented as mandala or indwellers of a mandala. Nowadays Marxism begins also to play a role which is not far from being a religion. Its Anthropos myth, however, is not projected onto a single person (Russia even condemned the cult of personality) except perhaps onto MaoTse Tung in China, but it is projected – as Robert Tucker has shown – onto a social class as a whole: the labour class, which is praised as representing the only noble creative uncrippled man, the giant who will master all difficulties, to quote Marx. He has no shadow. The latter is projected onto the capitalists and imperialists.

This one can clearly see for instance in the Utopia of the Chinese reformer K'ang Yu Wei who is still very much studied in communist China.[6] His whole system is based on the concept "Yen" which means humanness, social love, responsibility. But this must however, be realised only by outer social and political measures. Nobody seems to be aware of the obvious and simple fact that if the individual has no "Yen", society will not have it either. That we must first find the source of "Yen" within each of us, i.e. the Self, before we can relate to our fellow-men, is ignored. In other words, the humanness or love factor is projected onto a group and thus fragmented into infinite splinters.

This Marxist projection entails a collective pluralisation of the Self, which means its disintegration in the individual and in the community. To over-stress the idea of community produces general fear and mistrust. Even in small group gatherings the inner voice of the Self in the individual is muffled and the ego and its will to power accordingly reinforced. The coherence of the group accordingly regresses towards archaic animal patterns as we can observe nowadays, for instance, in the different youth gangs, who sometimes even revive a lot of totemic symbolism. On a bigger scale the mass-madness of National Socialism also showed all the symptoms of such a regression: the God image being Wotan, personified in Hitler, the black eagle and the skull totems, with its states of mass delirium and murderous consequences. Even small groups which tend as we know nowadays to remain more reasonable than bigger agglomerations of people can suddenly fall into states of emotional possession, as we all have seen time and again. In modern sociology one therefore tends to evaluate the masses negatively but groups positively; however this seems to me to be beside the point, because both can be reasonable or possessed. A dictator group can in itself be a small power clique and still act as dangerously as a blind mob. The real difference lies elsewhere: it all depends on how many individuals are conscious, are personally related to the Self within them and thus are not projecting their opposite, i.e. the shadow, onto others. That and only that can prevent outburts of mass-possession and mass-psychosis.

So we must return to the problem of the archetypes in their relation to consciousness or possession. I have already described what animus or anima-possession looks like in a woman or a man, but the archetype of the Self is not exempt from causing possession either: it makes the individual identify with the "great man" or "wise woman" within, and thus to become hopelessly inflated. In every asylum one finds a few Jesus Christs, Napoleons, Presidents of the United States and Virgin Marys. But when people are thus plainly mad, it is not so dangerous; there are many who only secretly over-estimate themselves through identification with a figure of the Self. Then they are just a bit too sure to be always right—and that is about the worst that one can be. They are secretly inhuman through some fanatical conviction or self-righteous attitude. That is what stands behind the many massacres of our time, much more than the outbursts of affect in single individuals which is the well-known other source of killing amongst men. Most of our people who explode bombs in our days have such a "righteous" conviction in mind which in their eyes justifies what they do.

All ideological fanaticism or overwhelming affect comes from the constellation of an archetype. And the archetype of the Self is no exception; it *too* can cause such affects. We must therefore respect those old Eskimo-shamans who already knew that one can only be a healer if one *knows* the ghost world but does *not* get possessed by its powers. Those who get possessed are the sick ones, in their view; those who disrupt the human community instead of helping it.

If we look now at our present day situation in the western hemisphere, we might draw the following overall picture: the western Anthropos figure, Christ, for a millennium and a half has united people. They were—at least in theory—all "brothers and sisters in Christ". Christ was—as the second Adam, also the primordial man, the God man and the innermost Self of the individual—according to the experiences of the mystics. But the fact that Christ is a good figure only—evil being excluded from him and either attributed to man or the devil—meant that he did not unite all the opposites. Whatever found no place in his wholeness was projected onto the heathen or some other people and powers outside. This fact and the rising and increasing over-estimation of rationalism, that late offspring of scholastic philosophy, has weak-ened the Christ symbol to an ever growing degree. Great masses of people have thus lost the religious symbol which held western mankind together in the past. Some look for it in Buddhism — others look for it in the regressive totemic symbolism hidden in Marxism, and still others just feel lost and attach themselves to more superficial values and ideas, keeping a kind of general Christian attitude towards their fellow-men, which is so bloodless that it just collapses in situations of distress and gives way to archaic barbarism.

But as in all neuroses, be it that of the individual or of the collectivity, the unconscious is revealing a tendency to unite the opposites again and to heal the split. We cannot at present predict how this will look on a great world-wide scale, but we can see empirically and assert for certain that a new Anthropos figure is forming in the collective unconscious, a figure which looks more like the "round or square man" or "true man" of the alchemists, not an anti-Christian figure but a more complete Christ figure, so to speak, which truly contains the opposites of the one and the many, the male and the female, spirit and matter, good and evil. It appears in every process of individuation which goes deep enough. Until now it only appears in the inner experiences of solitary searching people who stop outer fights by looking at their own shadow and try to learn a deeper and more truthful relatedness to the people who surround them. Towards the end of his life, Jung was not optimistic about our future; too much points to wars, mass psychoses and coming disaster, but he was sure of *one* thing: that only if enough individuals become conscious, in the way described above, will our civilisation be able to renew itself and continue to exist. Otherwise we will surely fall into barbarism, regressive totemic clan-mentality, endless wars and even possibly into final disaster.

One could say that Jungian psychology is not very widely spread amongst the masses — so if the process of individuation is the only help and compensation for these difficulties — how can this be of any wide use? To this we must answer that the process of individuation is not only brought about by a Jungian analysis because it is in itself a *natural process,* which can be realised by any person who is truthfully and consistently looking at himself or herself. Jung's achievement is mainly that he brought it up to consciousness and found how it can be supported consciously. In a way it does not much matter what name one gives to this process, as long as one lives it consciously. There is also, as far as I have seen, a strange way in which such people find each other and meet, with the help of the unconscious. The "Anthropos" brings them together. So perhaps the healing tendencies of the deeper collective unconscious of man might save us and bring about a new form of human coherence. But the disrupting powers of those who are possessed by demons, i.e. one-sided unchecked complexes, and the distorted ideas and emotions which such complexes engender, is also very great. It is no use denying or fighting them; the "true man" as Jung called the Self, will never take part in the game of shepherd and sheep, because he has enough to do in watching himself. He dives, so to speak, into a deeper layer of his psyche, where he is truly united with mankind, beyond its everyday struggles for power. From this layer stems all creativity — one can only be creative if one is connected with the "common man" within — and from this layer, therefore, we might be able to renew our culture.

NOTES

1. Public lecture given at the Royal Society of Medicine, London, on 27th September, 1974, under the auspices of the Analytical Psychology Club, London.
2. Mundaka Upanishad II.
3. Cf. C.G. Jung, *Collected Works* (London, 1954), Vol. 16 para. 454.
4. Cf. Ibid., para. 474.
5. Ibid., para. 444/45.
6. Cf. Laurence G. Thompson, 1958. *K'ang Yu Wei.* German: *Ta Tiung Shu, Das Buch von der Grossen Gemeinschaft,* Diederichs, Düsseldorf, Köln, 1974.

Transformations of the Persona[1]

by Faye Pye

FAYE PYE, B.A., M.A. Psych. (London), L.R.C.P., M.R.C.S. Royal Free Hospital) and late Psychiatric Registrar of St. John's Hospital, was a practising Jungian analyst in South Africa from 1948 to 1961, and in London, from 1972 until her death. She was also president of the Analytical Psychology Club.

Jung first formulated his concept of Persona in the two *Essays on Analytical Psychology,* the first draft of which appeared as early as 1912. As everyone knows, the word "persona" originally meant the mask worn by actors on the ancient stage, indicating their role in the drama. Jung gave the word a new technical meaning, as the outward form in which the personality is presented to society; to the world. In the two essays his evaluation of Persona is almost wholly depreciatory, and this view has remained as the generally accepted one in analytical psychology. The tone is apparent in the following examples:-

(1) Fundamentally the persona is nothing real: it is a compromise between the individual and society as to what a man should appear to be..... The persona is a semblance, a two-dimensional reality.[2]

and

(2) .... as its name implies, it is nothing but a mask for the collective psyche: a mask which simulates individuality, pretending to others and to itself that it is individual, while it simply plays a part in which the collective psyche speaks.[3]

The idea was already implicit in our language. We 'lose face', 'save face', 'face an ordeal', and so on. I think myself that there are historical and social reasons for Jung's depreciatory emphasis, but I would like to return to this point later.

First, looking at the matter quite naïvely, how does it come about that human beings need and acquire Persona?

It is useful, in seeking answers to this question, to start from a position which illuminates by contrast — a position which is perhaps the antithesis of Persona. This is the sense of unique intrinsic being which most people possess. Everyone longs to communicate his essential being to another, but seldom feels that it is possible. There are certain situations in which the boundaries of separateness may seem to have been broken. "Falling in love" is one of them, and probably the greatest pain in falling out of love or being rejected in love is the return to the situation of separateness. The prototype of the unconditional union for which we long has been said to be the pre-natal experience of the child in the womb. It has also been suggested that the ultimate and true goal of the longing is union with God, in which, in St. Paul's words, "We shall know as we are known". Plato has given us another symbol of the desire to return to a lost wholeness. He described an all-round being with four arms and four legs who was divided originally to make male and female. These two halves are always seeking to reunite. Yeats voiced yet another aspect of the essential self that longs to be known, when he wrote:

> Only God, my dear,
> Can love you for yourself alone,
> And not for your yellow hair.

The relation of the intrinsic inner being to the persona is expressed in the myth of Adam and Eve. Having eaten of the fruit of the tree of the knowledge of good and evil, they lost their innocence, covered their nakedness and as a result of their disobedience were cast out of Paradise. They were condemned to the arduous task of adapting to earthly reality. Similarly, every child, when it is born, is cast out of the womb of unconditional union into a separate existence, and into a family group or substitute for the family. With varying measure of success, the parental environment provides an approximate substitute for the lost intra-uterine paradise. It can of course never be perfect, and the most obvious and inevitable difference is the intermittence of personal contact and the variety of changing sensations. Touch, support, warmth, light, sound, emotion, smell, presence, perhaps also the quality of the libido generated near and towards the child — many factors and persons contribute, and at best they come and go.

As the child grows, it is called upon to exert itself, to contribute and to conform in increasingly complex ways — in cleanliness, eating, sleeping, playing, loving. Many such adaptations are learned before the ego is present, and it seems to me that this early conditioning represents the first persona formations. Persona, in this view, appears developmentally as prior to the ego, having the same function at its first appearance as it has later when the ego is also present. This is the function of achieving and maintaining union with the human environment.

In contrast to Persona, the ego when it first appears is a disturbing and dividing element. It exists only through its separateness and otherness. It can only be a rebel and a breaker of bonds. This emergence can create a tense and complex situation, because not uncommonly the mother has herself rediscovered her own primal union in relationship with her baby, and suffers severely from the psychic separation.

Once the ego is present with some degree of continuity, ego and Persona can cease to be in opposition, and enter into a liaison. Persona then becomes not only a means to union, acceptance and belonging, but also a protective covering for the secret life of the child. This dual role has probably contributed a good deal to the discredit of Persona. It makes possible a reservation, a sort of "counter-espionage", which is in part a means of keeping the grown-ups out, and in part an identification with them. This is necessary in order to maintain the balance of inner and outer security.

The secret life of the child is the germ of future independence and individuality. Parents who resent or fear it and gate-crash through Persona defences, or who depreciate the secret life and load it with excessive guilt, interfere illegitimately not only with the child's happiness and development but also with the future adult. Seminal independence may become renegade or defeated; Persona function may be lost or proliferate excessively. Both can happen.

Major changes in the environment call forth transformations of the persona. This is an important part of growth and adaptation made possible by the plasticity of Persona and its ability to compromise. The first transition of this kind is usually from home to school. Not only is there a new society to adapt to, but familiar habits, persons and authorities once absolute become relative. The ego's capacity for relativity is limited and the experience of it painful if not threatening. The conservatism of children is an expression of this. But the psychic function which can pioneer in a strange or divided environment is the persona. It leads the way into new situations, to be followed later by the less flexible ego when the demands and authorities have become familiar. Probably all major transitions follow this pattern: a persona transformation followed by an ego adaptation, from home to school, school to university, from being a student to doing a job, from lesser to greater status and responsibility. Persona unites, protects, compromises, and transforms, and as such is an essential aspect of the growing human individual-in-environment.

Now it seems to me that we take this all very much for granted. But is it not an essentially human characteristic, lying so deep in our nature that it must be considered to have a biological and even an archetypal basis?

An extraordinary degree of flexibility distinguishes man from all other animals. How great this is becomes apparent if we compare ourselves with termites who are born each with its inherited task that is necessary to the life of the community, or migrating birds sensitised to season, direction and ordered flight, or male weaver birds who build a number of intricate spherical nests and offer a choice to their mates. All are highly-skilled, remarkably adapted, determined by instinct.

To a far greater extent in human life the world begins anew with each individual. Persona is one of the means by which the human being achieves his human status. This is so, not only because Persona is necessary to ego development and to group belonging — but also because together with Persona the individual acquires the forms of behaviour which contain the cultural values of his people. In this sense Persona makes an historical link between the generations as well as the cement which holds society together in the present. Whether and to what extent the ethos contained in the forms is questioned, developed and made conscious is a matter for the maturation of the individual psyche. Ancient Chinese wisdom laid great stress on social form, probably for these reasons. (It is of course also true that other sources of Chinese wisdom emphasised formlessness.)

This brings me to the inevitable problem of opposites in the psyche. It would be false to present a picture of the persona which did not include its shadow side. To do justice to this at length in all its subtlety is more than I can attempt here. But at least let me say that Persona may indeed be a mask which covers with a fair semblance a personality that is in reality totally other than it appears. It can offer politeness as a substitute for good feeling, respectability in the place of morality, collective judgments in the place of insight. It can foster class-consciousness and "Keeping up with the Jones's" and any other form of intellectual, spiritual and materialistic snobbery and hypocrisy. It is not infrequently an instrument of power and seduction in public and in private life, "a poor player who struts and frets his hour upon the stage", playing a role not only to the world but also to the inner auditor. It is the most transient of psychic forms, the cheapest substitute for the "treasure hard to attain", and in its arrogance it is an impertinence in the face of the cosmos and the Ultimate.

Nevertheless, in spite of the undoubted importance of Persona as shadow aspect, its positive values remain. Why then was Jung moved to emphasise the negative? I think that the reasons are largely historical. In the first place, it is evident from *Memories, Dreams, Reflections* that the period in which he was formulating the *Two Essays* coincided with his preoccupation with his own intense fantasy experiences. This would have given him a heightened awareness of the contrast between the inner and the outer world, and the mask-like qualities of the persona. Secondly, he was a psychiatrist and analyst working with individual patients in the society of Europe before and during the first world war. This society was sophisticated, spuriously secure and on the brink of violent transition. In such circumstances the unconscious of his patients would contain disordered elements in strong contrast to their society and their social order. As *Essays on Contemporary Events* show, the unconscious foreshadows coming collective phases. On both personal and collective grounds, the psychic material of his patients must have given Jung a particularly clear view of Persona as mask. There is a parallel with Dostoievski's description in *The Idiot* of the prince's first encounter with polite society. He was charmed with their poise and manners, which seemed to him to be an expression of refined feeling and spiritual grace, but, as the author points out, their manners were purely mechanical and habitual, and in no way an expression of their inner being.

It is interesting to see the development of Jung's view of the "compromise between the individual and society". In the *Essays on Analytical Psychology and Education*, published in 1924, he wrote:-

The human being must be adapted on two fronts, firstly to external life — profession, family, society — and secondly to the vital demands of his own nature. Neglect of the one or the other imperative leads to illness. Although it is true that anyone whose unadaptedness reaches a certain point will eventually fall ill.... yet not everybody is ill because he cannot meet the demands of the outside world, but rather because he does not know how to use his external adaptedness for the good of his most personal and intimate life, and how to bring it to the right pitch of development. Some people are neurotic for internal reasons, others for external ones.[4]

This essay was written after the effects of the first world war had broken on Europe and Russia. There is a change of emphasis and tone, no longer dividing inner and outer as incompatibles, nor devaluing the means of bridging the two worlds, but rather stressing the need to make the bridge as part of the human condition.

Baynes, writing during the second world war, when the pace of social change and the ferment in the unconscious had vastly increased, wrote of Persona as "a legitimate social form belonging to an integrated order of society".[5] The point that I would like to bring out is expressed in the words "social form" and "integrated order" — we can only become conscious of something if we are also conscious of its opposite. To realise Persona as form means also to be aware of social disintegration and its consequences.

For an individual to find the proper place of Persona in his relation to an ordered society is one thing, but what happens if society disintegrates around him, or if the rate of change is so rapid that it is felt as disintegration? Persona then loses touch with traditional values and becomes a means of protection and belonging at all costs: in this sense we are all "displaced persons."

Since the beginning of the century the structure of society and also of our universe as we know it has undergone extraordinary changes. We are in the age of rapid transport, the exploration of space, computer intelligence, television and radio, the dissolution of matter to elements beyond form, a fearful capacity to interfere with the human body and psyche. We are also in the age of a ferment of cultures, shifting populations and a mixture of races on a global scale. These things are perhaps only in their beginnings, but the impact on the psyche is terrific.

In the generation of young adults the symptoms vary. A middle-class young woman, mother of three children, who has a secure home and apparently structured life tells me without embarrassment: "I don't really mind what I do. I only mind about being found out." A man who is a cultural leader in the arts, holding a public position says seriously, "The thing I am really fascinated by is futility." A teacher who is responsible for adolescents and who takes his teaching seriously says of himself and his colleagues, "We are the cream of the scum". For people who are "afloat" in society without established values, like a sea without landmarks, Persona may be not so much a mask as an instrument of navigation.

NOTES

1. Adapted from a talk given to the Analytical Psychology Club on October 10th, 1964.
2. C.G. Jung *Collected Works* Vol. 7, p.156.
3. Ibid Vol. 7, p.276.
4. Ibid Vol. 17, p.92-3.
5. Baynes *Analytical Psychology and the English Mind*, 1949.

Healing the Child Within[1]

by Culver Barker

CULVER BARKER was born in 1891. He studied engineering before embarking on a career in medicine which turned towards his real interest in personality disturbances, and child psychology. He met Jung in 1927, and worked with him in Zürich, where he afterwards lectured at the C.G. Jung Institute. He also took up a private practice, and was the author of Healing in Depth.

In speaking about what I have called the child within, may I remind us of the significance of the child as an age-old symbol that carries with it, or evokes, in all who are in a condition to be moved by it, the sense of wonder, awe, hope, redemption, creative possibilities, the richness of becoming, of the future, the sense of adventure, zest, discovery, courage, spontaneity, undoubtedness, wholeheartedness and meaning — in other words, all that the wise men felt after their long intuitive journey, when, guided by their eternal star, they found the Christ Child. It brings with it the sense of individuality, eternity and immortality.

The child, as Jung's researches have found, is a symbol which has been experienced again and again in different eras from the earliest times of human history. In other words, it represents a crucial, age-old experience and hope of mankind which is ever with us yet ever young — one of the archetypal experiences — and therefore carries and evokes fascination and numinosity.

On the other hand, when the eternal image is seen in an earthly child, one must never forget that besides all the wonders, there are also the little devils who at times can outwit the most sophisticated adult, especially when he, as it were, gets above his own nature; then, in an impish way, they may take control of the situation, quite amoral and irresponsible, and ruthlessly get what they want.

When I talk about the child within I mean that aspect within us adults which still reflects some of the qualities of the divine child, such as wholeheartedness, zest for life, awe, sense of wonder, etc.

When we are too unconscious of it, for whatever reason, and so do not mediate it, this force contains all the potentialities for constructive and destructive activities. So it can hold the creative dynamics of the human personality, its motive power. From this we can realise how important it is to become aware of it, because then there is a chance to relate to it consciously and be reinforced by it and carried along without detriment to our adult judgements and responsibilities. Otherwise we may identify unconsciously with it and thus be run or our adultness even swamped by its highly charged potential.

As a therapist, however, one is confronted mainly with the difficulties of the child at various levels of its development within its environmental setting; in short, with the problem child. We also find the problem child within the adult patient, very often as the central core of the problems and difficulties that bring him to seek the therapist's help. In the adult, because of its usually early root and decade-old reaction pattern, it requires a deep analysis to trace this problem child within and bring it back into the stream of life. This is what I call healing in depth.

The Stem of the Personality
I would like now to introduce an image which helped me greatly in tracing and recognising such wounded aspects of the personality which in the course of treatment we hope to link up with, to restore and help to reintegrate within the total personality. I find it useful to look upon the personality as a stem in which every unit of time from birth to old age is represented, just as every season of a tree's life from its earliest sapling days is represented within its stem. In the case of the human being this stem can be thought of as crowned with the glow of consciousness of the present moment. To me this makes a vivid image of the spiral of the growth and development of the psyche.

To continue with this image, the roots are sunk deep in the unconscious, the most recent ancestors closest to the beginning of the stem. At the base of the stem is the Mother-Child phase, and then comes the first budding of the child's individuality. At this early time the child's sense of himself reaches a certain definiteness; his differentiated consciousness begins to flower off from his unity with nature, his containment in the parents and in himself. It is a critical time of great sensitiveness, and in an ideal setting, acceptance and the warmth of parental love will bridge over from the early contained state to the more differentiated and less secure one which prepares the child for adult life. If the parents accept and affirm the value of his individuality and he can respond to this, the sense of his basic values becomes rooted and he will be able to make a more or less easy relationship with his environment into and from which he is growing. His experiencing of a fair share of loving acceptance of his basic nature is fundamental to his healthy being and living. Then, with sufficient security, he will go forward to the subsequent stages of development with the zest, self-confidence and sense of inner integrity which are his birthright as a human being, and so the sap of his energy will flow freely in his personality.

But if the parents, because of their own insecurity or for other reasons, do not or cannot accept sufficiently his basic nature, of if the child's inner or outer environment is such that he cannot receive enough of what he needs, then at this point where consciousness is so sensitive to the instinctual basis of being, his personality may be severely damaged. Beyond the normal bruising, he becomes estranged from his centre of being. Unknowingly he feels forced to twist or even abandon his natural pattern of unfoldment, and by trial and error he learns a way of behaviour that is more acceptable to his surrounding world, and which brings him the acceptance and security he so badly needs. Here we have the beginning of what may later become a very damaging distortion of natural expression, a mental formation replacing natural relationship.

With the differentiation of consciousness, selectivity evolves and certain aspects of his nature unacceptable to the parental authority and environment are not allowed to be spontaneously expressed. The quality of a severe or repeated early experience lays down a reaction pattern for subsequent phases. This may include anxiety, apprehension and guilt, particularly when it comes to the expression of his instinctual self and being. Because of the distortion of his personality he will doubt his own validity and basic natural meaning. Consciousness gets out of tune with his nature, and he may grow up, in part at least, at war with his basic self. I call this area of damage, with such deep wounds in the personality, the place of 'critical hurt'.

If now we turn to *types of traumatic experiences* I would distinguish between two different categories: *sudden and acute* on the one hand, and *repetitive or recurrent* on the other. Before we concentrate on those which have a deep-reaching or lasting effect and which we can approach by means of psychotherapy, I would like for the sake of completeness, to pause for a moment to note the fact that there are incisive experiences which do *not,* or need not, have a damaging effect in later life. Having to go to hospital for an operation may bring a traumatic experience to one child that calls for analytical treatment later on, but to another child, as I recently heard, it brought a reinforcement of his feeling of value and significance. Peter, aged six, previously indifferent to food and boyish games, came back radiant and rapidly became a robust little fellow. The cause of this remarkable transformation, which held its effect over several years, only revealed many years later during analysis, was that the surgeon after the operation called him a little hero and the nurses he felt had treated him as such. Again, one can readily see the difference between someone losing his leg by jumping from a moving bus or, say, at the battle of Alamein: the first may be damaged in his attitude to himself, while, in the second case, the feeling of a hero may well increase his morale rather than lower it.

We might further differentiate between predominantly external, physical causes and internal, psychological ones. In both cases the effect depends first of all on the actual depth of the threat to health and life. It is of the utmost importance to separate that which is objectively and biologically traumatic and differentiate it from the subjective intensity of reaction which may be disproportionate to the objective data. In less severe cases, such as, say, a fall from a horse, a bite from a dog or violation by an adult, the traumatic effect depends not so much on the event as such, but on how it is experienced and dealt with, or whether and how it links up with an already existing pattern. A fall from a horse, to one, may reinforce his inferiority and lack of achievement, but another may lose his fears of falling by falling 'safely' without the fearsome result anticipated and increase his feeling of security. As you may know, in learning to ski you have to learn how to fall securely and get up again, on your very first day of tuition. Again, on being stricken by polio, the extent of the trauma depends on the appropriate handling, for instance whether it is experienced as a challenge or as a punishment. I remember one stricken individual who, from his interest in movement arising from the damaged leg, became a good athletic instructor at a boys' school.

Still within the category of sudden and acute types of damage, I would like to point out that this extent has to be judged by whether the outer event produces a sensitized critical area, so that, whenever afterwards that area is activated, the response is that to the original threat and hurt. This may be very concealed, so that ten to fifty or more years later, an apparently innocuous event may send the individual into a spasm of despair unexplainable by the actual context as such. The possibility of this reaching back to infancy may help us to get nearer to the realization that an early trauma, even a birth trauma, may give the foundation from which a pathway of special sensitivity might extend up through the years into adult life.

We come now to the type of traumatic experiences which are caused not by a sudden, single or acute event but are brought about by a *sequence* of what in themselves would be minor experiences. I have found that it is rarely a single event but a *recurrent* everyday experience that may accumulate like certain drugs and become equivalent to a severe single trauma. So, in searching for damaging or traumatic agencies, it is necessary to look not only for the outstanding isolated trauma but for the influence of a demoralizing atmosphere or milieu or inhibiting environmental conditions which one might call traumatically sensitizing. As a steady drop of water may wear away a stone, so a repeated 'nag' can undermine the morale of the most stout-hearted child. Such adult dilemmas need to be understood, appropriately treated and brought nearer to health by tracing them down the spiral of growth back to what I call the area of critical hurt and the original traumatic experience. We can begin to heal from there.

NOTES

1. This paper is from Dr. Barker's Collected Papers entitled *Healing in Depth*, which the Editor has kindly put at our disposal. (Ed.)

Woman as Mediator[1]

by Irene Claremont de Castillejo

IRENE CLAREMONT DE CASTILLEJO was born in 1896. She studied history and lived with her family in Spain and France before returning to London in 1940. She became interested in Jungian analysis, and went to study feminine psychology with Emma Jung and Toni Wolff in Zürich. She practised as a psychotherapist in London for several years, and was the author of I Married a Stranger *and* Knowing Woman.

An interesting study of personality types in women was made by Miss Toni Wolff, one of Dr. Jung's first and most important collaborators. She gave a seminar in Zürich some years ago on this subject.

During many years of analysis of all kinds of men and women she observed that, quite apart from Jung's four psychological functions of Thinking, Feeling, Intuition and Sensation, woman can also be characterised by one or more of four distinct types of personality. She emphasized that the younger generation tends to combine at least two of these main types in contrast to older generations who seem more often to have been limited to one and she contended that the process of individuation in women demands a gradual assimilation of all four characteristic attitudes.

She calls these four basic feminine types, maternal, hetaira, amazon and mediumistic and describes their respective relationship to man.

The maternal type is the most obvious, but I find it illuminating that in her view this type not only cherishes all that is young and tender and growing but relates to the man principally as father to her children. One can, I think, see this also in the intellectual realm where a wife looks to the husband as the source of her ideas, and readily accepts his notions on politics, religion or whatever it may be, with the same blind wholehearted acceptance with which she accepts his child. The 'mothering' which tends to become smothering and which we so deprecatingly attribute to mothers is, if I understand aright, the negative side of the maternal which cherishes where it is no longer needed and is more likely to arise from the unconscious in women who are actually not mother types.

There is a good parallel here to the functions. Bad thinking is not the sin of thinking types, nor is bad possessive mothering likely to be the sin of differentiated mother types. The compulsive mothers are those whose maternal instinct comes rushing up from the *un*conscious in a most *un*differentiated way. It is then that the mother archetype takes charge and the woman feels like killing anyone who touches or criticises her offspring, and is quite unable to distinguish between mothering and smothering; and yet in the same way that thinkers, who have no function other than thinking, fall down badly when they use cold logic in situations which demand warm feelings, so likewise a mother who can only mother, although she does it well, may cause a nauseating feeling of surfeit in those to whom she ministers needlessly.

It seems doubtful whether the maternal type as such acts as mediator between a man and his *un*conscious though she may mediate between father and children. She does however care for and protect whatever is new and growing in the man which may enhance his position or influence in *outer* life, as such things are important in his role of husband and father to the children.

On the other hand any aspect of his personal development which is outside the family boundary, or does not accrue to the family's benefit, is frowned upon as a dangerous menace to the family's welfare. The poor man's danger from a wife who is such an extreme maternal type is that he feels spiritually imprisoned, and only valued as a financial provider or a useful piece of furniture.

The extreme opposite and furthest away from the maternal type is, according to Toni Wolff, the *hetaira* or companion. This type relates to man for his own sake, not as father to her children. She can be a companion of any level, intellectually, spiritually or sexually or all three at once, but not necessarily all three. She may in extreme cases be a *femme inspiratrice*. One frequently meets her in marriages where the children are only of secondary importance. Outside marriage she constantly fills the gap which a maternally orientated wife may leave in a husband's psyche, giving him value in *himself*, not only as husband and father.

To the hetaira the personal relationship with the man is all important. It is frequently the only thing in life which matters. Everything else can be swept aside as irrelevant. She does indeed give value to the man but she also reflects his personal anima, with all its inspiration and its flattery, to such a degree that she may lapse into the role of seductress. If so, she may lure him away from his real destiny, or the practical necessities of outer life, in favour of some illusory anima ambition, and so ultimately ruin him.

It is of the utmost importance that a woman should know her hetaira potentialities both in their positive and dangerous aspects, for if they are repressed she may turn her sons into secret lovers and her daughters into close girl friends thus hampering their ability to make their own relationships.

Though readily carrying a man's anima it is to his *personal* unconscious that the hetaira type relates and so it is his *personal unconscious which she can be said to mediate to him.*

The hetaira is not an easy role for a woman to play as it does not fit into accepted patterns of society. Nor do the women of this type always realise that they have a definite role to play; so they continually try to change their status of mistress to that of wife, mistakenly believing that marriage is the inevitably desired goal.
To quote once more from Toni Wolff:

> Everything in life must be learned, also human relationships; and it is therefore only natural that the hetaira cannot begin with it on the more differentiated levels. But once she has learned it, she will carefully observe the laws of individual relationship; she will notice what belongs to it and what does not, and she will if necessary know when a relationship has become fulfilled and complete.

The hetaira woman who breaks other people's marriages in order to become the wife herself has not yet learned what belongs to her particular form of relationship.

The third type, the amazon, is historically the product of today. She is independent and self-contained. She is primarily concerned with her own achievement. She claims equality with men. Although she may have love affairs or even marry and have children she is not dependent on the man for fulfilment, as are both the maternal and hetaira types. She meets man on a conscious level and in no way acts as mediator for him. She frequently lives her love life like a man, sometimes even misusing her relationships to further her own career.

The suffragette was of course the unadulterated amazon whose emergence filled men with horror. But today she has ceased to be the hard masculinised woman of yesterday and, having found her own level, no longer behaves as a menacing rival to man. Consciously he accepts her as a comrade, a pleasant workmate and a worthwhile challenge which stirs his own endeavours. Nonetheless, I am pretty sure that in the unconscious of men, the appearance of the amazon is still both feared and hated. I can find no other explanations for the persistence of the inner voice in every woman I have ever met which dins into her ears the words, "You are no good". Is not this her negative animus picking up man's collective unconscious fear of woman's rivalry, and his passionate desire to keep her in her place? If man could become more conscious of his inner disdain for women they might become less aggressive in self defence.

The relationship of the amazon type to man is like that of sister and brother. They understand one another, participate in similar activities and act as mutual challengers and rivals. There seems no place here for the amazon type to play a mediator role.

Toni Wolff's fourth personality type is what she calls the mediumistic woman and here we have *par excellence* the woman whose principal role is that of mediator.

To mediate is to be a connecting link between two things. Now, to begin with, what are the two things or states between which woman is supposed to stand, holding out a hand to each as it were, helping them to come to terms? We can think of mediators in any field. Let us begin at the circumference of our lives and work inwards, seeing at which levels women do in fact play this mediating role.

On the world stage mediation between conflicting powers or opposing ideologies is often called for, but I have not noticed that women take any particular part. In such spheres as these, women as yet seldom play any role at all, for in the realm of ideas and power politics women as women have not learnt to function. There are occasional exceptions but on the whole they join the ranks of men, adding their moral weight to his through numbers, not through any different quality of being.

The same is true within our nation states. Industrial disputes, the quarrels of political parties, dissension between rival churches, show no sign of any woman's mediation to soften their bitterness. There are indeed associations of women's groups but I doubt if they do more than exacerbate the situation.

The first glimmer of any such thing as real mediation appears within schools, and that but sparsely. The child who finds a teacher who can actually help him to pass from childhood into the adult world is fortunate, for teachers who have the gift of standing halfway between the child's mind and that of an adult are rare, and they are just as likely to be men as women — perhaps even more likely. The ones I happen to have known have all been men.

Drawing our circle closer we come to the family, and here at last we arrive at the fundamental, archetypal pattern in which we are all nurtured, where father is Father and mother, Mother.

Now what does this mean? For in actual fact it is often all mixed up and mother's animus frequently plays the role of Father, wielding the stick of authority over children and husband alike; while the children run, not to her, when they are hurt, but to father, sometimes even calling to him in their distress, "Mummy, Mummy."

Nonetheless it is here, within the family, that woman has in outer life her first real opportunity to play her role of mediator.

When father is in fact Father he stands for law and order and authority. It is he who represents the big world outside and can lead the children to respect and obey its forms, and finally to take their place in adult society.

But the world is harsh and wholly unpredictable to the child who has only half emerged out of the mists and timelessness of the great unconscious. Fiery dragons of his imagination are far easier to deal with than the irate grown ups of outer reality. In the boundless realm of fantasy one can take a sword and kill the smoking monster, emerging as the hero that man really is. Even if the giant enemy is too strong, or has a hide too thick for one's sword to penetrate, one can always render oneself invisible, or spread one's wings and fly over his head with a mocking laugh and sail away to the next adventure.

In the prosaic world of everyday a mocking laugh is more likely to produce a scolding. How bewildering a child's life must be! He is assailed on both sides by two completely different sets of values.

When already in my forties I had a dream which most aptly described the predicament of my own childhood, or that of any other small child caught between these opposing worlds.

In the dream I was a shy little girl aged six who went to visit the House of Lords. I opened the door and crept in. There they all were in a large square hall, dressed in black and all jabbering at once in Latin. I was much too small for them to notice me so I slipped round the edge of the hall and up the great wide stairs to an imposing gallery where sat still more rows of black-clothed men. I looked round carefully. Yes, there he was, the man I was looking for, the Archbishop of Canterbury. I ran towards him and flung myself upon his neck weeping with a cry of protest: "But the *Queen* doesn't believe in God!" Indeed she could not believe in the God of these black-clothed Latin-mumbling men, for the picture of the Queen, full-sized before my eyes, was not that of the reigning Queen Victoria, nor of my own mother, but a glowing colourful Queen of

Hearts.

Heart and intellect had different gods even at the age of six, and the child was in tears in her bewilderment. I woke from that dream in actual tears.

Heart and intellect, love and thought, prosaic reality and the poetry of mystical insight, were all opposites, hardly on speaking terms.

How badly the child needs a mediator, someone who can understand both worlds and help to bring them a little closer together. This can be and often is, the role of woman, for women, more easily than men, can stand with one foot in either world, and can ease the child's heartbreaking predicament.

But not only the child's, for it is the adult's predicament as well. Woman as mediator can restore to him a world he has lost, a world that he needs if he is not to become as mechanical as the machines of his own invention, and as dessicated as the synthetic foods with which he is vainly trying to nourish himself.

It is to Neumann, more I think than to anyone else, that we owe the realisation that consciousness, which has been so hardly won by man over the centuries, liberating his mind from the primal unity of all things, is not the only kind of consciousness. There is also a more diffuse awareness which is yet far removed from a state of unconscious mist, and cannot be called *un*consciousness. Neumann calls this "matriarchal consciousness" as distinct from the patriarchal consciousness of man's world. By matriarchal consciousness he means feminine diffuse awareness, in contrast to the masculine focused consciousness under whose aegis we normally live.

In his Essay *On the Moon and Matriarchal Consciousness*[2] Neumann says:

> It is in the act of understanding, that the peculiar and specific difference between the processes of matriarchal and patriarchal consciousness first becomes apparent. For matriarchal consciousness, understanding is not an act of the intellect, functioning as an organ for swift registration, development and organization; rather it has the meaning of a 'conception'. Whatever has to be understood must first 'enter' matriarchal consciousness in the full, sexual, symbolic meaning of a fructifiction.

By this Neumann means presumably that it must be personally experienced before it can be understood. The idea must be received and allowed to gestate.

He continues:

But this feminine symbolism does not stop here, for that which has 'entered' must 'come forth'... 'to come forth' marvellously expresses the double aspect of matriarchal consciousness, which experiences the light of consciousness as a seed that has sprouted. But when something enters and then even comes forth again, this 'something' involves the whole psyche, which is now permeated through and through with the full-grown perception that it must realise, must make real, with its full self. This means that the *conceiving and understanding have brought about a personality change.* The new content has stirred the whole being, whereas in patriarchal consciousness it would too often only have been filed in one intellectual pigeon-hole or another. Just as a patriarchal consciousness finds it difficult to realize fully, and to merely meet with 'superb' understanding, so a matriarchal consciousness finds it difficult to understand without first 'realising' and here to realise means to 'bear', to bring to birth; it means submitting to a mutual relation and interaction like that of the mother and embryo in pregnancy.

To carry a knowledge and allow it to ripen means at the same time to accept it; and acceptance, which here includes the idea of 'assimilation', is a typically feminine form of activity, not to be confused with passive submission or drifting. The comparative passivity of matriarchal consciousness is not due to any incapacity for action, but rather to an awareness of subjection to a process in which it can 'do' nothing, but can only 'let happen'. In all decisive life situations, the feminine, in a far greater degree than the nothing-but masculine, is subjected to the numinous elements in nature or still better, has them 'brought home' to it. Therefore, its relation to nature and to God is more familiar and intimate, and its tie to an anonymous transpersonal allegiance forms earlier and goes deeper than its personal tie to a man.

You will have noticed that Neumann speaks of this feminine matriarchal consciousness as 'it'. He does not speak of 'she'. He is indeed most emphatic that this type of consciousness, which I prefer to call diffuse awareness, can also be found in men, just as patriarchal or focused consciousness is also found in women. It is not a question of sex at all, but rather of a masculine or feminine attitude of mind, the possibilities of both being latent in every individual. Artists and poets of necessity have both.

Nonetheless, woman tends to be more naturally guided by an inborn diffuse awareness than is man, and although she is seldom able to formulate the things of which she is aware, her very presence in a close relationship with a man will open the door, as it were, to the wealth of the collective unconscious in the man himself. So he also, in contact with his own diffuse awareness, finds the unity of all growing things.

I cannot stress too strongly that matriarchal consciousness or diffuse awareness is *not* identical with the formless chaos of the unconscious. It is emphatically *not un*consciousness. Its difference in quality from masculine focused consciousness with which we are all familiar, lies in its whole unbroken state which defies scientific analysis and logical deduction, and it is therefore not possible to formulate it in clear unambiguous terms.

Woman's supreme role as mediator is here: between a man's clearcut intellect, and the awareness of wisdom and wholeness lying latent within himself.

How woman achieves this mediation is a mystery. She certainly will not succeed by attempting to explain. At best her words will only bemuse. At worst they will sound ridiculous. Inability to formulate the unformulatable is a hurdle she cannot jump. But instinct has its own unerring ways. The seed sprouts in the dark and ideas are germinated in the silence.

I have tried to depict in a poem how this particular process of mediation works. I call it:

Eve

When Eve uncovers on the salt sea bed a pearl,
She does not claim her ownership
Nor break it up to find the speck of sand within,
Spoiling its opaque loveliness,
But softly lets it fall in man's quiescent mind
To save it from forgetfulness;
And when one day it comes to light unsought,
She marvels at the pearly iridescence of his thought.

Whether or not a woman knows that this is what she does, that it was she who brought the pearl up from the depth of the unconscious, will depend upon the quality of her own *focused* consciousness. It takes a high degree of focused consciousness in a woman for her to be able to observe what she is in fact doing instinctively.

But please notice that Eve in the poem has not opened the door to chaos, nor has she handed her man the bare ingredients of a grain of sand and an oyster shell.

The pearl has been created, rounded and perfected. She did not create it, but it was she who found it because it is she who is at home in the sea of the unconscious and can dive more easily without being drowned. She brings up this symbol of wholeness, unbroken and still opaque. Such pearls are her jewels of awareness, her values which are utterly destroyed by man's dissection. A dissected pearl is valueless for it has ceased to be.

Now do all women behave like this? I think not. I am convinced that only a particular kind of woman plays this role, mediating to than the mysteries of his own psyche.

The mediumistic woman is permeated by the unconscious of another person and makes it visible by living it. She may pick up what is going on beneath the surface of the group or society in which she lives, and voice it. I have known women who were working in a group, dream dreams which seemed unmistakeably to be messages to the group as a whole. The mediumistic woman may become permeated by a religious creed and put herself at its service. She may express in her own person the spirit of an epoch. Joan of Arc was such a one. Her voices from the Collective Unconscious, speaking to her with the lips of saints, impelled her to live in her own person, and almost to bring into being, the spirit of nationhood which was trying to emerge in France. To quote Toni Wolff, "The mediumistic type is rather like a passive vessel for contents which lie outside it, and which are either being simply lived or else are being formed." In this sense she is immensely valuable in giving shape to what is still invisible beneath the surface. Women like Florence Nightingale or Elizabeth Fry were instrumental in bringing to consciousness a humanitarian spirit which had been lying latent. Toni Wolff suggests that women writers sometimes have a flair for mediating to their own time some wholly other epoch. Mary Renault is surely one of these. *The King Must Die* and other novels by her seem quite miraculously evocative of the spirit of ancient Greece.

On a more personal level I know one woman who dreamed a whole series of dreams pertaining not only to the man with whom she was in intimate contact but to his whole family. When she recounted them they were so dramatically relevant to his family situation that the man's attitude was changed and he was enabled to undertake a difficult task with his father which, before he was told the dreams, would have seemed utterly impossible.

I know other women who seem able to help men to die as their time approaches. These women may be aware that they do this. Sometimes the man in question also knows that the woman is fulfilling this strange role for him. But it is not always necessary to have an intimate relationship for such a thing to happen, and the emergence of such a mediator role may be as complete a surprise to the woman as to the man. I have met this in my own experience.

On one occasion I visited a man in hospital whom I did not know at all well, but who was a member of a society to which I belonged and with whom I had always felt some affinity. I visited him again when he was sent home to his wife to die. To my surprise he told me intimate things of his life which he had never before mentioned to anyone. I said almost nothing but when I rose to leave I kissed him lightly on the forehead. To my bewilderment he burst ino tears. Without knowing at all what I was doing I had freed him from the dry prison of his intellect in which he had been immured and put him in touch with his own unconscious feeling with its promise for the future. Next day, though extremely ill, he asked to see me. I sat by his bed and listened to his delirium. But it was no longer guilt-ridden. He had already embarked on a journey. He died that night.

Such a mediatory role was entirely unconscious and unforeseen. But I have known other women who appear to realise what they are doing. One of these was the wife of a modern high-ranking scientist, newly working in one of the old universities to the ways of which he was finding it difficult to adapt. She told me one day that she was haunted by a male figure in black mediaeval clothes who appeared every night in her dreams, and her task was to help him dress. (He wore a high pointed hat from the apex of which poured a cascade of fine black lace falling to the ground. Black lace covered his face and it was her business to encircle with small white feathers the point of his hat from where the black lace fell.) He held in one hand a money box raised to the level of his head.

As she woke each morning she clearly saw him standing by the bed. She was used to dreams but the insistence of this figure troubled her. I could not tell, from what she told me, whether he was a part of her psyche, which she needed to contact, or if she was picking up some unknown figure in the unconscious of her husband, of which he was unaware. I suggested she should draw him. She did so and showed the picture to her husband. He had learnt to respect her imagery. He looked carefully at the drawing. "Yes," he said, "that belongs to me." The dreams and the hallucination ceased. She had been the means of giving her husband an image from the collective psyche which concerned him and which he had needed to contact before he could feel at home in the mediaeval setting (the old university in which he actually found himself).

The mediumistic woman is, as Toni Wolff makes clear, not easy to discover for she seldom appears in public, and is not publicly recognised as having a definite role to play; yet it is she more than mother, hetaira or amazon who renders the unique service to man of mediating to him the contents of the Collective Unconscious. She is also less visible than other types because today a woman is seldom only mediumistic. She may also be a hetaira or a mother type and then it may appear that it is the wife and mother, or perhaps a lover or woman friend, who is playing the mediating role. So considerable confusion reigns and I think it is popularly believed that, with the exception of the amazon, women as women tend to be mediators. Even the amazon is seldom in this generation nothing else than amazon. She may combine in outer life maternal functions or be the gentlest, most feminine mistress. Her amazon personality will only show in her inability to commit herself to any dependent physical or spiritual relationship to the man. But the amazon, whether coupled with mother or hetaira, is still unlikely to be mediumistic, for medium and amazon are extreme opposite types as are hetaira and mother.

The mediumistic woman is elusive also because she has greater difficulty than the other types of knowing who she really is. All personality types, even the amazon, are related in some way to the masculine psyche, for it is of the essence of the feminine to be related to the male. But the mediumistic woman is always in danger of losing her own ego in the personality of the man she loves, or in the group which claims her interest. She literally *does not know* whether it is her own interest or feeling she is expressing or that of the other.

I met one remarkable case of this seeming loss of identity in a mediumistic woman who realised that in the absence of her husband or her son she felt completely vague, unfocused and at a loss. She went to an analyst in the hope that he might help, but was shattered by the following dream: She visited her analyst and looked into the mirror he held up for her, but to her horror there was no reflection. This dream convinced her, as nothing else could have done, of her paramount need to learn to exist in her own right and not merely as a mediator for other people.

Indeed it is vitally important for a woman who is to handle images from the Collective Unconscious to have a strong ego, if she is not to get lost in its mazes and cause confusion to herself and those around her. She must be able to know the difference between the world of images and the world of everyday if she is to stand in the middle and mediate one to the other. So the task of acquiring ego consciousness, or patriarchal consciousness as Neumann would call it, is for the mediumistic woman, though more difficult than for the other personality types, even more imperative.

Moreover, it is not enough today for any woman to be limited to one personality type any more than it is enough to have only one psychological function at one's disposal. The inner process which demands wholeness is vividly at work. When stuck in one personality type something forces a woman to develop a second, then a third and finally a fourth.

I should not like to give the impression that the mediumistic woman, mediator as she is, is wholly positive for man. She not only suffers more than most women from ego uncertainty but she can also be extremely dangerous. She may see too far and too deeply into the unconscious to be comfortable for those around her. As the mother of a family she may work havoc. She is apt to know what is happening before it has become visible in outer life and she is seldom wise enough to keep her knowledge to herself. Even if she does not voice her findings, she conveys them whether she means to do so or not.

This may be bearable in her relationship to a man but it can be disastrous for her children. The supreme need for growing youth is ability to experience for themselves, free from prying eyes, perhaps even from their own. Growth takes place in the dark places of the psyche in the same way as a seed needs the darkness of the earth in which to sprout. The unknown flower which will emerge is the delight of discovery. The mediumistic mother may, without any effort on her part, already know the type and colour of the flower still bedded tightly in its bud, for, in the unconscious, time has no meaning and all things are already known. If she mediates her knowledge to those around her, though she speaks no word, she will have robbed her young of the fullness of their own experience.

I know one mother who was constantly having dreams warning of this danger. She had considerable psychological insight and constantly feared that she was being over protective to her children. But the dreams always pointed to a wholly other danger.

In one dream there was a great mastiff guarding the door of her house. Little chicks were climbing all over him without his moving a muscle or showing any desire to pounce on them, or crush them with a paw.

A voice said, "Your dog will do your chicks no harm. He is their legitimate protector. Look in the back yard for the marauder." and there she saw an owl feeding peacefully with the hens, no-one noticing that he is the enemy of little birds and eggs.

The dreamer digested this as best she could but some years later had another far more frightening dream. She saw an enormous hollow tree, an entrance near the base. Outside the entrance was again an image of small animals, but this time they were kittens lying peacefully in a kind of nest.

She peered inside the hollow tree and saw to her surprise all sorts of animals big and little. As she looked, a lioness strolled out and walked among her own children outside the tree. The lioness moved among them easily without the shadow of a menace and it was clear that the children neither did nor had need to fear her. Then the dreamer looked higher within the tree, and at the top of it she saw fiery luminous snakes reach out from the sides of the tree twining together in the centre. It was the light they emitted which made the contents of the whole tree visible. Alarmed at their dangerous proximity to the children she stepped back. "That tree must be smoked out immediately," she said.

Whether she was right that the tree should be smoked out seems highly doubtful. But these fiery snakes, which, being at the top of the tree, stand presumably for spiritual insight, do appear to be shown as the dangerous element in contrast to the harmless lioness. To smoke them out would, for the woman, have been to lapse into a state of semi-consciousness and forego the fruits of years of analysis. The dream was perhaps telling her to close the door of the tree so that the snakes could neither emerge, nor the children wander inside inadvertently.

To sum up: I have tried to show that woman's role as mediator lies in her capacity to mediate the unconscious to others, but that not all women do this. The hetaira type will reflect the attitudes of the personal anima, but in order to mediate the contents of the Collective Unconscious, a woman needs to have in her make-up an ingredient of the medium type.

Moreover, if she is to be a good mediator and not just open the door to that very chaos man has left behind him, woman needs to have, along with her own diffuse feminine awareness, enough masculine ego consciousness to be able to discriminate between these two forms of consciousness. She needs to know which world she is in at any given moment, patriarchal or matriarchal, to use Neumann's terms, never confusing one with the other. She needs to know that one world cannot be expressed in the language of the other, but that the more she herself is aware of who she is and where she stands the more likely will she be to hand man not the chaos of the Collective Unconscious but pearls, opaque yet formed, from the realm of diffuse awareness.

NOTES

1. Reproduced from *Harvest*, November 1965.
2. *Eranos Jahrbuch* xviii. It also appeared in English in Spring 1954.

The Medusa Archetype Today[1]

by Andrea Dykes

ANDREA DYKES studied painting in South Africa and London. She gained the diploma of the C.G. Jung Institute in Zürich, where she practised as an analyst, and lectured at the Institute. She returned to England in 1976. She is now a member of the Association of Jungian Analysts in London. She has translated from German The Grail Legend, *by Emma Jung and Marie-Louise von Franz.*

Not a great deal of notice has been taken psychologically of the story of Medusa and her gruesome power to petrify all those unfortunate enough to behold her. This is in full accord with her life and character. She lived in a remote land, beyond human habitation, and seems to have spent her time asleep; not a type to obtrude herself into discussion or even into consciousness.

This unresponsiveness does not mean, however, that she plays no role in human life; it simply means she plays her part unnoticed in the background, and it is this retiring quality that contributes so largely to her power in our lives. Much of this power resides precisely in the fact that she provides a wellnigh invisible backcloth against which the more noticeable aspects of the psyche, anima, animus and personal shadow, play their parts and attract attention to themselves while deflecting it from her.

Just as in Greek mythology Medusa's home was almost inaccessible and its whereabouts known only to the other dwellers in that desolate realm, so likewise her place in the psychology of the individual is far out on the borders of the collective unconscious, whence she unobtrusively infiltrates into personal life.

In this study I hope to show that where there is a problem relating to this type of witch figure the animus, however powerful he may seem, is really entirely subordinate to the witch in the background.

Cecilia came into analysis in her mid-thirties in an effort to find some meaning in life and hoping to overcome the horrible depression she was in as often as not. She was the only child of her widowed mother who was extremely possessive of her daughter, and also wildly ambitious for her. The wretched girl was expected to make a world-renowned name for herself—and for her parent.

First of all, though, I will sketch a brief outline of the story of the Gorgon Medusa. When Akrisios king of Argos sent to inquire of the Delphic Oracle whether he would ever have a son he was told he would not, but that he was destined to die at the hand of his grandson. On hearing this he promptly had his only child, Danae, immured in a prison of bronze, where she was quite alone with only her nurse to care for her. But destiny was not to be cheated, for Zeus espied the lovely girl and visited her in the form of a shower of gold from which she conceived and bore the hero Perseus. When he discovered this, Akrisios refused to believe in the divine paternity of the child and caused mother and son to be set adrift in a chest which was eventually washed ashore on the island of Seriphos. This was such an obscure small place that it was perfectly natural for the fisherman who opened the chest and befriended Danae and her son to be a brother of Polydektes, the king of the island. When Perseus was grown to manhood Polydektes invited all the men of the island to a feast to which each had to bring the gift of a horse. The penniless hero, being unable to comply, either offered or was told to bring the head of the Gorgon Medusa instead. (In one of the oldest renderings of her she is depicted with a horse body attached to her buttocks.) This suited Polydektes admirably; he had fallen in love with Danae, who did not return his feelings and whose strong young son stood in the way of his using force. This detail shows the archetypal nature of the story; it is unlikely the king would have developed such a passion for the mother of a grown son, and why should he not have done so years earlier, when Danae first came to Seriphos?

Space does not permit us to discuss the unusual fact that Perseus' quest was undertaken in order to save his mother's life, for Polydektes means 'Receiver of Many', one of the many synonyms for death. As a positive mother Danae was unintentionally instrumental in causing her son to undertake the quest which transformed him into a hero.

Perseus, who would otherwise have perished in the attempt, was assisted in his task by Athene, who gave him a shield in which he could see Medusa reflected, thus avoiding having to see her directly and be petrified in consequence. She also guided him to the nymphs who lent him the winged sandals, helmet of invisibility, and the bag in which to transport Medusa's head. Hermes gave him the sickle with which to cut if off.

Medusa was originally a beautiful mortal girl with two immortal sisters, and was one of the many nymphs or humans who had the great misfortune to be loved by a god. In her case it was Poseidon, who made love to her in Athene's sanctuary, which so enraged the virgin goddess that she transformed Medusa into the most hideous creature imaginable, with a great gash of a mouth, boarlike tusks, a huge lolling tongue and, most frightful feature of all, snakes in lieu of hair. The effect was so horrible that all who beheld her were turned to stone on the spot.

The name Medusa is variously translated as 'Queen', 'Ruleress', or 'Mistress'. At first glance it seems strange the one mortal sister should have this name while the immortal ones were Euryale, 'The Wide Leaping', and Sthenno or Stheno, 'Strong' or 'Strength'. But since all three obviously form one figure the names refer to a strong queen with widespread powers. No archetype can be killed, but it can be depotentiated from a dominating to a more relative position, which still leaves a strong and widespread power which is immortal.

When Medusa was decapitated her two children by Poseidon, the winged horse Pegasos and the hero Chrysaor, sprang from her severed neck—a clear enough indication of the drastic help required by the children of the witch in their efforts to be free of their mother.

To return to Cecilia; her main problem was twofold. Firstly there was an unusually strong sense of inferiority, an unshakeable certainty she would never be able to achieve anything at all in her life. This feeling was certainly exacerbated by the mother's exaggerated expectations for her, but the roots of the complex reached deeper than that. The real problem lay in the girl's total and deadly lack of desire or driving force at all. She used to say: "I cannot want, I can only want to want." This extreme apathy is, in my experience, a sure sign of a basic witch problem. Where the animus is the foremost negative figure he does at least impart some sort of desire for something or other, however unrealistic it may be. Cecilia's total disparagement of herself first manifested itself when, at the tender age of four, she suddenly knew with absolute certainty that she would fail at anything and everything when she was grown up. Needless to say her expectations were fulfilled. As far as I could get the picture she grew up a limp and lost sort of person, finding it extremely difficult to make friends although she was very lonely and longed for companionship. But the knowledge of her inferiority robbed her of the modicum of self-assurance required for making relationships. Her life with her mother became ever more ingrown, and her connection with anything beyond that narrow circle ever more limited.

When Cecilia first entered analysis her then analyst expressed considerable irritation that she dreamt almost exclusively of her mother and hardly at all of any male figures, known or unknown. This was attributed to the workings of her formidable animus, who was blamed for all her difficulties, especially for her sense of inadequacy. Personally, I cannot help thinking that when almost no masculine figures appear in a woman's material the possibility of causes other than the animus should at least be considered. Also, however wearisome it may become having to listen endlessly to one exclusive theme in analysis, it must be remembered that when the work is taken seriously, as it was in this case, the unconscious must be trusted to produce material relevant to the problem that should be dealt with at that moment of time.

One of Cecilia's very first dreams actually points to a different and deeper origin of her troubles, only she knew no Greek mythology or literature and her analyst did not believe in interpreting his patient's dreams. She dreamt she was lying in bed in her room in the flat she shared with her mother; it was all so exact in every detail she assumed she was awake. As she lay there her mother's head without any body attached, came floating towards her in the darkness. When it was about a foot from the dreamer's face the mother's long hair (she had long hair in reality) drifted silently forward and attached itself, as if with suckers, all round Cecilia's face and neck, so that she was looking at her mother's face through a tunnel of the latter's hair. As soon as the hair had attached itself to her Cecilia felt first her strength and then her very life ebbing away, being sucked out of her by her mother's hair. In spite of frantic efforts to struggle against it and break the spell, she felt her life and consciousness draining away and was unable to move a finger or utter a sound. When she felt she was on the brink of extinction she just managed to gasp out the silent prayer: "Jesus, save me", whereupon a dagger in the form of a crucifix with a black Christ upon it was interposed between her and the head, severing the deadly hair. Cecilia awoke drenched in sweat and terrified. Although she did not know this at the time the dream bears a really striking similarity to one aspect of the Medusa legend. The Gorgon's head continued to possess life and to dispense death after it was cut from Medusa's body; Perseus made use of it on occasion and in the *Odyssey* Odysseus feared Persephone might send it against him when he descended to the Underworld there to seek guidance of Teiresias. It also survived on Athene's aegis where it acted on the goddess's behalf against her enemies.

The head in the dream is also a horror from the underworld of the unconscious, while the life-sucking hair tallies remarkably well with Medusa's snake locks, always considered her most horrible attribute. The effect is the same in both cases, namely total paralysis. Admittedly, paralysis is a common accompaniment of most true nightmares so it might be argued that not too much significance should be attached to this feature. On the other hand this is a Medusa dream, and paralysis or petrification is her particular effect, and it seems likely that some aspect of the witch is behind those nightmares in which paralysis plays a part. It is a typical witch weapon, not limited to Medusa, as may be seen in many of the Grimm fairy tales. Just as the Gorgons lived in a land of darkness, so too it was night in the dream. The most significant similarity to the legend appears, however, in the nature of the saving weapon: in the dream a crucifix, the symbol which since the dawn of Christianity has been held to be the most potent of all against the black powers, and in the legend a sickle given by a god for the depotentiation of an archetypal dealer in death. The common denominator of both weapons will show the meaning of the one in the dream. This must be of Christ as the Way and the Life and of Hermes Psychopompos, the guide of souls. The dagger crucifix is therefore symbolic of the whole way of Cecilia's life in a religious sense. As a portrayal of the intensest suffering it also indicates the pain Cecilia would have to undergo when she was forced to break with her mother in reality. It is a reminder that Christ said He came not to bring peace, but a sword.

Her serpent hair is the one thing everyone remembers about Medusa, and it was the only part of her that was at all alive. We are told that at the time of her death a few of her snakes were keeping guard while she slept. All the authors agree she was slumbering when killed, presumably an intuitive awareness that this was Medusa's true mode of being. In one version her hair was Gorgo's chief beauty, of which she boasted so much that Athene, in a rage, transformed it into snakes. As that which grows out of the head hair stands for autonomous thinking and the natural mind; if Medusa's was so beautiful it suggests her natural mind was ripe for further development.

Now though Cecilia was quite an intelligent person she had been so inhibited by her childhood certainty of failure that she had done nothing at all to try to develop her mind, being convinced it would be futile even to try. Thus a vicious circle arose: the less she developed her mind the more she fell into the paralysis of the witch, and the more she fell into the power of the witch the less she could do about her intellect. Her failure to grow in consciousness might be equated with Medusa allowing herself to be made love to by Poseidon in Athene's sanctuary. We have not space here to follow all the arguments testifying to Athene being the archetype of emerging consciousness, while Poseidon, the ruler of the sea, stands for the downdrag of the unconscious. But if Athene's role be accepted, Medusa's presence in her temple looks as if the girl could have and should have done something about developing her mind. Whereas her union with Poseidon shows she went the other way, allowing herself to be overcome by the unconscious and by blind instinctuality, for as one who frequently mated in horse form Poseidon represents instinct and not relationship in his unions. Athene's exaggerated ferocity towards Gorgo shows what a fragile thing the newly emergent consciousness was at that time, something that had to be guarded at all costs, with no mercy shown to backsliders. As well as snake-hair Medusa is sometimes shown as wearing a girdle of two serpents knotted and rearing angry heads over her diaphragm. The diaphragm is also where Athene wears the gorgoneion, Medusa's decapitated head surrounded by a pattern of rearing snakes. This latter was supposed to act as a terror-inspiring device against the goddess's enemies, but I think it also served another purpose. Medusa's effect was to petrify, which means concretisation run quite out of control. The positive effect of concretisation is to impart form, which is the feminine function at every level, from the maternal womb up to Sophia who imparts the form of true understanding. Primitives think not in their heads, but in their stomachs. We can take Athene, who was born direct from her father's head after Zeus had eaten Athene's mother Metis, 'Wise Counsel'; he had literally tucked Metis away in his diaphragm, as the emergence of cerebral thought from the more primitive type of thinking in the midriff. This midriff-thinking would consist of the vague images and notions that chase each other across the periphery of consciousness when thinking is quite uncontrolled and undirected. If Medusa be taken as the over-concretisation of the purely materialistic attitude, a homeopathic dose of this force would serve to impart form to those vague, chaotic, imperfectly registered shadow thoughts, so that they could be more clearly apprehended and used as tools of the thinking mind, for nothing can be clearly determined until it has been clearly seen by the inward mental eye.

In one passage in the *Iliad* the midriff is associated with the seat of the soul in the body: Patroclus hit Sarpedon with his spear ". . . where the diaphragm comes up against the busy heart", and when he drew the spear from his enemy's body, "The midriff came with it: he had drawn out the spear-point and the man's soul together." The diaphragm is in the central position between the consciousness of the head and heart, and the unconsciousness of the visceral region, and is also the seat of depression. The two angry snakes which guard this portion of Medusa's anatomy represent the cold-blooded murderous unconsciousness which here rules over the soul enclosed in the diaphragm. In her terrible depressions Cecilia used to say it felt as if a giant black snake was coiled up in her plexus.

Shortly after the dream of her mother's head Cecilia dreamt she was standing in front of an old-fashioned fishmonger's shop. All sorts of beautiful fish and other sea-foods were arranged in a circular pattern on the marble slab, but right at the back of the shop, half hidden yet wholly visible, a huge black constrictor snake was reared up on its tail. It seemed to reach higher than the roof of the shop and was swaying gently from side to side. The effect was extremely sinister, and when the dreamer dropped her eyes, unable to bear the sight any longer, it was only to find she was wearing a black snake round her waist as a belt. Its head hung down by her right knee and it was swaying to the same rhythm as the large serpent in the background. Cecilia felt too frightened to move and woke up. The identification with the great archetypal serpent is shown in the fact that the one round her waist was swaying to the same rhythm, so a difficult situation is indicated. Though luckily the dreamer only had one snake instead of Medusa's two, and its head was hanging down as if it would like to return to its native element, the earth.

The lovely fish on the slab represent the riches of the unconscious, and the circular pattern in which they were arranged suggests the order and harmony they could bring the dreamer, and also that she could impart to them. Right from the beginning of her analysis Cecilia did have very meaningful insights into the unconscious, by means of dreams, fantasies and, later on, active imagination. But none of them ever lasted any time at all. After a very few days the most meaningful inner experiences that should really have marked milestones on her analytic progress would just slip away as if they had never taken place, and she would be left without any benefit from them.

In reality snakes sway as a means of hypnotising their prey, so the swaying of both dream snakes shows how deeply Cecilia was under their baneful influence. The belt snake might be said to be the link on the personal level with the archetypal constrictor which was waiting to devour the positive fruits of the unconscious, the fish on the slab. In both this dream and the one of her mother's head Cecilia was too frightened to move; she was responding to Medusa's petrifying influence.

Snake venom is Medusa's own poison on the physical level and it is curious how similar its effects are to hers. The poison of all kinds of viper, the European snake, causes intravascular clotting if introduced rapidly into the circulation, while cobra venom induces paralysis of the tongue and larynx and is said to extinguish the functions of the various nerve centres of the cerebro-spinal system. (From their dealings with Egypt the Greeks would probably have known about cobras from very early times.) Clotting of the blood is the symbolic as well as actual solidification or petrification of the streams of psychic and physical life, while paralysis of the organs of speech well illustrates the very great difficulty experienced by the witch's victims in expressing themselves. Cecilia used to find it almost impossible at times to give a reasonable account of herself in analysis, because there was so little to describe, just one vast flood of misery without any interesting landmarks. There were times when she felt as if an external force was preventing her from speaking.

Paralysis, though terrible for the sufferer, is not highly dramatic. Both actually and symbolically it indicates being caught helpless in the rigidity of dense matter. It suggests what does not, rather than what does, happen. This was accurately reflected in Cecilia's life; her story was of things which did not happen, of disappointments and hopes deferred, rather than of tragic happenings. This nullity of life was accurately reflected in her remark that she could not want, but only want to want. This shows a really deadly lack of that desire which is one of the springs of life. The same kind of fate overtook the Argonaut Mopsus who, according to Ovid, was bitten by one of the serpents that were bred from the drops of blood that fell from Medusa's severed head when Perseus was flying from the scene of the killing with it. Morpus did not feel any great pain, but was straightaway overcome by a paralysing numbness. Needless to say he died of the bite.

Curiously, Cecilia never minded snakes at all although she had a violent phobia of earthworms. She dreamt of worms, she painted worms, they filled her with horror beyond expressing. Her reaction on seeing one would be of such fascinated horror she would be unable to tear herself away—she would become petrified into inaction. None of her efforts to understand the meaning of her phobia brought any relief, but after becoming aware of her Medusa problem Cecilia was told in active imagination that they stood for Medusa's snake hair and for total unconsciousness. After this the phobia simply faded away.

One very important landmark in her analysis, though we could neither of us make head or tail of it at the time, was when Cecilia had the truly horrifying experience of losing her soul. We are familiar with this hazard of primitive peoples, but do not really expect to have to undergo it ourselves. Cecilia did not know it was that, she simply felt 'as if she were her own corpse', as she phrased it. Not only was she dead, but the whole world around her was dead too, and with it all meaning and value. Her efforts to make a picture about it were unavailing, though she was well used to painting from the unconscious. All she could achieve this time were a few wisps of very pale grey writhing across the paper. We could neither of us see anything in them. She did not discover much more in active imagination; at first she was met by a brick wall. But after many hours of persevering, spread over many days, she elicited the information that *of course* she could not make a picture of how she felt, nor hope to talk to whatever was behind it, because the thing she was experiencing was the absolute evil behind all the manifestations of evil; it was the essential reality behind all the manifestations, the ultimate evil which could never be symbolised. This felt so absolutely true that Cecilia judged prudence the better part of valour and made no further efforts to contact whatever it might be. All she could be sure of afterwards was that the motive power behind the experience was feminine. After about six days she gradually began to feel human again.

Nine months to the week after this unusual experience, though she did not notice this significant time interval until much later, Cecilia began the decisive encounter of her whole analysis, when she first began to realise beyond any doubt that her problem was a serious witch-possession. This began with an active imagination in which she tried to find out about the worse than usual depression that was enveloping her. It turned out to be the witch, who boasted she was the residual dross left over from creation, that for which no use could ever be found. She claimed to be the hard core of unredeemable materialism, the nullity of life. Her strength was said to lie in her total passivity, she was the basic inertia that is always sucking all life back into itself. In the many talks Cecilia subsequently had with this figure the negative voice was usually through the mouth of a lesser witch, or occasionally of the animus, because the chief witch in the background was so inert she hardly ever spoke directly herself. This first talk turned into a fantasy in which Cecilia descended into a sinister and horrible underground town, all huge concrete box buildings and not one tree or blade of grass. She entered a building in which white-coated eunuchs were in charge of enormous steel filing cabinets containing endless punch-card records of love and emotion: how they worked, how long they worked, when they worked, and their intensity. Everything was there except the reality of those states. Presently she went into a room on a lower level, where she saw a magnificent man, larger than life, who had been ripped open across the shoulders and back of his neck. Smaller figures were engaged in pouring molten metal alloy into the gashes, the purpose being to 'metallify' him into a metal statue of himself, a modern technological version of Medusa's work of petrification. (This was two years before Cecilia identified her witch with the Gorgon.) When the metal was on the point of solidifying the man was stood up against a wall with his arms out in the attitude of crucifixion. An ancient witch-hag then murdered a tiny baby at his feet. Cecilia then summoned up her remaining courage and penetrated into an inner, windowless room where she sensed, though she could see nothing, an invisible female mass from which emanated all the other horrors of the place. The only other figures she saw were two prostitutes unsuccessfully wandering around in search of custom. Naturally they failed, since the only men present had been castrated.

The central figure of the fantasy, its power-house, is the invisible female mass in a windowless room. This is a significant detail, epitomising the cut-offness of the witch from everything symbolised by air. As with the classical Medusa here too the evil thing is hidden away in the background. Naturally the men were castrated—this is the effect of the witch both on men who come into contact with her and also on what might otherwise be a woman's creative animus. Here they symbolise Cecilia's purely intellectual understanding of the meaning of love; as the victim of a very serious witch possession how could it be otherwise? For of all the psychic figures the witch is the most utterly incapable of love. The lack of ability to love is also indicated in the two prostitute figures. Both animus and shadow figures being doubled, shows they are on the threshold of consciousness; as a result of the decisive encounter Cecilia gained some essential though painful insights into her own emotional shortcomings.

In a later talk with the unconscious Cecilia was told the metallified man was not just her own animus—he was far larger than life—but that he also represented the creative power of society that was being petrified by the materialistic attitude of current science and technology.

To be turned to stone is literally to become imbedded in the mother, matter most commonly having a feminine connotation. This was clearly stated by Cecilia some years previously, when she painted a series of three small spontaneous pictures, a sort of strip cartoon. In the first a young child was sitting on its mother's knee, in the second it was being absorbed back into her body, not orally but straight into her torso, in the third the mother was sitting looking very large and complacent, while of the child nothing was visible except for a small black animal-like head dimly showing through the mother's breast, and small black animal paws showing through her upper arms and thighs. Cecilia was told it would require psychic surgery to cut her out; at the time she had never heard of the child-eating witch Lamia who could, however, be made to regurgitate the child if she was caught and held fast. In his very learned book *Python* Professor Fontenrose makes an interesting comparison of the figures of Medusa and Lamia, showing how extremely similar they are. The image of the child-eating witch is a perfect picture, not only of the devouring parent, but also of the witch-dominated woman who unconsciously devours every new opportunity that life presents to her. Her own inner children, her new creative possibilities, find their way down her gullet with depressing regularity. This does not mean such women have to be outstandingly witchy themselves, what it does mean is that they seem to be in direct unconscious communication with what can best be termed the 'universal gullet', the throat of anti-life which is always waiting to devour whatever comes its way.

One of the interesting things about Medusa is her distant dwelling place. Its actual location is contradictory enough, being situated to the north, the south, the east and the west respectively, which is the same as saying it is everywhere and nowhere. It is, as Fontenrose points out, placed near each of the Greek paradises, which shows it is a pre-conscious condition. This is born out by Aeschylus' description of Kisthene, the Gorgons' home, in *Prometheus Bound*. It is ". . . towards the east/where the sun stalks in flame," a place where ". . . no ray of sun/ever looks down, nor moon by night". It is noteworthy that the land of eternal darkness should be so close to the sun, showing that in these far reaches of the soul the most decisive opposites of all, eternal darkness and perpetual light, are not so very far apart, presumably owing to the lack of any consciousness that knows they are opposites and which consequently would hold them apart (until they can be consciously brought together again by the acceptance of paradox). That Kisthene is right outside of time is shown by there being no light of sun or moon, for time is measured by the passage of the luminaries and where this does not take place there cannot be time, only duration, and neither can there be growth and change, which can only take place in time. Just as the positive paradise can be a death-dealing trap for those who seek to linger too long in its timeless peace, so equally its death-dealing counterpart, Kisthene, can become a source of regeneration to those, such as Perseus or Cecilia, who penetrate its horror of great darkness in order to gain some understanding of its central meaning.

Early in her analysis Cecilia started painting pictures, sometimes whole series of them, of absolutely desolate arid wasteland in which there was no other sign of life apart from her own small figure which might be shown either struggling painfully along or else collapsed and apparently on the point of death. She never had any inkling of the parallel to Kisthene, of which she had never heard. In one such picture, painted when she was really in despair, there appeared, quite without her conscious will, an enormous coal-black funnel leading down into unnameable depths of horror below. Appalled, Cecilia put in three little figures trying desperately and vainly to cling to the smooth side of the abyss, but her feeling of horror increased until it was borne in on her that this was not the way, and she added a fourth figure which was swallow-diving down into the depths, going willingly, whereupon her spirits rose and the despair abated. Her then analyst was horrified and said that on no account must she descend to that unknown region; which was quite possibly correct for then, but the picture, taken in conjunction with its effect on her, was certainly prophetic of the way she would have to go at a later date.

If Medusa's cave be taken as the entrance to the land of the dead, as indeed it was, and which was thought of as being below the earth's surface, then the funnel in the picture shows beyond doubt the direction Cecilia would have to take. She would have to go very near to death in her search. One version attributes a different dwelling to the Gorgons, saying they lived in Sarpedon, a rocky islet in Ocean Stream. This also stresses Medusa's antiquity for, in the *Iliad*, Ocean is spoken of as the forebear of the gods, which agrees with the reiterated claim of Cecilia's witch to be anterior to all manifestation, while the location in the all-embracing stream which surrounded the world conveys a sense of her ubiquitous power. Whether the Gorgons lived in a cave leading to the underworld or in the river dividing the world of the living from the archetypal world of the gods, it is either way a place of transition, a no-man's-land belonging to neither realm. This relates to a phenomenon I have noticed in other witch-influenced persons, as well as in Cecilia: where there is an overridingly strong witch-influence there is a feeling of belonging nowhere, of having no real roots anywhere. Such people really do seem to live in a state of suspension, a land of limbo between the worlds. This is not a psychotic symptom (as it might be in other cases) but an accurate response to the preponderant influence in their lives. It is all part and parcel of the total nullity symbolised by the witch. One of the most vital necessities with such people is to help them find meaningful roots in this world as well as trying to establish a connection with the creative levels of the unconscious.

In some versions of the story Medusa's power was said to reside in her eye or eyes; at times she had two, at others one. There is an Irish version of the Hansel and Gretel tale in which the witch is one-eyed. In what she subsequently said was the most terrifying experience of her first encounter with the witch, before she had identified her as Medusa, Cecilia had a vivid fantasy that she was in hell, quite literally the place of the damned. Hell took the form of a dubious suburb on the outskirts of an industrial town. It was night and badly lit and many doubtful looking characters were wandering around. The whole atmosphere was unspeakably horrible and worst of all was a café in which Cecilia found herself. A waitress brought her a cup of coffee she had not ordered. This woman seemed not to have any face, but on the left side of her abdomen she had a terrifying 'eye', a bright round disk of light, rather like a car's main beam. This eye glared at Cecilia in a way that seemed to see right through her and yet to be quite blind at the same time. Nothing could convey a clearer picture of total unconsciousness than an eye that glares but cannot see, cannot register what it beholds. Cecilia did not drink the coffee, which was probably just as well since partaking of food or drink in the other world ensures that the visitor will never be able to leave it, the best known instance being of Persephone who, by reason of the pomegranate seeds she ate while there, had to return to Hades for part of every year.

Concerning Perseus' equipment for his task, the best known is the

mirror shield given him by Athene. Greek shields were round, so
here we have a totality symbol as the essential means for the
accomplishment of the deed. According to Pausanias shields were
first used in the war between the twin brothers Akrisios and Proteus,
Perseus' grandfather and great-uncle respectively. When the Self is
symbolised by an inanimate man-made object such as a shield this
must be used in a manner consonant with its own nature, if its
intervention is to prove effective; it is dependent for its efficacy on
the proper attitude of the ego. As a weapon of war, albeit a defensive
one, the shield shows that strength and courage are essential
requirements. Here the mirror shield acts as the mediating element
between ego and archetype; it both protects from and establishes
connection with the witch, for it must not be forgotten that it works
both ways: whatever an observer can see in a mirror can also see him
in it. It is thus the place where each side can become conscious of the
other. As a Self symbol it must contain every aspect of the whole. It is
natural it should be Athene, the archetype of developing
consciousness, who gives the shield, for anyone who has to approach
that type of witch needs sufficient consciousness not to be sucked
down by her.

Once, after things had improved a great deal, Cecilia had a feeling
the witch was gaining strength again, so she painted a picture which
she hoped would mollify her persecutrix. She started off, quite
intentionally, by placing an offering in front of the witch who was
completely non-human with huge tentacles. The offering, which
Cecilia had intended should be a honey cake, one of the traditional
offerings to the underworldly powers, turned instead into three
things two of which were a pair of eyeballs. The witch, who appeared
to be blind, hovered her tentacles over them, and Cecilia feared she
might use them to see her, Cecilia, with, for she had included herself
in the picture. She therefore put the third offering, which had
turned into a small silver mirror, into the hand of her own pictured
image, where it was held between herself and the witch, with the
reflecting side facing the latter. The picture combines the motifs of
the independent eyes, like those sometimes attributed to Medusa,
and of the mirror. Being of silver suggests that Cecilia needed to
develop her own feminine nature more, as a safeguard against the
witch. Though it is also noteworthy that in the picture she was
putting it to a masculine use, as a shield, whereas in the legend
Perseus had to use his shield as a mirror, a feminine article. Each sex
must bring in something of the contrasexual element, otherwise the
personality is not whole enough to achieve the task.

After she had recovered from her first witch-encounter Cecilia dreamt she was shown quite an ordinary wall mirror by another woman, who then lifted it up, revealing another identical mirror beneath it, except that the second one was of gold-coloured glass so that everything was reflected golden-yellow. At first the dreamer saw her own face, but this then disappeared, and coming up from the depths of the mirror, as if from a very deep pool of water, there appeared a golden blob which slowly materialised into a white grinning skull which seemed almost to be alive and to possess an active malignancy. Cecilia found it horrible and was overcome by a sense of unutterable evil. The other woman then replaced the original mirror and Cecilia woke up. The golden colour and the death's head do seem very contradictory in meaning. The juxtaposition suggests that for Cecilia the greatest boon the positive aspect of the unconscious, symbolised twice over, by both mirror and water, could confer would be further insight into her problem. The skull is the basic form of the gorgoneion, that which lies behind the various modifications which appear in the head itself. She clearly has to reach to the bare bones, the very roots, of the problem. Since the image appeared in a mirror and her own face showed first, it refers to the painful necessity of accepting her own direct connection with the malign skull. But it must not be taken as only the personal shadow, because it came up from such depths of water; it is therefore contaminated from the collective unconscious.

As to the invisibility-conferring Helmet of Hades, Hades was the ruler of the underworld, the abode of the dead, which was known as the House of Hades. But he is not to be equated with the Christian Devil, the tormentor of evil-doers, which office belonged to the Erinyes and other grim figures. Neither is the House of Hades analogous to the Christian Hell; Tartaros was the abode of the damned. Hades was one of the ruling triad of gods, whose name means "The Invisible". When Perseus donned the helmet he was putting himself under the protection and into the power of Hades; he became as one dead, for they too are invisible. Medusa is an archetypal figure and it may well be asked how it is possible to become invisible to an archetype. The nearest I can get is to the idea of inner stillness, of quieting the innumerable ego thoughts and desires and fears that make such an unnecessary chatter. True stillness, the "Be still and know that I am God" of the Psalmist, suggests setting aside the ego's chatter and getting as close as possible to one's true reality, and this is certainly a needful state if any approach to the basic witch is to be made. On the reality level, if one can keep absolutely still, wild animals, which symbolically represent something of the divine as well as of the instincts, may approach quite close, but one movement and they are off. The helmet of invisibility can also work very negatively. Cecilia once had a dream that a man she was extremely fond of invited her out to a meal. Delighted, she went to a mirror to tidy up and was thunderstruck to see she was wearing a metal helmet that reached right down to her shoulders and had not even got a slit for eyes, nose, mouth or ears. No image could convey more clearly how completely the dreamer was enclosed in her problem nor how inhibited she must be in the matter of self-expression. In the dream she thought she looked like a man from Mars.

The obvious interpretation is of a severe animus-possession, especially in view of the dreamer likening herself to a man from Mars; more particularly so in that at the time of the dream all Cecilia's problems were attributed to her animus. A closer look at the dream helmet casts severe doubts on its meaning as an instrument of animus oppression, however. The absence of a mouth aperture is a strong contra-indication for this interpretation. The animus is the lord of words and needs the woman's capacity for speech in order to express himself, whereas it is the witch who keeps her victims silent. Mention has already been made of Cecilia's problem in analysis, when she sometimes felt as if a physical force were preventing her from speaking. Since a helmet is an almost exclusively masculine accoutrement it looks more as if both she and he were doomed to silence. This is not to say that Cecilia did not have an animus problem; of course she did, but it was secondary to the silent witch. It is possible the image also refers to the strong animus projection she was carrying at the time; as already mentioned her troubles were all attributed to him. If a person's problem is persistently misunderstood and attributed to the wrong source this could have a very separating effect on the sufferer. Had the dream helmet had a mouth aperture Cecilia would not have experienced the almost insuperable difficulty she had in expressing animus affect. Even when she/he was longing to rage she suffered from an even stronger inhibition which forced her to stifle the rage, to her own extreme discomfort. Again the possessive witch is refusing to part with even a negative affect! This stifling of affect was naturally attributed to Cecilia's 'sulky' disposition and she was blamed for not letting the negative rip and for the consequent damming up of negative emotions which she found almost impossible to discharge.

The reason Cecilia was only able to respond to the negative and separative effect of the helmet was probably because at the time of the dream she was quite frantic and hopeless, running round in small circles of despair, and therefore quite unable to achieve true stillness. Early in her first analysis Cecilia dreamt of a woman who went everywhere accompanied by her small daughter whose whole face was covered in a white plaster cast. The mask had tiny slits for eyes and nostrils, but no opening for the mouth. Because the eyeholes were so tiny and set at the wrong angle the child could not see the ground at her feet and had to be led everywhere by her mother. The whiteness of the plaster shows the far too white attitude imposed on the child by her Theosophist mother, and being unable to see the ground at her feet hints at the lack of roots in this world which has already been mentioned as one of the problems of the witch-dominated person. In the dream the mother is the mediator of reality—the ground at her feet—for the child, with the inevitable distortion which occurs when reality is apprehended through another consciousness, and not directly. This dream is the forerunner of the helmet one, although separated by many years. In some ways the situation has deteriorated, for in the later dream there are no apertures of any kind in the helmet. It would be inevitable that if the condition of the first dream was not dealt with in a positive manner it would get worse. An effort was made at the time; her analyst suggested she fantasise taking off the child's mask. This she tried to do, when, to her horror, just as she was gently inserting her fingers round its edge, the whole mask came away, bringing all the skin of the child's face with it, so that nothing was left but a bleeding pulp. The shock jerked Cecilia right out of the fantasy, which had been extremely real. A slower approach was needed. The positive aspect of the helmet dream compared to the earlier one is that now the dreamer wears the helmet herself and is her actual age. The problem has reached that much closer to consciousness, which it could only do when the unconscious pressure (the lack of apertures in the helmet) has become so intolerable that it forces its way through into consciousness.

To turn to the kibisis, the wallet in which the severed head was to be carried away: fairy tales are full of magic containers out of which anything from food to soldiers may be summoned, and there is at least one tale of a knapsack into which things may be wished. The bag given to Perseus is, however, the only one of which I have knowledge that was destined to contain just one specific object. It was a very necessary piece of equipment, considering that the head retained its deadly property even after decapitation. It symbolises the ability to contain a vital experience; the more profound an experience, the more essential that it should be contained, both in order that its full benefit be retained and also that others should not be injured by it. There is often a strong temptation to talk inadvisedly about an impressive archetypal experience, partly from a need to dissipate its powerful mana, but also frequently out of sheer boastfulness. This wrong attitude towards an archetypal event can result in the subject losing whatever meaning it originally had for him. It can also prove dangerous to others who may be less well equipped to face such matters, even at second hand. Mention has been made of the Argonaut Mopsus who died of the bite of one of the serpents bred from Medusa's blood. No mention is made of the kibisis in this version; the happening was broadcast in a heedless manner, with disastrous results.

Some time after Cecilia had realised the nature of her persecutrix she dreamt she was with a young couple she knew in reality. They came to a wayside stall where tourist trash was on sale. The young woman wished to buy a semi-transparent white plastic bag. The mother and daughter who owned the stall said that *if* she bought it she would either die or fade away. At that moment she became as white as the bag and lost her human identity, becoming like a wraith, with no substance or reality. The mother and daughter then seized her and ran off with her. The dreamer now knew they were witches and told the girl's husband they must get her back at all costs, though he seemed to be taking his wife's abduction extremely calmly. Somehow they got hold of the girl, and Cecilia said they must string her up from a tree, as though she were going to be hanged, with only her toes touching the ground. This would frighten her into returning into her body. Under the dreamer's initiative they were looking for a suitable tree with a branch of the right height, when she woke up. The witch element makes it clear that the plastic bag is a debased kibisis. The girl who wanted it was years younger than Cecilia and not overburdened with brains. She is therefore an immature shadow who no longer takes the threat of the head seriously enough, as if it could be contained in a man-made substance. This would equate with thinking the whole problem could be controlled by consciousness. But as soon as the witch threat is taken too lightly it becomes threatening again. A positive development is that the witches said that *if* she took the bag she would suffer, as if there was now an element in them that did not necessarily desire this outcome. The strange motif of stringing the girl up so that only her toes touched the gound suggests the need for greater tension, as if Cecilia had become too slack in her attitude, or at least her shadow had. The toes only just touching the ground also diminishes contact with the chthonic element, in this case the materialism of the witch, to a minimum. The most striking message of the dream is the passivity of the man, the animus figure. Cecilia described him as being rather an aggressive personality in reality, who would brook no interference in his affairs; he was also very fond of his wife and had she really been abducted he would not have waited for the police before going after her. In the dream he is entirely passive, only acting under the dreamer's instructions. Cecilia admitted she had been feeling rather browned-off with all the work on the witch, and wishing an animus figure could come and do some of it for her. The dream shows her that he cannot. What is good about the dream, in spite of its inconclusive outcome, is the way the dreamer, the dream ego, took the initiative. She knew what had to be done and tried to do it.

Although Cecilia had a fair proportion of dreams about shoes she never had any of winged ones and, as far as I know, only once dreamt of being in the air. Although that dream is relevant to our study it is very long and complicated and would take too long to discuss here. I only mention it to keep the record accurate. Perseus flying to the killing probably indicates the need to approach the witch from the element opposed to her own materialism.

The only dream Cecilia ever had connected with the sickle is the one I mentioned first, of the dagger-crucifix which saved her life.

Since I have spoken so much of the unconsciousness of the witch let me conclude by relating two out of the many dreams Cecilia had which dealt with the subject. In one she was sitting on the ground in a circle with many other women. She then left the circle and her mother was with her. To her horror her mother suddenly leant over her and prised open her jaws, and injected a paralysing fluid behind her tongue. It all happened so quickly she was unable to protect herself. She tried to protest in anger, but the drug took immediate effect and she became unconscious, although still dimly aware of what was happening. Sitting on the ground indicates a close connection with the earth, here to be equated with the life-giving mother, while the circle is always a protective formation as well as being a totality symbol. The moment the dreamer breaks this protective constellation she falls victim to the witch working through her mother.

In another dream she was sitting in a café patronised by very dubious looking customers. To her great relief a decent looking couple came in and sat at her table; they all three talked together. Then she saw an old woman creep up behind the couple and pour something into their coffee. Before Cecilia could utter a word of warning they had both drunk the stuff and immediately fell forward, completely unconscious. The dreamer was then seized and bound and laid on the ground, preparatory to being dispatched. She was unable to utter a sound until the moment her body touched the ground, when she was able to scream and woke to the sound of her own cries.

Once again Cecilia had been to naïve; instead of warning the others at once, she waited until it was too late. The sight of the old woman creeping up should have been enough to put her on her guard. The couple represent quite positively intentioned, but not powerful, aspects of the shadow and animus. With all the work Cecilia had consciously done on the witch the responsibility for action against her has quite definitely shifted over to consciousness, to the dream ego; the initiative lies with Cecilia, which means greater vigilance than she showed in the dream. Coffee is the stimulating drink which induces wakefulness, so it is appropriate that it is precisely this beverage that was drugged to induce unconsciousness. Just as in the previous dream Cecilia fell into her mother's negative power the moment she rose from the ground, so there it is contact with the ground that enables her to scream, to break the spell. One must be grounded in reality in order to resist the witch.

Over the years Cecilia had had dreams which seemed to confirm her growing feeling she should become an analyst herself, so I will end by quoting one which was, to my mind, the final confirmation that this was the right course. It ran: "There were many people, and a terrible woman was working for the death of all of them. It was very subtle; she cast a mysterious influence over certain places, and if the people went and stood on those places they would die. I seemed to be guiding the group. We were managing to escape when I suddenly realised the spot where we were now standing was one of the dangerous ones. I told everyone to get out quickly and had the feeling we had all reached safety, when I woke up." The dream can be interpreted subjectively, with the people standing for Cecilia's inner figures, or objectively when they would refer to actual people whom she would be in a position to help. What matters is that the dreamer is able to detect the witch in her absence and to take the requisite action.

NOTES

1. Lecture given to the Analytical Psychology Club, London, on 16th December, 1976.

Opposites and the Healing Power of Symbols[1]

By Molly Tuby

MOLLY TUBY *is a member of the International Association for Analytical Psychology. She is a past chairman of the Guild of Pastoral Psychology and current chairman of the Analytical Psychology Club, London. She was the editor of* Harvest *for nine years. She practises in London. She is also an accomplished cook and contributed a chapter towards the book* A Taste of Heaven!

Some time ago, I promised to give a talk on the opposites. However hard I tried, I was unable to settle on the way I would treat the subject. The day of the lecture was drawing alarmingly close, and after a series of unforeseen interruptions, I wondered if something was badly out of gear and if I would do better to keep still and not go against fate. I was so puzzled that I threw an *I Ching*. In this Chinese *Book of Changes* we are told that there are times of Increase and times of Decrease; times of Progress and times of Retreat. We are advised to heed the time of darkening of the light and warned when "it is not well to strive upward, but is well to remain below." I was fully prepared to abide by the oracle. Well, what came up was Hexagram 27 where the commentary reads: "When things are held fast, there is provision of nourishment. Hence there follows the Hexagram of Corners of the Mouth", made up of the trigrams Ken, the Mountain, or Keeping Still, and Chen, Thunder, or the Arousing. "An image," it adds, "of providing nourishment through *movement* and *tranquillity*".

This paradox brought me at once to the heart of what I wanted to express: the movement of the ego, bound by space and time, and tranquillity of that which is unchanging and outside the categories which govern our conscious everyday life.

Further on, I read in a lighter vein: "From the hexagram as a whole, as representing an open mouth, are derived the movements of the mouth: speech and the taking in of food." This pleased me much because I have always been partial to speech and food, especially when they are combined!

The *I Ching* speaks on many levels. Its profound wisdom is imparted in poetic images which go straight to the heart and appeal to the imagination at the same time helping to see clearly and often concretely what is cut off or only confusedly apprehended. In other words, feeling and thinking, intuition and the reality function, which within themselves form two irreconcilable pairs, were transcended by the symbolic meaning of the message. I was then able to extract from the profusion of half-perceived ideas, which were swamping me, some definite themes for my reflections on the opposites; from the unconscious chaos, order emerged and I decided to concentrate on certain important stages of human growth and development.

When I read that "words are a movement going from within outward" and that "eating and drinking are movements from without inward", I thought of energy flowing towards objects in the outer world and energy flowing into objects of the inner world. I understood that the wholeness of this open mouth was concerned, among other things, with bringing together those two opposing directions of extraversion and introversion which divide man from man and man from himself, unless he finds a creative balance between their dynamic interplay.

The constant polarity between the ego and the unconscious goes on all through life; for a positive unfolding of the personality, the ego has to become aware of many existing opposites: the duality between light and dark; the coming to terms with the masculine and the feminine principles within; the making conscious of the attitudinal and functional types; and finally, the relationship between instinct and spirit.

In this paper, I would like to look at a few traditional attitudes in the past, then at some spontaneous ways of coping—or not coping—with the problem of the opposites in our present day. After that, I shall try to show how the opposites in the psyche, and their union, become more and more central for Jung, and how he approached this problem by putting, as he so modestly said, old truths into modern words. In the light of his discoveries, I shall try to convey my personal reflections on the particular sets of opposites I had so much trouble in selecting, and on the emergence of the healing symbol.

Traditional Approaches

We live in a world of opposites, and from time immemorial

religions and philosophies have attempted to find ways by which their resolution can be achieved.

According to Chinese teaching particularly concerned with this problem, the whole Cosmos obeys the law of complementarity between the two primal opposites of Yin and Yang, the male and female principles. The two are combined in the T'ai Chi, which is completion. But Yin has the seed of Yang in it and Yang has the seed of Yin, and they are perpetually turning into each other. The Chinese way is based on recognising and accepting these contradictions, putting up with them somehow, so as to be in harmony with the ever-changing cosmic forces; a sort of inaction, allowing the creative activity of the Universe to operate. It is the Middle Way, or Tao.

The Indian's approach is different: he seeks to liberate himself from the opposites by achieving *nirvandva* (free from the two). He believes in a power within, the Atman, which can bring deliverance but is reached by the extinction of all desires: *neti-neti* (not this, not that); a state wherein he is untouched by the opposites of either pleasure or pain.

The people of the West have never been so consciously aware of the problem of the opposites as have those of the East. Nevertheless, there have always been philosophers who have referred to it, but purely intellectual attempts are bound to fail. In the West, it is Christianity which took up the problem with all its crucial implications. The anguished dilemma that seems to ring through the centuries is that of body and spirit, stemming from original sin. Redemption can only come about through the saving power and love of Christ who willingly suffered crucifixion. On the personal level, surely this means an acceptance of Calvary, which is a holding of unbearable conflicts; and it is through death of a part of ourselves on our inner cross that resurrection can take place: born from the greatest pain we can possibly endure consciously, a strange and miraculous renewal can come about.

I have reminded you very briefly of varying religious attitudes to show that the experience and knowledge stemming from the world's highest teachings seem to have one point in common: whether the path is through love, selflessness or the middle way, the only solution for man faced with conflict is his willing surrender to a power greater than himself. And this, we know, is the key not only to holiness for the saints and the mystics, to creation for the poets and the artists, but the way to wholeness and healing for all human beings. On the other hand, if we speak of surrender we must have something to surrender, so our first task is to ensure that the ego is free and strong enough to undertake a holding of the opposites which in turn may lead to its death and rebirth on a more spiritual level.

Modern Ways of Coping

Today, when few people are satisfactorily contained in a traditional religion, the fundamental contradictions and conflicts of life are dealt with in ways which are rather destructive to the individual. Of course there are people with good instincts who grow and develop spontaneously, but there are others who by ignoring the real issues pretend the problem doesn't exist, which is essentially an escape from facing up to life. These are usually the people who sneer at any hint of a search for meaning through art or prayer or an individual way of life. They are the negative, uncreative ones whose joys and griefs do not quite reach down into their guts. They remain on the surface. Bored and frustrated, they can't grow unless some saving neurosis pulls them out of the morass. They tend to belong to the over-rational, materialistic category of people. Not always, though. There are other ways of running away.

I remember an endearing old lady, a spinster, who lived for her cat and her flowers, and looked at the world with frightened blue eyes, saying she wondered why anybody was afraid of death. *She* wasn't. Her dead father visited her regularly and told her not to be afraid; that everything was the same on the other side—exactly the same; nothing would change; even her little garden would be there . . . the Garden of Eden she had never been able to leave . . .

Another very common way of dealing with contradictions is to identify with a cause outside and project the conflicting element on to the "enemy". Unfortunately, we have all too many examples around us. It would seem that our time is particularly vicious in its rejection of the middle way, with people fanatically clinging to one point of view and arriving at insoluble dichotomies in the social and political spheres.

An equally frequent mode of reaction is to swing from one extreme to the other. On a collective level, we can observe that the course of history has always been governed by the law of enantiodromia, or swing to the opposite: a classical age succeeds a romantic one; an authoritarian regime follows a liberal one, and so on. On the personal level, the people who swing from one extreme to the other are those with weak egos, who pick up the possibilities and potentialities of every given situation, throwing themselves in, body and soul, or who are incapable of coming to any decision. They are driven, like leaves in the wind, and finally feel utterly dissatisfied, with a sense of failure and a taste of ashes in their mouths for all the abortive attempts at living, loving and creating. If this goes too far, they come to a standstill, like Buridan's ass who starved to death between two equally appetizing bundles of hay because he couldn't make up his mind.

This is how I made my *entrée* into the world of psychology, at a time when I was totally paralyzed by conflict. Basically, I belong to the Buridan type as was demonstrated by my block about the lecture.

I first arrived in Zürich for rather dubious reasons having little to do with Jung. Psychologically, I was at the end of my tether, so much so that when in a last gasp of outside effort I was going to start yet another something-or-other, I was stopped dead in my tracks by a fit of anxiety which was so acute that I couldn't leave my room. An analyst was brought to see me, and after an hour and a half's conversation the anxiety vanished and I was committed to the analytical way for life! This was quite extraordinary and proved to me both the reality of the psyche and its purposiveness.

During that first session I explained to the analyst why, for me, there was no solution but death. I drew a circle which I divided into eight equal parts; four at the top, and four at the bottom. And I explained that each section of the circle was one possibility of life for me: for example, I wanted to be a great actress, expressing the most beautiful poetry in the world. But on the opposite side of the circle was expressed an equally compelling urge . . . to be a cook. I could so easily become a nun. Or, equally easily, a courtesan, and so on. What made matters worse was that the four on top of the circle were lofty and spiritual and the four below were earthy and dark, so the poor little point in the middle was torn between two forces that could never meet. In those days I had no knowledge of symbolism: I had no idea that the circle could express the Hermetic vessel of transformation; that the quaternio of opposites coincided with the usual quaternary structure of the mandala; nor that the point often symbolized a mysterious creative centre in nature . . .

. . . This primordial image, or archetype, of unity was activated in the unconscious to compensate the distress and confusion in consciousness.

When I told my analyst that I would *have* to choose either one way or the other he made a statement which turned the tide. He said: "Or, you could take a third course: you could hold the opposites . . . ". I didn't understand. How could I? But I was stirred in a way I had never been before and I knew somehow that it was the beginning of a course I had always known. In the storm of inner turmoil I had experienced, at the same time, a brief moment of perfect tranquillity, which was the first fleeting awareness of the beneficial effect of holding contraries in consciousness.

Now, what was the part of me which heard and understood the message which the ego, certainly, had not grasped? I have come to the conclusion that very often in the darkness of the inner journey we catch a glimpse of something we half recognize, which fills us with hope and faith, and then we lose it; but it gives us the courage to go on until we find it again and are able to keep it. With growing self-awareness a shift takes place from an alienated ego-bound position to a deeper center of gravity, rooted in areas reaching far beyond repressed personal elements into those regions of the psyche which are timeless and universal.

It is often at the moment of relinquishing that we become aware that the wilful ego, making blind and collective demands as well as legitimate ones is only one of the protagonists in a dialogue with another important part of ourselves—a part which is ready to accept responsibility for our fate, whatever that may be. It is this paradox which brings food to the soul and turns the sterile "neurosis" into a genuine sacrifice which enriches and transforms.

Jung and Alchemy

When Jung realized that certain fantasy or dream images could not possibly be explained by individual experience, he postulated the concept of a collective psychic substratum which he called the collective unconscious. Later on, it was *The Secret of the Golden Flower*, a Taoist text of Chinese yoga and alchemy which lead him to explore the field of medieval alchemy and to find in it the connecting link between gnosticism and the processes of the collective unconscious observable today in modern man. From this Jung evolved his concept of a true centre of the psyche, including conscious and unconscious, which he called the self, opposed to the ego, which is the centre of consciousness. This centre is surrounded by a periphery containing everything and is itself a generator of energy. This energy is the source of an almost irresistible urge to become what one is, not what one would like to be, but what one is really. That is the individuation process and it proceeds from the self. The stages it follows are comparable to the stages of the *opus alchemicum*. Jung has developed these parallels in several of his volumes. In *Mysterium Coniunctionis*, his most exciting book, he summarizes the whole idea in the following lines:

> Today we can see how effectively alchemy prepares the ground for the psychology of the unconscious, firstly by leaving behind, in its treasury of symbols, illustrative material of the utmost value for modern interpretations in this field, and secondly by indicating symbolic procedures for synthesis which we can rediscover in the dreams of our patients. We can see today that the entire alchemical procedures for uniting the opposites could just as well represent the individuation process of a single individual.

The synthesis Jung refers to here is the relationship of the ego to the contents of the collective unconscious, to those visions which the alchemists were projecting onto the metals they were working with. This synthesis occurs at a stage of development when the integration of the personal unconscious has taken place. The transpersonal side of the process would have no meaning if there were not a strong and liberated ego to experience it, for, as the old alchemists used to say: "Only separate things can unite." The stage where synthesis begins is individuation proper, which may lead to the union of the ego with the self, experienced as enlightenment: Tao, Samadhi, Satori, or union with God for the Jewish and Christian mystic.

It is quite impossible to give even a succinct description of alchemy now, but there are a few points I would like to stress:

First, the purpose of the operation which was to transmute base metals into gold—gold that was not gold—in an attempt to transform the darkest and vilest into the highest value; an operation which the alchemists saw, literally, as being brought about by the spirit Mercurius; Mercurius duplex; the principle by which the lower and material is transformed into the higher and spiritual, and vice versa; the trickster; the animal spirit; the principle of life which effects the union of masculine and feminine; the spirit which quickens and brings about the union of opposites; the arcane substance; psychologically, the collective unconscious.

Secondly, to carry out the transformation it was necessary to make the stone, or lapis, which was also the tincture and the elixir of life; in Jungian terms, all symbols of the self as awareness of the wholeness of man, and also the archetype of the Redeemer.

Thirdly, the force that set the whole thing in motion, the central principle at work, the one which effected the change and brought about fulfilment, was the interplay of opposites, with no end of manner in which the various pairs were experienced: dog and bitch; sun and moon; fire and water; red sulphur and silver mercury, etc., etc. The problem of opposites in the world has always been expressed by the symbol of male and female. The object of the *opus* was to achieve the uniting of a succession of opposites culminating in the *hieros-gamos,* or royal marriage out of which was born the paradoxical *Rebis,* the Hermaphrodite, both male and female, and fruit of the mysterious *Coniunctio Oppositorum.* And to make the paradox even more difficult to understand, the Hermaphrodite was also the starting point of the *opus.* The supreme work was man's experience of being united with the whole world: the eternal ground of all empirical being, the assumption on which alchemy is based being the unity of all things. And this is very exciting. Alchemy is a protest against dualism. Alchemy asserts the unity of matter and the possibility of transmuting matter into spirit and spirit into matter. The transformation of the *prima materia* is undertaken so that the spirit imprisoned in it shall be set free and, as the world is one, as Microcosm and Macrocosm mirror each other, what happens on one level happens with the planets; what happens with the planets happens with man; man as body is also matter, and if the operation on matter is successful, man himself will be purified and redeemed.

Looked at from the deterministic point of view of chemistry, all this is nonsense. But what the alchemists were really trying to do was to solve a divine mystery. In our language, they were concerned with the relation of the unconscious with inorganic matter and with the unitary psychophysical reality which may be underlying both, as described by Jung. I am thinking, for example, of the much quoted vision of Kekule, the physicist, in which a snake grasping its own tale was whirling before his eyes and where this archetypal image of the Uroboros at the same time described the structure of the benzine ring. As time goes by, the discoveries in the physical sciences, especially in terms of energy, seem to support Jung's bold hypothesis. Based on this hypothesis, the insoluble controversies about determinism and indeterminism could be transcended by bringing in a third principle, that of synchronicity. This far-reaching concept is the one which rules the *Book of Changes,* the oldest alchemical text we know: the *I Ching.* In the forward to *Aurora Consurgens,* an alchemical treatise attributed to Thomas Aquinas, Marie-Louise von Franz writes:

The time may not be too far off when physics and depth psychology will really be able to join hands, and only then will the full significance of Jung's rediscovery of alchemy be appreciated.

Is it not possible that, like the mystics and some great artists, the alchemists had an intuitive vision into the truths to be established later by the scientists? Their casual explanations were naïve, but their knowledge was real.

Let us now turn to the analytical work: it involves a dialogue between two human beings which is a psychological relationship of a very special kind, based on the transference and counter-transference, the archetypal aspects of which are clearly recognisable in the alchemical symbols. The adept used chemical substances as a painter uses colours to express the images of his fancy and these visions represent the individuation process as can be observed in dreams today. But before coming to the dreamwork, concerning opposites and the healing symbol, let me first define as best I can, what I mean by 'healing', and what I mean by a 'symbol'.

Healing

By 'healing' I do not necessarily mean a cure, nor the elimination of symptoms. I mean something which has more to do with a subjective process, difficult to describe because, by its very nature, it is irrational, totally individual, and yet linked to a timeless and universal experience. By helping a person to understand what the unconscious is saying, and by encouraging him, or her, either to integrate this knowledge into the ego, or relate to the unintegratable, and accept it, the therapist hopes to promote growth according to that particular person's own inner laws, thus allowing the unfolding of the total personality. Neurotic symptoms may, or may not, disappear in the process. One hopes that they will: pain and frustration are never welcome. But to get rid of them is not really the goal:

1.   So often an analysis is terminated with the analysand declaring that the experience was unique and well worthwhile; he is feeling greatly enriched, and is able to look at his symptom in a completely different light. But the symptom there still is . . .

2.   Conversely, a patient may lose all pathalogical manifestations pretty quickly, and yet feel that the work has only just begun. He wants to go on: it is something else he is looking for.

3.   And, of course, there are those numerous men and women – I am almost tempted to say those numerous boys and girls – who know, confusedly, from the start, that there *is* something they are looking for. They don't know what it is, but they do know that their discontent stems from within themselves and that they are yearning

for an inner journey for which they need a guide.

The insights gained through therapy usually lead to a growing awareness of the relative position of the ego. The 'I' which is the centre of consciousness, whilst being freed from many unconscious identifications and projections, emerges stronger, less insecure, but more modest, so to say. It knows itself better, but it also knows that it is not the sole master in the psychic house. Of course, the patient always knew this, since compulsions, obsessions, anxiety or depression were constantly reminding him of the ineffectualness of his will-power.

The error lies in believing that one *ought* to be totally free to obey the dictates of the ego without taking into account the demands of the unconscious. In such a situation, the unconscious protests. The symptom calls attention to other forces, and only a change in attitude can bring about the ability to live life to the full. One's own, individual life, to the full. If we have the courage to accept our limitations and to acknowledge the inner gods, or universal, age-old archetypal forces within ourselves, then we live our fate, not crawling along grudgingly, but going with it, and more creatively. This is a difficult choice to make, and one which explains, perhaps, what Jung meant when he declared that ultimately, all neuroses are the non-resolution of a religious problem. Becoming conscious of one's individual fate, and going with it, is another way of describing the Jungian concept of individuation, a process which sometimes needs to be consciously encouraged by establishing a dialogue between the ego and the deeper layers of the unconscious. In this process, the emergence of symbols is of crucial importance.

We can perhaps define healing as a dynamic happening related to a deep understanding of the role of suffering; an acceptance to be what one is, totally: whole, rather than striving towards an image of perfection; and, ultimately, an awareness of, and a relatedness to, a power greater than ourselves. In other words, healing is discovering the meaning of our own life, and our place in the universe, not as a philosophical concept, but as an existential experience of inestimable value—the pearl of great price, hidden in the dunghill of unconsciousness, and pride.

Humility towards the powers within, and respect for the conscious ego which is responsible for receiving and interpreting the messages coming from the unconscious, are qualities which both analyst and analysand must cultivate. Jung thought that no therapist could lead his patients further than he had gone himself. I would like to put it slightly differently and suggest that no therapist can help his patient on the inner journey unless he himself is continuously grappling with his own unconscious material. The theme of the wounded healer is universal, and eternally valid. It is archetypal. From the most primitive shaman, to the Greek god Asklepios; from the healing heroes in the earliest ages of humanity, to Christ the Redeemer, it is through some divine injury that healing of man takes place. This mythological motif is no doubt behind the modern requirement that every analyst should undergo analysis, which I suspect is useful only in so far as the therapist discovers his own hidden wound out of which is constellated the healing power of the patient. It is as if the relationship between the analyst and the analysand were the vessel in which the healing symbols could be born. The greatest error a therapist can commit is to believe that he himself is the holder of the power to heal.

To illustrate this, I would like to tell you a dream, published by Dr. Jolande Jacobi. It is the dream of a brilliant French doctor, aged 35, who, although emotionally stultified and sick, possessed outstanding intellectual ability which led him to believe that when his patients got well, it was due to his own will and skill. . . . However, through an archetypal dream, his unconscious corrected and compensated the one-sidedness of his conscious mind which was badly threatening his psychic balance.

This was the dream:

The dreamer is sitting on a stone bench in an underground cave where the ceiling and walls are covered with stones that sparkle like jewels. He is dressed in an ordinary modern suit. Behind him, but a little higher, is sitting a noble priestly figure in long white robes.

A girl, in poor hospital clothes, is led in, to a bench in front of the dreamer. She is in a catatonic state, completely inaccessible.

The dreamer speaks to her very gently, and gradually she comes out of her stupor and looks at him.

The transformation continues: she takes on fairy-tale qualities and dances away like an elf.

Now, I quote the dreamer himself:

"All the while the high priest sat motionless behind me on his raised chair, and I knew that it was he who had cured the girl by his mana-influence.

The dream left me with a feeling of profound security and confidence in the figure of this man. It was he who had the healing power that had passed through me."

The dream speaks for itself: it is not the dreamer's ego that cures, but the power 'standing behind' him and 'passing through' him. Healing comes from the archetype of the spirit, appearing in the form of the wise and priestly figure (who dwells, somewhere, in each one of us). And if the dreamer truly accepts this corrective, then the feminine aspect of his psyche (which was sick and rigid) will come to life again, and his paralysed creative gift will be restored. Imagination allied to intellectual ability will no doubt make him a greater doctor, because a more complete person.

It has been suggested (by Prof. C. A. Meier, of Zürich) that the model for modern psychotherapy may lie in the ancient rites of incubation performed in the temple of Asklepios at Epidaurus, in Greece, and in various other places in the ancient world. There are certainly some significant parallels. First of all, only those *summoned* by the god (the god of healing, Asklepios) were allowed to take part in the initiation rites.

In a roundabout and very painful way, beginning an analysis *is* a sort of call, a summons. Writing of modern man, Jung says: "Anyone with a vocation hears the voice of the inner man: he is *called*."

As I suggested earlier, when the inner man cannot make himself heard, a neurosis develops, forcing the individual to change course and be true to himself, true to his vocation. Healing begins through the call of the symptom. In ancient Greece, a sign such as a dream, or a vision, had to indicate to the sick person (or to a relative) that he was *called* by the god of healing. The patient would then prepare himself with the help of the temple attendants. (Incidentally, those who dedicated their lives to the cult of a god were called *therapeutea*, and it is they who performed the preparatory ritual). Sacrifices were offered, and the *therapeutea* would bathe and purify the incubant, who would then be left to sleep, *alone,* in the sacred precinct of the temple. If Asklepios appeared to him, either in a dream or in "the waking state", i.e. in a vision, he was cured. An interesting detail: the god himself, or more often his serpent or his dog, touched the affected part of the incubant's body, and then vanished—think of the laying of hands as a healing practice, even today. Very often, the epiphany took the form of a beautiful young boy appearing in radiant light: an apparition of the divine child.

An important fact should be stressed: these dreams were never interpreted, either by the priests or the physicians. They just happened. The right dream *was* the cure, and the role of the *therapeutea* was to assist, to help the patient *be* in the best possible situation to receive the healing dream . . . in other words: to draw upon his own inner healing power.

Symbols

Now I am going to tell you a dream (which some of you might have heard already)—a dream which one of my patients dreamt at a moment of great inner stress—and shall then try to convey to you what, in Jungian terms, I mean by a symbol, and how, because of the symbol-forming capacity of the psyche, we carry within ourselves a creative power which may bring about not only the alleviation (or even the disappearance) of neurotic symptoms, but, more important, a broadening and an enrichment of the whole personality, that is to say, *healing* in the deepest sense of the word.

My patient, who was 23 when she first came for help, had been suffering from terrifying nightmares since the age of 12, nightmares from which she would awake carrying with her for several minutes, or even longer, the hallucinatory images of the dream. Her relation to outer reality was markedly distorted, her projections onto the environment being almost delusional. However, her ability to understand the language of myth and poetry proved quite remarkable and the horrific events of her dream-life were related to, symbolically, whilst their personal elements could be integrated into the ego.

The result was that very soon after starting treatment the terrors ceased completely, her dreams became the centre of intense interest, and she grew aware not only of the separateness but also of the link between inner and outer worlds. She began to take responsibility for her actions and for her relationships (marriage, of course, being the most problematic of all).

One day, she brought the following dream:
"You and I were sitting in a room. In front of us were two revolving circles, one for the male and one for the female principle. As each circle revolved, a series of images came up, each image giving way to the next one. You were explaining the male circle to me. After a number of images, there appeared a black and white snake which in turn gave way to a nun and then ... to a jar of jam. The snake was not the animal but the erection of the penis."

Obviously, we discussed this dream on a personal, concrete and reductive level, although the jar of jam defeated us completely, and I was rather reluctant to prod and probe into such a surprising creation produced by the unconscious. Also, I felt (secretly) excited by this small jar of jam, this concentrate of sugar and fruit, transmuted into something humble, but quite delicious, coming in as an unexpected *third* . . .

And I thought of Jung, and of his insights into the work of the alchemists (those masters in symbolic experience), teaching us that if a union is to take place between opposites—in this case between two intrapsychic components polarising as the inner masculine and the inner feminine—this union will come about through a *third* thing which will represent not a compromise but something *new*, an entity which can only be described in paradoxes . . . like gold that is not gold, or the stone that is not stone.

I felt I was confronted here with the transcending function. I shall explain: most great human problems are insoluble because they represent the polarity which belongs to life itself. They cannot be solved, but only outgrown, *transcended*. This transcendence of our personal problems leads to a raising of the level of consciousness, and by widening our horizon, the conflict loses its urgency.

A conflict cannot be tackled logically, but it can recede, leaving room for a different outlook. It is not repressed, but simply appears in a different light.

In his Introduction to *The Secret of the Golden Flower,* Jung writes:
> What, on a lower level, had led to the wildest conflicts and to panicky outburts of emotion, viewed from the higher level of the personality now seems like a storm in the valley seen from a high mountain-top. This does not mean that the thunderstorm is robbed of its reality, but instead of being *in* it, one is now *above* it.

The unifying of the opposites in a single entity means bringing the qualities of both conflicting poles into a unique "mixture" which becomes more than the simple sum of both.

This process of uniting conscious and unconscious into a synthesis, or symbol, is what Jung calls the transcendent (or transcending) function, by which he does not mean a metaphysical happening, nor one basic function such as thinking or feeling, but merely the fact that by this very complex process, in his own words, "a transition is made possible from one attitude to the other".

Now, let us come back to my analysand and to her jar of jam. A month later we were discussing another dream in which a young man was giving her a glass of water and *sugar* for comfort. Remembering the jam, I pricked up my ears and asked what she felt about sugar.

There was quite a long silence, and then she said: "The water of gold heals the heart."

She was surprised at her own words. I probed. She remembered a superstitious grandmother dipping her wedding-ring in a glass of sugared water and giving it to drink to anyone who suffered from shock or a weak heart.

By talking of sugar, and sweetness, and the heart, and of the fruit on the tree of good and evil, we came to the conclusion that sugar, and particularly that small jar of jam which haunted her and filled her with awe, had something to do with her feelings, that area which was her least differentiated side, infantile and autonomous, ruled by the inferior function which, when it *does* appear in consciousness, may have a precious quality of freshness and vitality, due to the fact that it stems, not from the ego, but from the self, that is, from the centre of the whole personality, hitting consciousness unexpectedly, like lightning, and thrusting the ego aside and making room for the totality of the person which extends far beyond the ego. It is the redeeming function.

For this young woman, the emergence and understanding of the unifying symbol was not only a turning-point in her personal development, bringing a dramatic improvement to all her relationships on the emotional as well as on the sexual level, but it liberated powerful creative forces which were able to be channelled into artistic expression and professional competence, thus relieving the personal conflict of a vast amount of psychic energy, because a symbol *is* a self-representation of the energic processes of the psyche. It is the vehicle by which one form of energy is transformed into another, and makes possible the transmutation (or true change) of psychological conditions.

In modern, western man, the ego is usually the more highly charged in energy, so when confronted with the unconscious *it* takes the lead. But what if each of these two forces has equal strength?

Then the ego's position becomes unbearable, movement is suspended, and consciousness is forced into a position beyond the opposites; when, from the depth of the psyche, from that area common to all men, springs the appropriate primordial image carrying the message from the unconscious into consciousness and forming a bridge between the two realms. The symbol acts as a mediator and is alive for so long as its meaning surpasses conscious comprehension.

Words tell us a lot about the ways of the psyche. The word 'symbol' derives from the Greek word 'symbolon' which combines two root-words; *sym,* meaning 'together', or 'with', and *bolon,* meaning 'that which has been thrown'. It was used to designate the two halves of an object which two parties broke, between them, as a pledge to prove their identity when they met at a later date. A symbol was thus originally a tally referring to the *missing* piece of an object which, when thrown together with its partner, recreated the *original whole object*. This corresponds exactly to the psychological function of a symbol.

When a symbol is fully understood it is no more a symbol, but a sign, which contains no more than what was put into it. When this stage is reached, the weight is once more on the side of consciousness but thanks to the self-regulating capacity of the psyche which counterbalances another natural tendency (that towards dissociation) the unconscious is activated again, bringing another imbalance, and a new symbol has to be found.

And so on . . .

In so far as a symbol is a living thing, it is an expression for something that cannot be defined in any other way. It is a paradox, giving shape to the inexpressible.

Symbols can be collective or individual. Those that the human spirit has created through the centuries manifest themselves in countless mythological themes which we can observe all round the world, and in the highest forms of religious dogmas and rituals (such as the hero conquering the monster, the night-sea journey, immersion in water, rebirth, and so on). Others arise from the symbol-forming capacity of specific individuals and are cloaked in their own particular imagery (like the appearance in a dream of a bewitching siren with the features of one's girlfriend; or the small pot of jam, a parallel to the quintessence, smaller than small, but more precious than all the riches in the world).

They are a personal creation having its roots in a primordial pattern and enabling the individual psyche to preserve its unique form of expression at the same time as merging with the universally human, collective psyche.

I have noticed that in times of great affliction, if the primordial images or themes can be linked to our personal predicament, it helps us to bear the pain which we are now sharing with the whole of humanity. Through imagination, we are lifted out of the prison of blind personal conflict into the realm of archetypal opposites, becoming one in the chain of universal, age-old experience which gives meaning to our suffering. Hence the value of steeping ourselves in myth, poetry, music—in *all* forms of symbolic expression.

And this leads me to the importance of art and the very special role of the artist in society. With the artist, symbols are not usually exploited for his own psychic development, but are the material and substance of his work, and make him the most authentic spokesman of the eternal vital forces in the souls of mankind, and also a leader into the future, particularly when he is groping to find expression in new and original forms.

I would also like to say a few words about the role of creative self-expression, so-called art therapy.

Working on the symbol gives a patient the invaluable advantage of helping the analysis with his own resources, and freeing him from over-dependence. Jung said something quite delightful on this. He said: "Often the hands know how to solve a riddle with which the intellect has wrestled in vain."

The process of unifying conscious and unconscious can, of course, take place spontaneously, but when it is consciously induced, the most effective method is one which Jung devised for himself when he was forced to face the confrontation with the unconscious. Many of you have probably read his account of it in *Memories, Dreams, Reflections*.

This method is an original exercise, which he calls 'active imagination' and which proves highly therapeutic for those who are capable of performing it. It has a different function from guided fantasy, so popular today, because the intitial image is always a personal one, and the role of the ego is paramount.

Active imagination consists in choosing a dream-image, or a fantasy-image, especially one conjured up by a bad mood, fixing it by concentrating on it and watching its alterations, which reflect the unconscious processes whilst the images themselves are made up of conscious memory material.

It is the combination of both images and alterations which constitutes the union of conscious and unconscious. Active imagination is like dreaming awake, except that for this inner theatre to have a cathartic effect it is necessary for the ego to participate, to be involved.

This is most important: archetypal images emerge from the collective unconscious, make their impact on the psyche, and sink back again into an undifferentiated form of energy. In this undifferentiated state, they are neither good nor bad; neither creative nor destructive; neither healthy nor sick. The aspect which will affect the psyche depends entirely on the conscious attitude of the individual in question: after all, man's capacity for consciousness is the hallmark of his humanity.

Creative self-expression and active imagination are a process of coming to terms with the non-ego, with the Other in oneself.

Paradoxically, this loneliest of ways may also prove to be a most effective way out of loneliness. And here I would like to digress for a few moments and dwell on this particular scourge of modern times: Loneliness.

Loneliness

Loneliness conjures up pictures of long, solitary Sundays; of frustrated housewives in stark and unfriendly tower-blocks; of old, retired men no longer needed; of ageing women; of unwanted immigrants. Loneliness has to do with the breakdown of the family; the breakdown of official religion; and the breakdown of all the structures which used to contain a human being from birth to death—structures which he may have disliked, but to which he belonged.

In these days of rapid change, some people are trapped in the values of the past, so they are disconnected from what is happening in the present.

Others live by a vision which is incomprehensible to their contemporaries because the symbols they are instrumental in bringing into being belong to the future, so they too suffer from spiritual isolation.

All of us, at some time or another, experience acute loneliness. Even if life has been kind to us and we are lucky enough not to fall into any of the socially under-privileged categories the idea of loneliness always strikes a chord, and fills us with fear. It is a subjective state which varies with each individual, but in every one of us there is ultimately an inner core of total loneliness and it is this aspect that I am going to speak about.

Loneliness is feeling cut-off, being unable to communicate; having no-one with whom to share essential experiences. In extreme cases, it becomes alienation, psychotic isolation that nothing can reach, so intolerable that it breaks into violence, or ends in suicide.

In the consulting-room, whatever the problem, loneliness always comes up, like a leit-motif. One young man says (pointing to his heart): "I feel it here, like a big black hole." A married woman, who lives and works with people (many people), describes her life as a desert, "a barren, arid desert", where no real meeting has ever taken place.

Most of modern art, literature and philosophy express the despair and absurdity of human existence: Kafka, Sartre, Magritte. The list is endless. The collective alienation of our time has been beautifully expressed by T. S. Eliot.

In *The Waste Land,* you can take any line, at random;

. . .Son of Man,

> You cannot say, or guess, for you know only
> A heap of broken images, where the sun beats,
> And the dead tree gives no shelter, the cricket no relief,
> And the dry stone no sound of water.

Arid, barren, a psychological wilderness. The waters of life have stopped flowing. The old symbols are dead: they no longer reach the soul.

When life has lost meaning, we invest our all in personal relationships, we make frantic attempts at human contact because *of course* we all know that the cure lies in relationship.

But what if we can't relate? The supreme aloneness is the aloneness we feel with the person we love most. And what if we can't even love? That must be the supreme horror.

The Cycle of Life and the Problem of Opposites

Personally, I have found Jung's insights into the fundamental pattern of the life cycle one of his most helpful contributions, and I shall now try to show how relevant it is to my theme.

The infant, perhaps already in the womb, starts the journey of life immersed in the images of the collective unconscious. He lives in a pre-personal world, a world where unity is not yet split into an outward physical reality, and an inward psychic reality. This is when he lives in a state of identification with the mother, a stage in which the ego has not yet separated from the self, or totality of the psyche. The first task for the child is to free himself from the powers of the collective unconscious which fascinate him and which he is most reluctant to leave. However, something in human nature urges him on, pushing him towards individual development, which means establishing a firm and separate ego.

This process is usually supported by education (at any rate by traditional education) and when all goes well, the emerging ego builds up a healthy connection with the previously unconscious processes and, to quote Jung: "thus separating them from their source in the unconscious, like an island newly risen from the sea".

Separating, yes, but not *severing* the now conscious processes from the source. This is the razor's edge between creative maturity and alienation. Here lies the pitfall and the root of all loneliness.

It is interesting that Jung was led to his vast research in mythology, religion, anthropology and alchemy through the unconscious material of a certain type of patient.

He had, in his practice, many middle-aged, well-to-do, socially successful people who called upon him for help because, having achieved what they had thought was their goal in life, surprisingly, they were now feeling discontented, bored or restless. In other words, they felt stuck and had lost all zest for life, or even suffered from deep depression. The words they used were strangely reminiscent of the barrenness of the desert and the sterility of the waste land.

It became apparent, in these particular patients, that the reductive methods of psychoanalysis did not apply: the problem was not the freeing and building-up of the ego. Jung came to believe that some people become neurotic because they are confined within too narrow a spiritual horizon; life has not sufficient meaning because the ego has lost touch with the archetypal background; it is dried up like a plant cut off from its roots and lying to waste in a psychic soil which is as dry and as arid as any physical desert. When this happens, the time has come to heed the unconscious and to understand its symbolic language.

With those particular patients, Jung observed a shift from the ego-bound centre to a deeper one, in which irreconcilable opposites are united, through the agency of such symbols as the mandala, for example.

Dr. Gerhard Adler, in his remarkable book *The Living Symbol*, gives a minute account of a case like this. The attitude required for this sort of development involves giving in to the spontaneity of the psychic processes, and firmly looking inside instead of only outside. It requires intense introversion, a willing acceptance of the wilderness and all the sacrifices which it entails.

It is this attitude which favours the emergence of the healing symbols, linking once again the alienated ego to the true regulator of the personality, the self, centre and sum of both conscious *and* unconscious.

Looked at in this light, the personal neurosis is transformed into the religious quest for wholeness.

This is the point where Jung discovered striking parallels beween the symbolic material of his patients and the universal symbols of myth and religion. It became evident that both manifestations expressed archetypal patterns of human development. In the individuation process, consciousness emerges from the sea of the unconscious, and then returns to it, *knowingly*, in a transformed state. In other words, the ego *leaves* the self in order to become aware of its uniqueness, and then must be allowed to *return* to the self consciously in order to experience its link with the totality of life and death, of time and timelessness.

Neurosis caused by the need to relinquish the ego in favour of the self was seen by Jung as the crisis of middle age. And indeed, it often is so, although today the problem presents itself differently: many young people need to find a metaphysical meaning to their lives, even though their ego-development is far from adequate. The stages of ego/self relation are not always so clear-cut, although the overall pattern still holds, and the right connection between consciousness and the unconscious is the key to the problem of alienation.

At this time of transition, we must be wary of old models, and *at the same time*, never lose sight of the eternal matrix of the everchanging archetypal images. In recent years there has been a frenzied reaction against the old ego-values of reason and self-discipline; an immense hunger for the repressed Dyonisian; so much so that we are witnessing quite astonishing experiments in instant ecstasy: sex orgies, drugs, esoteric mysticisms, all attempts at reaching back to the source, at bridging the gap. Unfortunately, the delicate ego/self axis has often got smashed on the way, and, with it, sanity and any sense of meaning.

But *is* it so unfortunate? Is it not out of chaos that new forms have always emerged? Instead of a straight axis, there is perhaps a need for more sinuous lines relating consciousness to the archetypal forces, to those gods within, all clamouring to be acknowledged.

Is it not possible that the mark of the new age will be a paradoxical sort of polytheism contained within the embrace of the total Oneness, with a much more fluid and flexible sort of ego consciousness in the centre?

And I suggest that it is through these new forms of *inner* relatedness that the meaning of the phenomenon of loneliness can be truly understood.

Looked at reductively, it seems that loneliness is connected with difficulties in the mother/child relationship, and many interesting discoveries have been made in this field. However, following one of Jung's most important concepts, we must never forget that the mother image does not only connect back to the beginnings, but may also point towards the unconscious as creative matrix of the future; and also, if we concentrate too exclusively on the infant we carry into adulthood, there is a danger of remaining encapsulated in infantilism, whereas to accept this infant as a part of our present wholeness may help to constellate the archetype: the archetype of the divine child, bringer of renewal and healing.

From this viewpoint, loneliness can be seen as an expression of the crisis of our age, which certain individuals are called upon to work through on the symbolic level.

Related to the problem of loneliness and alienation, a phenomenon of great significance is taking place, and that is the springing up of an incredible number of small groups, with an incredible number of varying purposes. Surely they are the outward reflection of a new inner happening, and are (usually) of enormous importance to those participating in them.

Compensating for the lost outer structure, for some of us, they represent a sheltered but exacting 'place' where we find the courage to explore new modes of being; where we can speak to others without shame or pretence; and where we draw the strength to acknowledge our *separateness*, our *uniqueness*, that inner core of total loneliness, so we can then bear to be *alone*, in the creative sense of the word, alone with ourselves, truly ourselves.

They are a 'place' we can go back to regularly, and this helps us find the courage to let go of the old and receive the new; the new which seems to be working its way into the consciousness of a multitude of individuals, painfully, frighteningly.

But that is the way of the psyche. The old symbols die, sink into the unconscious, and re-emerge in a new form, to become the living symbols of a new age. The Redeemer's face changes with every culture, but the archetype is always there, buried in the depths of our psyches, and will no doubt manifest anew in the hearts and souls of individual men and women, when and where it will, that is to say, when and where consciousness is ready to receive it.

As a psychotherapist, a large proportion of my daily task consists in looking for, looking into and looking after the more murky and shadowy sides of human nature, because like the cornerstone which is thrown away, it is usually the despised element which proves the most vitally important. Like the alchemists, we have to suffer the *nigredo*, the blackness, which is the indispensable first phase of the work.

Whenever we look inside ourselves instead of seeking for outer solutions we come up against repressed, unadapted elements which we find unacceptable, and they often appear in dreams in the form of the most ghastly people we know, of the same sex as ourselves, whom we have to acknowledge as partial pictures of our own psyche—the side of us which Jung called the shadow. Integrating the personal shadow is the most important happening in the process of growing up. Befriending it gives strength to the ego, keeps our feet on the ground, especially when more lofty confrontations might lift us into inflation, and finally, knowing the worst in ourselves stops us from projecting too wildly onto our environment. It is good for friendship because it makes relationships with our own sex easier and it is a reminder to be modest and tolerant concerning social and political issues.

At a deeper level, there may be quite ominous encounters with the dark forces of destruction which, at one point, have to be faced by those embarking on the journey of self-knowledge. Dreams can hint at the Dionysian mystery of bloodshed, dismemberment and dissolution. This can be a terrible and almost blissful experience, and one which humanity, hiding behind the illusion of culture and civilization, believes wrongly, to have outlived. The orgies of murder and violence are still with us. Where do they originate, if not from the subterranean regions of the human psyche? And when they do occur, why do we always blame the "other side" for all the horrors? Contents of the psyche which remain unconscious are projected onto the outside world. So each one of us is partly responsible for the evil around us when we fail to get in touch with our own inner darkness. It's no use pretending it is not there: all we achieve is to add yet another stone to the lynching of a scapegoat. The only contribution to universal fraternity, it seems to me, is to reach down into ourselves where we may possibly manage to get into contact with the self common to all humanity, the living archetype of Everyman. On the other hand, paradoxically, as well as ruthlessly throwing light on the buried contents of the personal unconscious, there is also the need for a certain dimming of awareness. We must refrain from thrusting too glaring a light onto those dark and mysterious areas protectively enfolding the seeds of psychic life. Like the hero of many myths, our ego needs to perform periodic night-sea journeys if we are to maintain our links with the hidden source of our being. Ill-timed interpreting interferes with the spontaneity of the creative processes.

Even more difficult than the coming to terms with the shadow is the reconciling of the masculine/feminine polarity. That "a girl has a masculine and a man a feminine soul" was a saying quite common among the alchemists of the 16th century. This knowledge was forgotten. Jung reintroduced it, and much has been written on the complications of the animus/anima relationship. When this contrasexual entity remains unconscious, whether it is projected onto an outside partner or not, it is always problematic, and more often than not, the source of untold suffering because it involves the most vulnerable part in a human being, the erotic. Integration of the animus or anima is obviously a great help in the relationship between the sexes. But it is the cultural implications which are less obvious. In alchemy, the masculine/feminine conjunction was expressed by the Hermaphrodite, which is also a symbol of the self. I often wonder if the Hermaphrodite is not, possibly, the primordial image at the back of the Unisex confusion which is a state of undifferentiation due to infantile fascination with mother, or the unconscious, but also a sort of inferior version of, or attempt at, reaching a new and richer sort of consciousness where every potentiality would be realised by relating knowingly to the masculine and the feminine *within*. Exceptional human beings have always been androgynous psychologically, and sometimes physically; the history of art, literature and religion is ample proof of this.

Another aspect of the cultural implications of the anima/animus problem is the unconscious investment of divine power on a human being. This gives rise to the most compelling ties a person can experience. He or she is completely possessed by the loved one who carries the totality of his or her soul. No amount of human exchange can ever be sufficient. Only complete incorporation would be satisfying. It is the most heart-rending situation and can be very destructive. It is a feature of modern society that no religious symbol can contain the intensity and fervour of these total love projections. In ages of faith, the Virgin, or Christ, or Isis, or other divinities performed this function. Now, there is so much psychic energy imprisoned in the deified "personal relationship" (which is no longer "personal" at all), that no space exists for ordinary, human intercourse, and no outlet can be found for individual development and religious fulfilment. The result is breakdown of marriages and the perpetual search for yet other soul-images to project onto. In this situation, withdrawal of the projection, with all the agonizing pain which goes with it, is a prerequisite for spiritual growth. Acceptance of defeat in love is difficult. Yet it is the best attitude for the miraculous birth of a new symbol and its healing power.

Symbols have a constructive and integrative function, not only individually, but for mankind as a whole. In the past, societies used initiation rites, or mysteries, to bring about the transformation of instinct into spirit. Nowadays, the religious symbols, as used in the outer forms of worship, seem to have lost their living power for many people. As with the alchemist, it is in the solitary experiences of analysis, or art, or individual prayer that the symbols of totality may be found; the symbols which truly contain the opposites of male and female, spirit and matter, good and evil, light and dark. May be, it is in seeking for the stone which is no stone, in allowing the archetype of the Redeemer to be reborn in each one of us that we can best contribute to the healing of the collective conflicts of our time—without ever forgetting to make outward decisions to the best of our ability: Movement and Tranquillity, as expressed in the "Corners of the Mouth", Hexagram 27 in *The Book of Changes*.

NOTES

1. This article is a combination of *Holding the Opposites*, given to the Guild of Pastoral Psychology and *The Healing Power of Symbols*, a public talk given to the Royal Society of Medicine, sponsored by the Analytical Psychology Club.

BIBLIOGRAPHY

G. Adler, *The Living Symbol*, London, 1961. *Studies in Analytical Psychology*, London, 1948.

René Alleau, *Aspects de l'Alchimie Traditionelle* (Editions de Minuit)

E. F. Edinger, *Ego and Archetype*, Baltimore, 1973.

M. L. von Franz, *Aurora Consurgens*

M. L. von Franz, *Harvest 1975* (Analytical Psychology Club)

Vera von der Heydt, *Prospects for the Soul*, London, 1976.

Vera von der Heydt, *Alchemy*, Guild Pamphlet, No. 105

R. F. Hobson, *Loneliness*, Journal of the Society of Analytical Psychology, Vol. 19, London, 1974.

J. Jacobi, *Complex, Archetype, Symbol*, London, 1959.

C. G. Jung, *Collected Works*, Vols. 5, 8, 9, 13, 14, 17

C. G. Jung, Forward to *The Secret of the Golden Flower* (Routledge & Kegan Paul)

C. Kerenyi, *Asklepios*, London, 1960.

P. W. Martin, *Experiment in Depth* (Routledge & Kegan Paul)

C. A. Meier, *Ancient Incubation and Modern Psychotherapy*, Evanston, 1967.

S. Vernay, *Into the New Age*, London, 1975.

The Beyond
(Death and Renewal in East
and West)[1]

by Barbara Hannah

BARBARA HANNAH studied with Jung in the 1920's in Zürich, where she has continued to practise, and teaches at the C.G.Jung Institute. She is a member of the International Association for Analytical Psychology and has contributed many articles to professional journals. She is also the author of Striving Towards Wholeness *and* Jung: His Life and Work.

It is, of course, quite impossible for me to say anything in the least definite about the subject I have had the foolhardiness to choose as my theme. But two special things urged me to do so, beyond and above the natural interest in the subject that grows on one more and more in old age.

The first is to be found in *Memories, Dreams, Reflections* where Jung says:

> A man should be able to say he has done his best to form a conception of life after death, or to create some image of it – even if he must confess his failure. Not to have done so is a vital loss. For the question that is posed to him is the age-old heritage of humanity : an archetype rich in secret life, which seeks to add itself to our own individual life in order to make it whole.[2]

And the second compelling reason was in a dream of my own. About two years ago I dreamt that I had passed through a door numbered 3 or 9. There was a numinous feeling and I was slowly wondering if this was death, when I was told to go back through the same door, because I had permission to return to the earth in order to write down all I knew about the life beyond death, as if I had been for a short time in that world.

The very evening after I had the dream, we dined with friends one of whom suggested a subject for a further book. The synchronicity of the dream and the outer event made me take up the suggestion, but the fact that, taken more literally, the dream said I should write all I knew about the 'Beyond' itself – combined with the just-quoted passage from Jung – has never quite left me in peace, so that, when Marie-Louise von Franz suggested that I should take up this theme, I knew at once that I must make the attempt, even if I must only confess my failure.

But – as is usually my custom when confronted with a specially difficult task – I took up the subject in active imagination, and was told that I should certainly try but only if I could find a material as a basis for what I said. I thought over many materials but none even began to satisfy me except a paper on *Death and Renewal in China*, by Richard Wilhelm[3], which Marie-Louise von Franz had given to me to read some years before. As she gives the most relevant part in her new book on numbers, I felt reluctant to use it but, with her generous encouragement, I at last overcame my misgivings. I must also thank her here for her patience in listening to my difficulties in writing this paper and for many valuable suggestions.

The paper in question is not an old Chinese text but rather Wilhelm's own summing up of the Chinese point of view on death and renewal seen from more than one side. The most important point of all seems to be held in common by their three chief religions: Taoism, Confucianism and Buddhism, but, I must own to my surprise, of all these three, Confucianism seems much the nearest to our own Western point of view. This is really because, as is well known, Buddhism is concerned with a long series of incarnations, which culminate in the goal of Nirvana, an achievement where the individual has at last fulfilled all his karma and may dissolve forever in an eternal impersonal bliss. The Taoists also seem little concerned with the ultimate fate of the individual or with how long he survives, but the Confucians put a much higher value on consciousness and on this human life altogether and thus indirectly on individual survival in the Beyond.

As is well known, the Chinese – in fact the whole East – have a very different attitude to the opposites than we have in the West. It is amazing how passionately – even after many decades of studying Jung – many of us still cling to the white opposite and condemn the black. In this age, indeed there seem to be quite as many or even more people who find the black opposite the more rewarding, but they thus as a rule carefully avoid the moral problem – that Jung always said was indispensable – and thus prevent themselves from realizing that they are repressing the white opposite. And as Jung frequently pointed out, it is not pursuing perfection but holding the balance between both opposites that is the vital thing now. In *Late Thoughts* in his *Memories,* for instance, he points out that: "Evil has become a determinant reality .... We must learn to handle it, since it is here to stay. How we can live with it without terrible consequences cannot for the present be conceived."[4]

And he continues: "Touching evil brings with it the grave peril of succumbing to it. We must, therefore, no longer succumb to anything at all, not even to good. A so-called good to which we succumb loses its ethical character. Not that there is anything bad in it on that score, but evil results develop because one has succumbed to it.[5] Every form of addiction is bad, no matter whether the narcotic be alcohol, or morphine or idealism .... Recognition of the reality of evil necessarily relativizes the good, and the evil likewise, converting both into halves of a paradoxical whole."

I have just reminded you of how Jung himself regarded the opposites, because it leads the way into the whole Chinese philosophy of life which – in contrast to the West – is all based on the equality of the opposites. Those of us who use the *I Ching* are well acquainted with the equal opposites of Yang and Yin, masculine and feminine, but perhaps we are less aware that Chinese philosophy regards life and death also as a pair of equal opposites on which all human beings are based. In fact if it tends to favour one of those opposites, it is rather death. Wilhelm points out that the Chinese simply do not prize life as we do and rate it so much higher than death; on the contrary, they do not regard life as quite real but more as a temporary illusion, so clearly it is easier and more natural for them to hold the balance between life and death than it is for us. Some of the oldest documents in China point out that the greatest good fortune which a man can meet is to find a death that crowns his life, his own specific death, and the greatest misfortune that threatens him is to find an untimely death that tears his life apart instead of completing it. Therefore the ancient sages in China absolutely refused to call any man happy till after his death.

As death is valued so highly in China, it is natural that the Chinese also regard fear of death as a great stumbling block and that one of the most important tasks of a well-spent life is to educate oneself in fearlessness toward death, a fearlessness, Wilhelm emphasizes, that is ready to look all that befalls us in the face and is anxious to come to terms with everything that the future could bring. Therefore they spend a great deal of time – already in life – in thinking about death; in fact they fulfil the task that Jung advises us to fulfil: they really do their best "to form a conception of life after death or to create some image of it."

Wilhelm tells us a good deal about how they set about this task, and this is the reason that I felt this paper might give us some hints for our own efforts in this direction. Although, as always when we are dealing with Eastern ideas, we must not forget that any imitation of the East does not agree with Western man, Jung says of this in his Introduction to *The Secret of the Golden Flower:* "The Chinese can fall back upon the authority of his entire culture . If he starts on the long way, he does what is recognised as being the best of all the things he could do. But the Westerner who wishes to start upon this way, if he is truly serious about it, has all authority against him. That is why it is infinitely easier for a man to imitate the Chinese way."[6] But "it is sad indeed when the European departs from his own nature and imitates the East or 'affects' it in any way. The possibilities open to him would be so much greater if he would remain true to himself and develop out of his own nature all that the East has brought forth from its inner being in the course of centuries."[7] Keeping this in mind we will see what hints for our own work we can find in this excellent article of Richard Wilhelm's, although I must emphasize that time forbids me to give you any idea of its rich content; I can only pick out a point here and there.

Wilhelm points out that this "long way," as Jung calls it, requires the most serious and concentrated thinking, but that this is something very different from what we understand by thinking in the West. Chinese thought is far more substantial than ours, an active thinking that even has an effect on the realm of objective existence. To sum up, they would not say "I think" but "it thinks in me" and they explore these objective thoughts as we might explore an unknown territory on earth.

Jung learned this kind of thinking the hard way many years before he knew anything of Chinese thought. I first realised how much of the "hard way" it was when he was struggling to find his way in the unknown labyrinth of alchemy. He explained how lost and near despair he often felt and added: "I have experienced nothing like it, since my first confrontation with the unconscious but that was worse, even much worse."

It was in a conversation with the figure he called Philemon that Jung first learned of this different substantial kind of thought. He writes: "He (Philemon) said I treated thoughts as if I generated them myself, but in his view thoughts were like animals in the forest, or people in a room, or birds in the air, and added: 'If you should see people in a room, you would not think that you had made those people, or that you were responsible for them.' It was he who taught me psychic objectivity, the reality of the psyche."[8] And exploring the unconscious with this kind of objective thinking eventually led Jung to the basic foundation – that is the same in East and West – of the human psyche, to the four square "mandala as an expression of the Self." So that when Wilhelm sent him *The Secret of the Golden Flower* in 1928 – more than ten yers after his own discoveries – he tells us that it "gave me undreamed of confirmation of my ideas about the mandala and the circumambulation of the centre. That was the first event which broke through my isolation. I became aware of an affinity; I could establish ties with something and someone."[9] It is with the kind of thinking, taught to Jung by Philemon, and which he subsequently taught us as active imagination, that the Chinese explore the Beyond and try to form some conception of it.

Wilhelm tells us that the Confucians hold that two opposite principles form two poles between which everything lies. They have many names for these principles of which I will only mention heaven and earth, because they hold that the human being has two souls, one belonging to each, as it were. At death the vegetative soul falls down into the depths of the earth where it then forms part of an ancestral deposit of death and rebirth. This is the reason that every Chinese wants to die in China, or at least be buried in his own soil. But there is another soul which at death soars into the heights. This is the soul which is capable of becoming spiritual already in life. Wilhelm points out that the spirit is not something that grows naturally in man, but something that he must make a great effort to acquire in the course of his life. According to the Confucian idea, this spirit has a kind of consciousness that can survive death. It never dissolves at once, any more than the body, and therefore the Chinese always speak in the death chamber as if the deceased were still present, in order that he may gain time to separate himself from the body.

This is certainly an archetypal idea, lying in the unconscious, which can come to the surface anywhere and at any time. If you will excuse a personal memory: an aunt I had never liked died when I was about seven or eight. Immediately I thought how careful I must now be not to say, if possible even to think, anything negative about her, because I took for granted that she would now hear everything I said and even probably what I thought. I instinctively kept this conviction to myself but I was nevertheless amazed years afterwards to learn that at any rate in my family it was not a generally recognized fact.

Wilhelm goes on to point out that a dynamic point of view is to be found everywhere in China. They do not emphasize the solidity of matter as we do but rather regard it as a dynamic condition. As the spirit undoubtedly exists but has no substantial existence, it is rather regarded by the Confucians as a tendency towards consciousness, it "naturally leads a somewhat precarious existence unless it has been so concentrated in the course of life, that it has already 'built itself a kind of subtle body of a spiritual nature', made as it were of thoughts and works, a body that gives consciousness a support when it has to leave its former assistant, the body. This psychic body is at first very delicate, so that only the very wisest men can preserve it and find their refuge in it after death." Ordinary people cannot achieve this, and therefore their existence after death depends on the thoughts of the survivors which is the underlying meaning of the whole ancestor cult in China.

This striking formulation of the possibility of building a subtle body during our lifetime, which would afford us the same refuge and home in the Beyond as our physical body does in this world, made an indelible impression on me when I first read the article several years ago. Of course the idea itself was not new to me, it is the central idea of *The Secret of the Golden Flower,* for example, but the penny at last dropped, so to speak, when I read this clear formulation of it in Wilhelm's article. It is not even an exclusively Eastern idea; the Western alchemists also often emphasize this quality of their *lapis.* To quote only one example, the *Rosarium Philosophorum* says: "We have seen it with our own eyes and touched it with our hands." And, in his Eranos lecture *On Zosimos* in 1937, Jung suggests that Christ was referring to the same thing when he said to Nicodemus: "We speak that we do know, and testify to that we have seen."[10]

What subtle substance exists that is as tangible and visible as these testimonies suggest? All I can think of must be something similar to the ectoplasm that mediums produce in seances. Numberless scientifically controlled experiments with the weight of mediums during seances – to say nothing of the many photographs that have been taken – have proved that this ectoplasm has a physical weight and is sufficiently visible to register on a sensitive enough film. But the results of such seances are usually exceedingly primitive and unsatisfactory, and most parapsychological phenomena are particularly frequent in the neighbourhood of adolescents who have not yet become conscious of the great change that is taking place in them.

In fact altogether parapsychological phenomena seem often to be the pre-stage, as it were, of a creative effort. Jung used sometimes to say: "There were loud reports in the furniture in my room last night, so evidently I have to make another creative effort but I am not yet conscious of its content." And you will all remember the dramatic account he gives in *Memories* of the parapsychological phenomena that took place all over his house before he wrote *The Seven Sermons to the Dead*.[11] The haunting ceased immediately when he took up his pen to write.

Altogether – although of course we are speaking of something which in itself is beyond our comprehension – parapsychological phenomena seem to point to a condition of the beginning, a condition in which the ectoplasm, so to speak, is still entirely autonomous. A creative effort, a becoming conscious, the "thoughts and works" mentioned by Wilhelm, seem to crystallize it, as it were, and thus to begin to form the "subtle body" which he speaks of here, a sort of mandala-like refuge of an enduring kind.

I admit that I thought concretely enough, when I first read this formulation of Wilhelm's, to think that this subtle body must necessarily resemble the physical body in shape. Presumably it has this aspect. Jung's dream of the Yogin – to which we will return later – who had his features, points in this direction.[12] And his experience in 1944 when he saw his doctor in his 'primal form' telling him he must return to earth – he evidently recognized him at once – is also similar evidence.[13] To say nothing of the Zen masters who sometimes say to their pupils "show me your face before you were born." But obviously as this body is thought of as our refuge in the Beyond, it must belong to a realm where we are entirely dependent on symbols as the best possible expression for something that is essentially unknown. In *Memories* Jung spoke of the yellow castle in the Chinese *Secret of the Golden Flower* as such a symbol, and calls it directly "the germ of the immortal body."[14]

There is really a great deal of evidence to be found in modern dreams that the Western unconscious is just as concerned with our building "a subtle body of a spiritual nature" already in our lifetime as in China. I will just draw your attention to two examples: A woman – who was still under 50 – had a particularly clear dream in this respect. She was at the time much occupied with the problem of whether to buy a certain house. She was very anxious for some comment from the unconscious before making her decision irrevocable but to her great disappointment she had no dream. Then, just before she completed the purchase, she dreamt that, though the house in question was quite suitable as a garage for her body, it was of little importance. Another house was of vital importance and she should give her whole attention to building it. Already in the dream she realized that this house was in the Beyond, for its site was quite close to the house of a great friend who had died two or three years before.

A few months before his death Dr. Jung told us that he had had a dream that the "other Bollingen" was now complete. I must explain that he had several dreams throughout the later years of the "other Bollingen" which was apparently built in stages similar to the stages in which he built his tower on the upper lake of Zürich, as he describes in his *Memories*.[15] From how he had always spoken of the "other Bollingen," we had no doubt that it was built on the boundary of the two worlds or even quite in the Beyond. So the news from his dream that it was now completed made us very sad, as one could not doubt that he himself felt that he would move into it entirely before long.

Wilhelm points out that the physical body itself is quite willing to die when its time comes but that there is an inner aspect of the body that possesses consciousness and it is this aspect which is constantly imagining how death will be before it comes. It is this aspect that gives rise in many, if not most, individuals to a profound desire for immortality, and which is constantly imagining how death itself will be. Wilhelm regards these fantasies as one of the strongest forces there is, that has created such buildings as the Pyramids but also – ironically enough – killed millions of people in religious wars between people who held conflicting fantasies as to how it would be. The old philosopher, Dschuang Dzi, held that the psyche can be taken apart, as it were, and that consciousness can learn to stand aside and watch the change in all things, an exercise that frees the ego from its body and immensely enlarges its range.

This taking apart of the psyche, and teaching the ego to stand aside and watch, seems to me very similar to what we do when we learn in analysis that the ego is *not* the master in its own house but only one of many inhabitants. Although we frequently try to manage the shadow, anima or animus, for instance, when we first learn how much they take upon themselves, it is really a good deal wiser and in the end more rewarding to stand aside and watch their behaviour till we know who or what they are. Moreover – as Jung was always emphasizing in analysis – the vital point is not what we are going to *do* about a thing, but whether we *know* it or not. Nothing could annoy him more than for us to ask: "What shall I *do* about it?" "*Know* it" he used to reply and sometimes remind us of *The Secret of the Golden Flower* saying: "Indolence of which a man is conscious and indolence of which he is unconscious are a thousand miles apart."[16] If one can learn to stand aside and watch the "taken apart psyche" – as Dschuang Dzi recommends here – we shall indeed see "the change in all things" for everything unconscious changes when it becomes conscious. This does indeed begin to free the ego from the body and to "immensely enlarge its range."

But this is not enough, as Wilhelm points out; the position must then be consolidated and that involves a separation from the corporeal altogether, and for that it is necessary to build up a new body for ego consciousness. This body is made, as it were, of energy, and can only be achieved by exercises in concentration and meditation to free these energies and to direct them to the support of the entelechy, that seed which is present from the beginning in latent form.

The seed that is present from the beginning but in latent form is in our language the Self. Jung has often compared it being there from the beginning with the lattice of a crystal which – though invisible – is present in the solution from the beginning. If for a moment we consider the making of this subtle body as if it were a crystal, the Chinese idea would roughly be that the crystal itself could never form in the solution unless we spent the most profound meditation and concentration upon it which would enable it to become visible, hard and strong in the shape predestined from the beginning for that particular crystal.

Wilhelm carries this analysis of the seed further and points out how in every seed there is the image of a new plant or tree, but that – through concentration of the energy inwards – this image has become invisible, yet surrounded by a kind of substantial husk which must decay in order for the entelechy – the new image – to take on substance, develop and become visible once more.

This image of the husk of a seed having to decay that the invisible entelechy may develop, again take on substance and grow into the plant or tree is really the problem of rebirth which – as Wilhelm points out – was regarded as so vitally important in the early centuries of Christianity but which no longer plays any role in the Church, at all events not in the Protestant Church. Yet, as Jung pointed out in his 1939 Eranos Lecture *Concerning Rebirth*,[17] all ideas of rebirth are founded on the fact that transformation of the psyche is a natural process. He continues: "Nature herself demands a death and a rebirth. As the alchemist Democritus says: 'Nature rejoices in nature, nature subdues nature, nature rules over nature.' There are natural transformation processes which simply happen to us, whether we like it or not, and whether we know it or not."[18] It seems to me that the Confucians especially made a great effort to become conscious of the natural process of rebirth, and to prevent it taking place unconsciously. That the latter can be disastrous beyond measure we saw in the last world war for, as I am sure you all remember, Jung pointed out repeatedly that the events in Germany were simply an individuation process taking place in the unconscious, with no one aware of it.

Jung spoke particularly plastically of the undeveloped seed idea in his 1932 seminar on Kundalini Yoga. He pointed out that the fact of our still being in Muladhara shows that we are still just seeds of what we could become, less than embryos, only germs in the womb.[19] These germs are the sleeping gods, what we should call the Self, which lie invisible and latent in us all. Jung even says: "What we take to be the culmination of a long history and long evolution would be really a nursery, and the great and important things are high above it and are still to come; exactly as the unconscious contents which we feel down below in our abdomen are slowly rising to the surface and becoming conscious so that we begin to have the conviction, this is definite, this is clear, this is really what we are after."[20] Jung goes on to point out that while this is only a germ, it is apt just to disturb our functioning, but that – if we persevere in concentrating on it – it becomes an embryo and even – when it really reaches consciousness – it becomes a full-grown tree. He points out that the whole purpose of the awakening of the Kundalini is to separate the gods from the world – where they have slept – so that they may become active, and with that we necessarily start a new order of things. He adds: "From the standpoint of the gods, this world is less than child's play, it is a seed in the earth, a mere potentiality, our whole world of consciousness is only a seed of the future. But when you succeed in the awakening of Kundalini, so that she begins to move out of her mere potentiality, you necessarily start a world which is a world of eternity, totally different from our world."[21]

As we shall see, the goal of all that Wilhelm tells us in this paper is really exactly the same as Jung describes here, it is becoming conscious of the 'world of eternity' but it adds the idea of forming a new body in which we can find a refuge in this world of eternity, just as the physical body is our home and refuge in this world.

We have learned so far that this subtle body is made of "thoughts and works" and above all of energy which we must detach from the earthly things – that have been our main preoccupation – and give to supporting and furthering this entelechy, this seed of the eternal that is latent in us all. Only a movement of retreat with the utmost concentration, Wilhelm says, makes it possible for the new growth to take root, and Jung pointed out in his Kundalini seminar that when this seed begins to move in us, it has "the effect of an earthquake that naturally shakes us and can even shake our house down."[22] We obviously need strong roots in the "here and now" to stand this and I think it is just here that the Chinese better consciousness of the earthly body stands them in good stead and has probably contributed a lot to their being more willing and able than we are "to form a conception of life after death or to create some image of it."[23]

The necessary concentration is expressed in China through many images. To mention only one: a sage is depicted in deepest meditation in whose heart a small child is forming. This little child is nourished and cared for there until at last it is ready to float through the cranial cavity out into the heights as the new divine birth. This, Wilhelm says, is an image that represents death already in life. It means emerging into another order of time, where we can see the whole of life as from another dimension and yet, at the same time we remain energically connected with our present life in our present order of space and time. Wilhelm says that this meditation engenders a concentrated latent energy which gathers everything to *one point* because it frees itself from transitory time. It is clear that no ordinary intellectual thinking would be of the slightest use here; in fact the only Western parallels that I know are the profound meditation of the mystic and the concentration on the unconscious that Jung learned and taught us in active imagination.

Wilhelm points out that this is a point on which all the Chinese religions agree: Confucianism as well as Taoism and Buddhism all hold that the most important task of a lifetime is to bring every physical and psychic disposition, that form the capital with which we are born, into harmony by assembling them all round a centre which then shapes them into a whole. He points out that if this procedure succeeds it represents the most unusually strong force. The danger in the East, which Wilhelm points out, of not being able to keep all these psychic components together, and of getting possessed by a force that escapes and becomes autonomous, is exactly the same as so often threatens us. An autonomous complex, such as the animus or anima, can gain the upper hand and even land us in a condition that is worse than before we made the attempt to reach our unconscious. Jung often used to deplore this fact and say that if people were not going to go through with it it was better that they should never begin.

Wilhelm points out that such incidents – which are depicted in numberless fairy tales – are only of secondary importance in China where the recognised goal in all three great religions is to *unite* the whole psyche round a centre by constant meditation and concentration. They say indeed that deviations from this goal make it possible, for example, to talk to the ghosts of the deceased. Although –as Wilhelm tells us elsewhere[24] – mediumistic seances are "widely prevalent" in China and we also learn that they are not valued at all highly by the Chinese who are concerned with the goal which we are considering. He also tells us that outpourings of the unconscious, such as we frequently reckon as works of genius, are also not highly valued in China. (I imagine he means such works as Nietzsche's *Thus Spake Zarathustra* which has all the characteristics of having burst forth from the unconscious with little or no control being exercised by the conscious.) Such works are regarded in China as wasted energy, undeveloped births, which finally – because they are not subjected to conscious concentration and thus related to the centre – flicker out and disappear.

It seems to surprise Wilhelm very much that, as he expresses it, something lower, like ego consciousness, should have to take the lead in the production of something so much higher than itself that it could even be called divine. Yet the Chinese take this fact very seriously, and say that at first this higher being needs to be educated and formed by consciousness, for it is powerless to develop without it. We are already used to this idea, for the alchemists also say that the god hidden in matter can only be liberated by the efforts of the alchemist himself. And it is an archetypal idea that quite frequently appears in the dreams of modern people. For example, Dr. Jung once told me that a woman patient of his had the following dream: There was a group of birds, all about the size of pigeons, and she had the task of teaching them to walk up and down stairs! To her great surprise, one of these birds was the Holy Ghost, who had to be taught the same thing, exactly like the other birds! Dr. Jung remarked that this only sounded extraordinary because of our Christian upbringing; it was really just a natural fact.

So the Chinese undertake the education, or one could perhaps rather say the liberation, of this seed that is innate in us all. This, as we have seen, largely consists of freeing the energy that is caught up in all our worldly concerns, and surrounding the entelechy with it. Or in other words, freeing our minds of the finite in order to concentrate on the infinite which – while we are still alive – accustoms us to the Beyond and its infinite, unlimited values, before the time comes for us to move over, or in other words to die.

Jung speaks just as strongly in his *Memories* of the value of realising the infinite. He even says: "The decisive question for man is: Is he related to something infinite or not? That is the telling question of his life." But he adds the warning: "The feeling for the infinite, however, can be attained only if we are bounded to the utmost. The greatest limitation for man is the 'Self,' it is manifested in the experience: 'I am *only* that'! Only consciousness of our narrow confinement in the Self forms the link to the limitlessness of the unconscious. In such awareness we experience ourselves concurrently as limited and eternal, as both the one and the other. In knowing ourselves to be unique in our personal combination – that is, ultimately limited – we possess also the capacity for becoming conscious of the infinite. But only then!"[25]

Here I think is the point above all where any imitation of the East can harm us. They are conscious of "their narrow confinement" but all too often we are not. And yet – as Jung makes so clear here – it is the *conditio sine qua non* of all realization of the Beyond. Therefore we cannot, as the Chinese do, fix our whole attention and concentration on the infinite – we get terribly out of ourselves if we try – but can only approach the same result by the paradox: "I am *only* that" and yet I can participate and to some extent realize the infinite at one and the same time.

The Chinese point out – and this probably holds good for us – that the best opportunity to realize the infinite is in sleep. The philosopher Dschuang Dzi says that "the spirit wanders in sleep, for in sleep it is in the liver". Wilhelm explains that he means that during sleep it is not in the brain, nor anywhere in consciousness but in the vegetative system. Deep sleep, they think, is very nearly related to the condition in which we shall find ourselves after death. But here their view is again different from ours in that they regard dreams as "remnants of consciousness" and think that they should be educated not to disturb us! This to them is the same thing as educating ourselves for life after death, and they maintain that great sages no longer dream.

This is always a great difference between the Eastern and our own point of view. They seem, for the most part, to be entirely blind to the value of dreams and to how much we can learn just from them about the condition they wish to establish. We certainly do not think it would help to educate our dreams (!), in fact we know we can do nothing of the sort without grave psychic loss. Dr. Jung dreamed up to just before his death and most particularly meaningful dreams. But that we are in the Beyond during sleep, almost entirely freed from the limitations of space and time, is certainly an idea that is founded on fact.

This is probably the reason why it is possible for us to "do our best to form a conception of life after death, or to create some image of it." Probably the Beyond is much less strange and far more familiar than we expect. I once heard of an English doctor whose experience during a bad illness brings us some confirmation of this. He was very near death, in fact the people round him had even thought he was dead, but nevertheless he recovered entirely. Afterwards he remembered very vividly that he had been in a place which was even more familiar to him than his own house and garden. But he had been astonished beyond measure to learn that this familar place was death! Dr. Jung – when he heard of this – said that exactly agreed with his own impression; he thought we should find the Beyond extraordinarily familiar to us. He added, however: "But I don't think the ego will like the change, we must reckon with a protest from it."

Wilhelm then goes into what he calls a third subject which is not individual but collective in character. As this would be rather long and complicated to explain, I would like to remind you of the better known and similar idea of the individual and universal Atman. Using that language, it is only through the existence of the universal Atman that it is possible for the individual Atman to experience the post-mortal condition in a way that no longer arouses the slightest fear. Therefore it is the task of life to prepare itself for death – *not* in the sense of chalking up a number of good deeds to our credit in order to ensure our later entrance to heaven – but in the sense of creating a condition that represents a detachment from the finite in favour of the infinite. This they regard as a journey or journeys into the universe.

A short time before his death, Dr. Jung dreamed that he saw a green, scarab-like beetle circumambulating his pocket knife, spinning a thread round and round it. Then it went on to spin a sail, and using the pocket knife as an anchor it sailed off into space. The pocket knife was one Dr. Jung had had for years and used daily for many purposes, so, if we take it as representing the ego mind and will, we might venture the hypothesis that – even in death – the ego does not just disappear but is put to a completely new use: i.e., it is used as an anchor to the individual which would prevent the soul from disappearing into the impersonal unconscious.

Wilhelm goes on to explain that detachment from the finite – whether it is in actual death or death in life for rebirth – is a repetition of the great psychical revolution of birth, when heaven and earth step aside and change places for the human being. If we think of Dr. Jung's dream of the Yogin who had his face and who, he realized, was the one who was either meditating or dreaming his present life,[26] we might say that at birth, the great figure of the Yogin, representing heaven, steps aside, or falls asleep, and gives over the action for its lifetime to the ego, representing the earth. And, as Dr. Jung realized in his dream, when the Yogin wakes up and takes over again, the ego will cease to function as before, either through actual death or by the ego's death for rebirth. The death of the ego for rebirth is really exactly what Meister Eckhart constantly advises when he says "leave yourself." He even says: "Remember, in this life no one ever left himself so much but he could find something more to leave. Very few can stand it who know what it really means. It is just a give and take, a mutual exchange: thou goest out of things so much and just so much, no more or less, does God go in: with all of his if thou dost go clean out of all of thine. Try it, though it cost thy all. That way lies true peace and none elsewhere."[27] In his own Western, medieval language, Meister Eckhart is advising the same thing here as the Chinese do when they say they should detach their whole attention and energy from the finite and give it to the infinite. Meister Eckhart sees it as giving up our own human way entirely, so that God may replace it by his divine will, whereas the Chinese sage sees it as giving up all interest in the world so that the divine entelechy, that is present in us all, may develop and grow into its own realm, the infinite.

That these efforts – difficult as they are – sometimes succeed in China is demonstrated by the fact that Wilhelm tells us the different ways in which the Taoists and Confucians live after it has succeeded. Both indeed now take eternal things much more seriously than temporal matters. It seems, however, that the Taoist develops a very ironical attitude to this life and is inclined to despise and laugh at the whole thing. But the Confucian, Wilhelm says, shows a "sovereign dignity" in his whole new attitude to this life. He descends from the high summits he has discovered to the place on earth where he belongs and most adequately fulfils every duty which pertains to that place. This is *not*, Wilhelm adds, because he feels any need to acquire merit by doing so, but because it is now the way in which it suits him to live. He can give himself fully to this life now because he no longer has any need to *go over* into the Beyond. Finite and infinite, here and Beyond, are no longer in any way separated for him, they exist simultaneously and are both penetrated equally by the Tao, the meaning, in which he now lives and has his being.

At bottom the idea of the Confucian now living his life in Tao is exactly what Meister Eckhart also means when he says that, if we can only give up our own ego way entirely, God will replace it completely by his will. It is really only a difference in language, for in both cases we live by something that is equally at home in finite and infinite, to such an extent that the two are no longer separated by space or time. Or – to put it in our own more modern language – the ego abdicates in favour of the Self. But – and this is very important for us – we, like the Confucians, must then live our outer lives more and not less fully. Dr. Jung said in his seminar on Kundalini: "You should leave some trace in this world which notifies you have been here, that something has happened. If nothing happens of this kind, you have not realized yourself, and the germ of life has fallen into a thick layer of air that kept it suspended, it never touched the ground, so could never produce the plant." And he adds later: "If you succeed in completing your 'entelechia', that shoot will come up from the ground, namely the possibility of detachment from this world."[28]

Only by detachment – that quality which Meister Eckhart values higher than any other[29] – can we "form a conception of life after death or create some image of it." But we can only afford this detachment by the utmost attachment to life and by a determination to live it as faithfully as possible, till we really come to the right time for what the Chinese call the greatest good fortune of all: namely finding our own specific death, which will crown and not tear apart our life.

NOTES

1. This paper is published by kind permission of the author and of Mr. David F. Marshall, manager-editor of *Quadrant* © 1969 by the C. G. Jung Foundation for Analytical Psychology Inc. New York.
2. *Memories, Dreams, Reflections* (Pantheon Books, New York, 1961), p. 302.
3. In *Wandlung and Dauer,* Richard Wilhelm.
4. *Memories, Dreams, Reflections*, p. 328 f.
5. The German (p. 331) is: "aber es entwickelt böse Folgen, weil man ihm verfallen ist." The English translation (p. 329) "to have succumbed to it may breed trouble" seems to me too mild.
6. *The Secret of the Golden Flower* (Routledge & Kegan Paul, London, reprint of 1965), p. 95.
7. Ibid. p. 85 f.
8. *Memories, Dreams, Reflections*, p. 183.
9. Ibid., p. 197.
10. St. John, 3:11.

11. *Memories, Dreams, Reflections,* p. 189 ff.
12. Ibid., p. 323.
13. Ibid., p. 292.
14. Ibid., p. 197.
15. Ibid., p. 223.
16. *The Secret of the Golden Flower,* p. 91.
17. *Collected Works,* Vol. 9, I, pp. 111 f.
18. Ibid., Vol. 9, I, p. 130.
19. *Hauer Seminar,* p. 154.
20. Ibid., p. 156 f.
21. Ibid..
22. Ibid., p. 158.
23. *Memories, Dreams, Reflections,* p. 302.
24. *The Secret of the Golden Flower,* p. 3.
25. *Memories, Dreams, Reflections,* p. 325.
26. Ibid., p. 323.
27. *Meister Eckhart,* translated by P. de B. Evans (London, John Watkins, reprinted 1952), Vol. 2, p. 6.
28. *Hauer Seminar,* p. 161.
29. *Meister Eckhart,* Vol. I, pp. 340 ff.

Reflections on Jung's Concept of Synchronicity[1]

by Rosemary Gordon

ROSEMARY GORDON, PhD., is a professional member and training analyst of the Society of Analytical Psychology. She is a fellow of, and past Chairman of the Medical Section of, the British Psychological Society, and also a fellow of the Royal Anthropological Institute. She is co-author of The Function and Nature of Imagery, The Study of Education and Art *and* The Forbidden Love, *and author of* Dying and Creating. *She is a part-time lecturer in the Art Department of the London Institute of Education, and also participates in the activities of the Jungian Group in France.*

When I was trying to write this paper, I found myself battling with it. So I stopped to ask myself what it was that had actually attracted me to the problem of synchronicity. I then discovered that the problem of synchronicity represents for me a challenge, a challenge to my tendency to look for bridges, or to build them. Bridges help me to see the world as one, as a totality, however intricate and complex its internal pattern may be. Such was the conclusion of my introspection; and I felt that this conclusion was confirmed when, a while later, I decided to consult the *I Ching* about the prospects of my attempt. I felt justified in consulting the *I Ching;* after all I was going to write about synchronicity. The *I Ching* answered me with Hexagram 20; this made little sense to me at first, until I noticed a sentence which seemed to me to express my basic concern; it seemed to me then that the *I Ching* had given me my *leitmotif.* It said:

> Thus also in nature a holy seriousness is to be seen in the fact that natural occurrences are uniformly subject to law.

Perhaps I do no more in this paper than expand or spell out Jung's ideas and arguments. But until one has for oneself discovered and experienced a problem as difficult and as baffling as synchronicity, one cannot really relate to it or handle it. I need not apologise, I think, for indulging in speculations which are essentially tentative. We are still very much in the dark, we can only grope around, and no-one was more aware of this than Jung.

I want, first of all, to summarise Jung's thesis. Jung developed the concept of synchronicity in order to provide a theoretical framework which might help us to deal with those strange and apparently inexplicable facts that defy the classical categories of time, space and causality. They are the facts and phenomena that most scientists try to by-pass or to ignore. They are the facts which appear to be random or haphazard, but which induce in us a feeling that something important is happening. Briefly the phenomena that aroused Jung's curiosity and concern are as follows:

1.   Clairvoyance. This refers to the perception of an event which takes place at such a distance from the observer that his ordinary sense organs cannot be thought to have transmitted it.

2.   Precognition. With precognition one perceives an event which does not yet exist, but which will only happen in the future. For instance in one of Rhine's experiments the subject is asked to guess a series of cards that will be laid out in either the near or distant future. As Jung reports, the interval was increased from a few minutes to two weeks.

3.   Telepathy. This is a communication between persons which is independent of the usual and sensory channels of communication.

4.   Psychokinesis. This is said to occur when a psychic state exerts an influence upon the physical world, again independently of known sensori-motor methods. Examples of this are the Poltergeist phenomena, or the results produced by Rhine in his laboratory when the subjects' will was shown to affect the throw of the dice.

5.   The coincidence of a psychic state in the observer with a simultaneous but objective event. The best example is again given by Jung: a patient was telling him a most important dream in which she was given a golden scarab. At that moment Jung heard a gentle tapping on the window behind him; he went to investigate, opened it and in flew a scarab beetle, or rather the nearest to a scarab beetle found in Switzerland.

6.   The duplication of cases. This is quite a familiar phenomenon in medical practice as well as in daily life. But the most dramatic and amusing example of this is Jung's story of M. de Fortgibu.
   A certain M. Deschamp, when a boy in Orleans, was once given a

piece of plum pudding by a M. de Fortgibu. Ten years later he discovered another plum pudding in a Paris restaurant, and asked if he could have a piece. It turned out, however, that the plum pudding was already ordered – by M. de Fortgibu. Many years later M. Deschamp was invited to partake of a plum pudding as a special rarity. While he was eating it he remarked that the only thing lacking was M. de Fortgibu. At that moment the door opened and an old, old man in the last stages of disorientation walked in: M. de Fortgibu, who had got hold of the wrong address and burst in on the party by mistake.

Behind all these phenomena there stands for Jung the general problem of the equivalence, or correspondence, between physical and psychic process, between external and internal events; the problem of the apparently meaningful configuration "formed by chance events in the moment of observation".[2]

As a result of study and reflection and collaboration with Professor Pauli, the physicist, Jung has proposed that the categories of space, time and causality, which classical physics had invoked in order to explain and account for events, should be extended; and that to these three categories should be added as a fourth dimension, the category of synchronicity. Synchronistic events are events connected by inconstant connections, while causal events are connected by constant and regular connections. synchronicity is thus a principle opposed to causality.

As a matter of fact, I think that in his essay on synchronicity, Jung has really given us not one, but three major explanatory principles. They are probably interdependent, but it may clarify the problem if we differentiate them. These three explanatory principles are as follows:

1. Acausal orderedness: Jung regards this as the major category; it would therefore have been more logical to oppose this to the causality principle rather than synchronicity, because Jung regards synchronicity as only a special instance of the acausality principle.

2. Synchronicity: This is a phenomenon whose essential quality is meaningfulness. Jung places the accent quite emphatically on this quality of meaningfulness when he distinguishes synchronicity, or, as he calls it, 'meaningful coincidence' from what he calls 'meaningless chance groupings'.

Jung ascribes the functioning of synchronicity to the activity of the unconscious psyche. He claims that only the unconscious psyche can have *a priori* knowledge, that such knowledge is usually in the form of images and that it is always based on archetypal processes.

3.   The third concept he produces is the concept of the 'psychoid'. This property he now attributes to the collective unconscious, and he describes it as that property which is found to be common to both matter and psyche. Jung feels that such a concept is absolutely necessary, if one is to account for the interaction between mind and matter. For how, so he asks, can there be such interaction unless ... "psyche touches matter at some point and matter is latent with psyche".[3] This is an extremely difficult and puzzling subject, and I shall return to it later.

Jung describes the archetype as "the introspectively recognisable form of *a priori* psychic orderedness".[3] This means, I think, that he regards the archetype as a sort of psychic sense organ, which enables us to perceive or to experience acausal orderedness.

The hypothesis of synchronicity provokes speculations in three different fields of study - physics, philosophy and psychology, which I shall try and discuss in this order.

Jung himself was obviously very interested and influenced by the recent developments in physics, especially by the speculations about probability. The modern physicist is in fact much exercised by the enigma of the co-existence of randomness and caprice in the individual particle with the statistical regularity of aggregates of such particles and their conformity to laws. For instance, if an atom is heated, it becomes self-luminous. But the light it emits is not continuous and the omissions are of different colours; no rule governs their sequence; yet every element has its own characteristic assortment of colours on being heated, and by this it can be identified.

This paradox inevitably tempts one to ask whether the behaviour of the individual particle is really truly random and unpredictable, or whether there is perhaps a certain order, which cannot be observed or measured, but which would explain the regularity of the aggregates. In other words is there perhaps a "configuration formed by chance events in the moment of observation"[2] that underlies the apparent randomness of the individual particle; does the 'caprice' of the individual particle in fact conform to some acausal orderedness, so that, paraphrasing Jung about synchronicity, the coincidence of events in space and time means something more than mere chance?

I feel that valuable help in dealing with this paradox comes from Professor Margenau, who in 1961 published his book called *Open Vistas*, in which he proposes a scheme that seems to me to be an interesting parallel to Jung's scheme of causal and acausal orderedness.[4] Margenau proposes that we distinguish between what he calls 'physical reality' from what he calls 'historical reality'. 'Physical reality', Margenau suggests, covers those events and processes which are governed by the statistical regularity of the aggregates; it refers therefore to the macroscopic world, to the enduring entities of classical physics. It is the world of high probabilities, the world in which one asks how and why such and such events evolve out of such and such antecedent events; it is the world of essences, in which we are concerned with 'chairness' or 'tableness', rather than with this or that chair or table. This then is Margenau's 'physical reality'. 'Historical reality', on the other hand is the "reality of the bare and given facts and immediacies of our experience". For instance, if one makes an observation in microphysics, one may see a particle at a definite place. Therefore, at the moment of the observation, and at that moment only, the object was surely at the place were it was seen. But the observation bears as much on the question of the physical behaviour of the particle as on the psychology of perception. In the realm of historical reality, therefore, the dichotomy between spectator and spectacle is undone, and the partial fusion of knower and known is recognised. Historical reality, therefore, concerns itself with individual events, with single observations, with the total pattern in the "here and now", with existences. Margenau's 'physical reality' is therefore the contemplation of the world in terms of the causal laws, or in terms of what Jung has called the 'dramatic story'; while his 'historical reality' could be thought of as functioning in accordance with Jung's principle of synchronicity, that is in terms of the perception of a meaningful, existing and present pattern.

This is perhaps the point to discuss briefly the status of the concept of causality at present. Causality is a concept that has undergone considerable evolution. According to the classical theory of causality there is a necessary connection between events in a time series; cause and effect need not be different in character, but they must occupy different moments in time.

However, Hume has lifted the problem of causality out of the field of the logician, and has placed it into the orbit of the psychologist. Hume has suggested that the concept of causality does not repose on any logical argument, but that it is an idea which men form as result of habit. The experience of a uniform recurrence of events creates in them a compulsory anticipation and they form the belief in a necessary connection; this then becomes the foundation of the principle of causality. Thus, the concept of causality springs, not from logic and experience, Hume would argue, but from man's congenital need to assume order and uniformity.

Since Hume other philosophers and psychologists have suggested that man creates for himself the concept of causality by extrapolation of the experience of his own subjective activity. If, for instance, I now turn my head to the right, I experience that my intentions, my thoughts and my will have caused my head to turn right. Causality, on this view, is therefore the projection upon the external world of experiences noted in the internal world.

In more recent times philosophers and scientists seem to be more concerned with the relativistic quality of causality. Bertrand Russell for instance, suggests that in the well developed sciences the causal laws are so complex, that they are merely elaborate inferences from the observed course of nature.[5] For de Broglie the causal laws of mechanics are simply a "macroscopic illusion due to the complexity of objects and the lack of precision of measurement".[6] And in support he quotes von Neumann who wrote already in 1932 that ...

> it is only on the atomic scale in the elementary processes themselves that the question of causality can be really put to the test; but on this scale, in the present state of our knowledge, everything tells against it. There exists today no reason which allows us to affirm the existence of causality in nature.[7]

On the whole, the idea of probability has replaced the idea of causality.

The concept of probability, however, provides a framework, not of an 'all-or-nothing', but of a 'more or less'. It is a concept that seems to me to be akin to Bergson's idea of 'weak' and 'strong' causality. Speaking of 'weak' causality, in "continu et discontinu" Bergson writes:-

> If, therefore, we decide to conceive the causal relation in this *weak* form, we can affirm, a priori, that a relation of determinism between cause and effect will no longer be necessary, for the effect will no longer be given in the same cause. It will reside there only in a state of possibility and as a confused representation which will not, perhaps, be followed by the corresponding action.[8]

De Broglie explains Bergson's view as follows:-

> Weak causality allows us to suppose that the same cause can

produce one or other of several possible effects, with only a certain probability that such an effect will be produced and not such another. Physicists no longer succeed in finding anything except this weak causality on the very small scale.[6]

Margenau, so it seems to me, discusses the concept of causality with an understanding of man's emotional needs of it when he writes that ...

it does no harm if the physicist tries to explain the erratic behaviour of the atomic world by a reference to causative agencies; it affords him comfort and makes the microcosm seem less strange; the fact is, however, that he is then indulging in a bit of metaphysical speculation, and he ought to be aware of it.[4]

On the whole then, ever since Hume, it is no longer asked: does causality exist? but rather: why does man need such a concept? The answer to this lies probably in the fact that man needs such constructs as 'essence' and 'causality' in order to create for himself order and meaning. As Margenau says:

. . . facts clamour to be explained; they do not carry within themselves the elements of order which reason desires to bestow upon experience ... The facts alone are meaningless. Only when they appear at the end of a deductive chain do they take on richness, perspective and significance. The deductive chain is called an explanation; its links, together with other concepts, form a theory

and he quotes with approval Kant's succinct remark that

Concepts without factual content are empty; sense data without concepts are blind.

In concluding his essay on synchronicity Jung remarks that to him synchronicity seems no more baffling or mysterious than the discontinuities of physics, and he proposes that we should think of causeless events as creative acts, as ... "the continuous creation of a pattern".[3] Am I too speculative when I suggest that perhaps Jung thought of the psychic as manifested in the randomness of the individual particle? for 'randomness' might indeed be regarded as a 'creative act'.

This possible link or analogy between the psychic and the random brings me immediately to the question of what Jung meant when he proposed the idea of the 'psychoid'. Here seems to be the germ of a theory about the relationship between body and mind; it is, however, not quite clear to me whether Jung regards the 'psychoid' as something additional to mind and to body – a hypothesis that would offend the 'canon of conceptual simplicity' – or whether, as I believe is more likely, he regards the psychoid as the basic substance, which is only differentiated into mind and matter for the purpose of examination, observation and thought. In other words, does Jung propose here a fundamental monism? Does he conceive the 'psychoid' in much the same way in which Spinoza conceived 'substance', that is as 'God or Nature' – soul and matter being merely attributes of this one substance – 'the divine substance' as Stein has called it in a personal communication.

This second interpretation seems to tally with remarks that Jung has thrown out in some of the other essays. In *Spirit and Life* for instance, Jung writes:-

> This living being appears outwardly as the material body, but inwardly as a series of images of the vital activities taking place within it. They are two sides of the same coin, and we cannot rid ourselves of the doubt that perhaps this whole separation of mind and body may finally prove to be merely a device of reason for the purpose of conscious discrimination – an intellectually necessary separation of one and the same fact into two aspects, to which we then illegitimately attribute an independent existence.

And in *Nature and Psyche* Jung also says that:

> psyche and matter are two different aspects of one and the same thing.

Later in the same essay he argues that if his reflections are justified, then it must be assumed that psyche is intimately connected not only with physiology and biology, but also with "the realm of atomic physics." Perhaps I was not excessively speculative when I suggested that Jung himself may have related together the psychic and the random.

I have wondered whether, in developing the concept of the 'psychoid', Jung had not in fact tried to align himself to Bohr's principle of complementarity. Bohr believed that the limitations of man's understanding made it inevitable that he should need dual types of description of the world and of his experiences of it. Robert Oppenheimer has pointed out examples of such dual or complementary reasoning in such pairs of theories as the kinetic theory of gases versus the dynamics of molecular motion; the biological theory of life versus the physico-chemical descriptions of life; the introspective analysis of consciousness versus its behaviouristic description; and then there is, of course, the corpuscular theory of light versus the wave theory of light, a controversy which had in fact led to the formulation of the principle of complementarity.

If it is indeed Jung's view that the 'psychoid' is the wholeness out of which matter and psyche differentiate, then the psychoid can also be thought of as encompassing microcosm and macrocosm, and causal as well as synchronistic processes and events. But if the 'psychoid' is such a totality, then it is essentially irrepresentable. Understanding and experience of the totality can be gained only through differentiation, that is through the constellation of the opposites and through the elaboration of theories that are opposed to each other, but whose complementary character is recognised. If, as I have suggested elsewhere, and in another context, we regard the archetypes as "pieces of the self", then it is natural that it should be their function to mediate to consciousness the psychic experience of the 'psychoid'.

As I have already pointed out, synchronicity is distinguished from acausal orderedness – its superordinate principle – by its essential quality of 'meaningfulness'. In whatever sense Jung wanted to use this term 'meaningfulness' – and I suspect that he meant to convey with it the perception of order and the experience of significance – the concept of meaningfulness refers to the intimate relationship between subject and object, between knower and known. Meaningfulness is surely that quality of an experience which has been contributed mainly by the spectator in the spectator-spectacle interaction. As I have mentioned, Jung insists on this distinction between a 'meaningful coincidence' and 'meaningless chance groupings'. The difference between these two seems to me to lie in the difference of the involvement or in the state of preparedness of the person concerned. It is the involvement or the preparedness which determines whether a series of events shall be merely chance groupings or whether they shall be synchronistic. It follows that, in order to decide whether a particular event is or is not synchronistic, we must explore the person-event interaction: Does the event touch on matters that are intensely experienced? Is it the concern of some major interest? Is it the focus of some deep conflict? If the answer to these questions is 'no', then the coincidence will probably pass by unnoticed; it will remain 'coincidence'. Jung, Rhine and others have in fact described some of the psychological conditions that favour a synchronistic occurrence. They are: interest, excitement and heightened emotions; boredom is definitely an obstacle.

Analysts take the problem further. Fordham in his paper on *Reflections on Archetypes and Synchronicity*[9] supports Jung's belief that "synchronicity depends upon a relatively unconscious state of mind, i.e. on an "abaissement due niveau mental". Fordham describes in his paper the misadventures of one of his patients in an ocean boat race. The boat had been given to the patient by his father, who hoped that the son would realise his ambitions for him and win the race. The son, however, was in the middle of a period of acute conflict with his father. Quite unaccountably, and for no apparent reason, the mast fell overboard in the middle of the race. This surprising accident had put an end to the patient's conflict. Fordham describes a whole number of other coincidences on this trip which seemed to express further the patient's conflictful relationship with both his mother and father, and of which he seemed to have been relatively unconscious at that time. But, Fordham goes on to describe, for months afterwards the patient looked for and found 'significant coincidences' – two people wearing the same type of hat, or looking at him in a similar way, etc. – but these coincidences lacked any real meaning and were merely echoes of the original and true synchronicity.

This 'echo synchronicity' suggests that acausally ordered phenomena may in fact be happening around us all the time; it is only under certain conditions that we attend to them and that they then assume meaning for us. Fordham's patient continued to report apparently synchronistic events, though they lacked intrinsic meaning. Had they not perhaps a meaning in terms of the patient's needs in the relationship to his analyst?

Michael Balint, in a paper on parapsychology[10], has suggested that ESP phenomena – which Jung subsumes under the heading of synchronicity – occur in analysis when the patient is in a state of intense, positive and dependent transference, a state which is not, however, fully appreciated or understood by the analyst. ESP phenomena represent, according to Balint, the patient's effort, bordering on despair, to win the analyst's attention. Consequently, he argues, the dynamic interrelationship between transference and counter-transference is one of the most important contributory factors in ESP.

Balint's suggestion seems to me to be very important and of much practical use. It creates a state of mind in which synchronicity is not an event that fascinates, but it is a challenge. Balint's approach is not opposed to Jung's or Fordham's. On the contrary. All three of them point to unconscious needs, affects and complexes as factors that favour the occurrence of a synchronistic event. But Balint's suggestion is very precise, and definite, and so provides a focus for one's attention. It also helps us, I think, to understand a phenomenon like echo synchronicity, a phenomenon where the event itself has no intrinsic meaning.

However the transference-counter-transference situation is perhaps even more complex and intricate than the dimensions of 'attention' and 'inattention', 'positive' and 'negative' suggest. Perhaps I can make clearer the intricacy of the pattern that exists between synchronicity and the transference–counter-transference situation by giving some examples – two of my own, and one from a paper by Mary Williams.[12] In these examples I shall try to draw attention to the complexity of the interaction between synchronicity and the unconscious mechanisms and to the technical problems that this poses.

The first is a case of a telepathic dream produced by a patient coming from a large family but who feels herself to be a dark and sad Cinderella, the very unfavourite daughter of her mother.

She has had a recurrent dream in which she comes to me for her session, but she finds me over-burdened with domestic affairs – the housekeeper has left or I am moving furniture – or else I am swamped by the demands of a large and clamorous family. In consequence I have no time for her. She feels sad and rejected, yet it is almost not my fault. It is often another, an elderly woman, who tells her that I am too busy. The projection of her family situation into our relationship is evident.

In actual life one of my best friends had died. The funeral was on a Friday. This patient was the last patient I was going to see before setting off for the funeral. In the course of the session she suddenly remembers the dream:

I am in a department store. I am going along a corridor and suddenly come upon a group of people, assembled round a coffin. There is sadness. But I don't really have anything to do with it. It is not my dead, it is not my grief; I don't really belong there, and I leave.

The dream was quite right in many respects. There was "a dead", there was a grief and it did not really belong to her. This seemed, therefore, to be a telepathic dream. Naturally I was impressed and moved and for a brief moment I wondered whether to tell the patient about the synchronistic character of her dream; whether to let her into my secret; whether to admit her to the group of mourners. I desisted. I felt that the need for absolute union and the fear of such absolute union might be made almost unbearable for her were I to let her know about this secret communication between us. I feared that she would experience such telepathic communication either as me invading her – this would create terror – or as her intruding into my private life – this would create guilt. I feared that the ever-present desire for magic and the ever-present apprehension of magic might be supported and nourished. I decided that it was enough that I should know what had happened between us and try to become aware of all that it might express.

This telepathic communication seemed to me to be primarily an expression of her great need for togetherness, a need to sweep aside all the barriers that were between us. It seemed to me possible that my own sadness had somehow leaked, though I had not seen the patient in between my friend's death and her funeral. However, the dream, telepathic as it might be, seemed also to belong in character to the type of dreams she had had before about our relationship. It repeated once more the theme of finding herself excluded from a group. This sense of exclusion is undoubtedly a deep fear in this patient; it creates unconscious expectations which colour all her relationships, particularly the analytical relationship. It is a complex, which of necessity makes her sensitive to any event that fits into the complex. I felt that it was better to work out this problem between us in terms of her own feelings and fantasies, rather than introduce what might have seemed to her magical or miraculous.

My second example is, if anything, even less dramatic than the first. Another woman patient had had several dreams in which I was instrumental in her meeting a man. The wish to be married was uppermost in consciousness. But for many months she had experienced strong homosexual desires for me and often complained bitterly that I would not go to bed with her, that I would not let myself be seduced. She felt she was bad, ugly and utterly unloveable. She is in fact a very attractive and elegant woman. Her need of me was intensely jealous and exclusive. To her sharing means losing. However, while expressing strong sexual wishes for me in the sessions, she also produced dreams in which she seemed much afraid of being seduced by a woman - the woman was either quite undisguisedly myself or else somebody who was readily recognised as being me. In her actual behaviour with me I had already noticed a need to protect herself against any possible physical contact or closeness between us. For instance on leaving my room at the end of the sessions she would always close the door carefully behind her. I felt that she needed to imprison or to cage me in as soon as she could no longer rely on the boundary of the analytical situation to protect her.

The major ingredients in this patient relevant to the point I want to make are therefore:

1. The wish for a satisfying heterosexual relationship in marriage.
2. Jealousy.
3. Overt homosexual desires in the transference.
4. Fear of homosexual seduction.

While the patient was able to gain considerable insight and emotional experience of the first three affective patterns, she has never been able to experience or acknowledge her fear of seduction.

However, a series of coincidences dogged this patient, which became so regular and so predictable, that I became almost accustomed to them: this is the only one of my patients who has met me together with my husband in a pub. Whenever a patient rings up and my husband happens to be answering the telephone, it is certain to be this particular patient. One day, on leaving me, she met another patient, a young man, who was bounding up the stairs, carrying, for the first, and I think only, time a bunch of flowers to bring to me. This coincidence created such anxiety and fury that she broke off treatment for a few weeks.

Some time ago the patient became depressed. For many months she had not been able to come to me more than once a week. I now arranged to see her three times a week – Mondays, Thursdays and Fridays. This worked well for three weeks. In the fourth week she cancelled the Monday session, because of the school's half term. In the fifth week she again cancelled the Monday session, but for what seemed to me a much less valid reason. On Thursday morning I had a date to go out. I was late. My maid happened to look out of the window and saw my husband. This was quite unexpected. I quickly decided that he might give me a lift in the car to where I had to go; I called out of the window to him and signed him to wait for me – little knowing that my patient was waiting on the doorstep. I gathered up my shopping basket and went downstairs. On the stairs I met the patient, who had been let in by the housekeeper ... The session, as you can imagine, was extremely tense and disturbing. I had had a quick look into my diary only to find that I had not in fact noted down this extra appointment with the patient.

I do not, of course, claim that my forgetting this patient's session was a synchronistic phenomenon. Later introspection led me to realise that I had felt that my good offering of the extra sessions had been rejected or dealt with in a somewhat cavalier fashion; I had felt annoyed, though unfortunately, I had not made this sufficiently clear and conscious to myself. No, my forgetting is explicable in terms of what we know about unconscious mechanisms. However, the circumstances around this forgetting seemed to be tailor-made for this particular patient. Once more the third person, the man, had intruded into our relationship and threatened to separate us, leaving her alone and deserted. As we worked together on what had happened and on her feelings about it, she suddenly admitted that she had felt almost a little pleased, because it confirmed to her that she was free. At that point I took a risk. I decided to call her attention to the pattern of coincidences that had formed itself between us. This pattern, I suggested, expressed for her what she could not feel consciously, that is her fear of too great a closeness with me and her fantasy and wish that the mother surrender to her the man, whom she holds captive inside her.

I feel that in this second patient a reference to the synchronicity in our relationship helped to create a greater consciousness. It did, in fact, succeed, because the patient has become more able to face up to and to experience the fear, hostility and rivalry that is between us. In her case synchronicity, I feel, took over the function of the analyst's interpretation; it made explicit an unconscious emotional experience.

The synchronistic events in Mary Williams' *Poltergeistman* are very much more startling and dramatic than those that I have been able to produce from my own experience. Mary Williams' patient, a man of 32, arrived for treatment together with his Poltergeist. Phenomena of raps ... "loud and sharp like something hard cracking" were heard by both patient and analyst and both of them saw a cupboard door open "slowly and silently". The Poltergeist "made a positive crescendo of raps" when the patient and his girl-friend discussed anything to do with dreams or psychology, and he tormented the girl-friend even in the patient's absence. The Poltergeist also caressed the patient, stroked and tickled his face, twitched his hair, and of course, appeared in dreams. Mary Williams sums up her interpretation of the phenomenon as follows:-

It seems to me that the appearance of the Poltergeist coincided with the rise of the unsolved mother-child complex, which lay behind the father identification, and which was split off from the ideal male personality. It had the mother's puritanical yet fiercely jealous and possessive nature and tended to act as she would in the original mother-child relationship....What he was up against was an archetypal power transmitted through the mother, which produced the phenomena and affected all those who came into contact with him.

The Poltergeist, she suggests, "behaved like a succubus, but its loving intentions were usually masked by its forbidding, moralistic nature, so that he felt he had to fight it." When, as a result of the analysis, the patient succeeded in de-identifying with the parents, and in making conscious his puritanism as well as his intense incestuous longings for the mother, then the Poltergeist departed.

The Poltergeist case raises, of course, the whole problem of the relationship between mind and matter. It raises the question of how unconscious complexes can project and manifest themselves in the physical world. It also raises the problem of patient and analyst sharing and participating in a joint unconscious drama.

And then there is the further question: why does the unconscious complex express itself here in synchronicity, in a spirit manifestation, when in other and similar cases it shows itself in symptoms, dreams and fantasies? Is there anything special about the sort of people in whom complexes take on this particular, this synchronistic form? There are some studies of the personality of people with well developed psi functions – as the capacity to experience synchronistic phenomena tends to be called. Rhine reports some of these. It is usually expansive rather than constricted people who have a well developed psi function, so he claims; and he believes that psi is distributed along a normal curve, like most abilities; that is to say the majority of people have an average amount, a few people have outstandingly high and a few outstandingly low psi ability. But on the whole research and information on this point is meagre and unreliable, and so far the more promising approach is really that of the analysts, who like Jung and Fordham, relate psi to an 'abaisse- ment du niveau mental'. In support of this view I would like to mention another patient of mine. She had toyed with the idea of analysis for a while, until a synchronistic event made her enter analysis precipitately and in a great panic. She had always been liable to experience telepathy and apparently precognition and clairvoy- ance. As a result of an accident she saw a great deal of her G.P. and fell in love with him. As her feelings for him became stronger, so her jealousy of his wife became more intense. One evening she indulged in her feelings of jealousy and hatred of her doctor's wife and wished her dead. That night she dreamed that she saw the doctor's wife laid out on a stretcher; she was dead. The patient then tried to console her doctor and started to look after him. On the day following this dream, the patient was told by a colleague that the doctor's wife had unexpectedly died that night. You can imagine that the patient's horror and guilt were intense, though there was also some secret triumph at her apparent power and witchiness.

As the analysis proceeded, fewer and fewer synchronistic phen- omena occurred or were reported. It seemed as if the patient had lost her fascination for them. Strangely enough, as far as I know, there have never been any synchronistic phenomena between the two of us.

Observing this patient I began to realise how difficult it must be to develop efficient ego functions if one possesses high psi. Confusion is so likely to result, because reality, fantasy and synchronicity cannot be easily distinguished one from another. There may also arise the question of course – particularly urgent in the case of my patient – whether one merely receives information about a certain event, or whether one has perhaps oneself produced it. In other words, was my patient a medium or a magician?

Thinking about the few examples I have given, I have asked myself whether it is really true that synchronistic events are 'acausal'. We seem, after all, to find some sort of explanation in terms of unconscious complexes and unconscious inter-personal relation-ships. We seem to be able to define some of the conditions that are favourable to synchronicity, and we can ourselves create other conditions – such as a greater consciousness – which are, apparently, unfavourable to synchronicity. It is therefore possible to make some predictions about synchronicity.

It would, of course, be misleading to suggest that consciousness and synchronicity are always antagonistic to one another. Perhaps the most important difference lies in the way the synchronistic phenomena are experienced. Where there is much unconscious-ness, synchronicity is either denied, or else it provokes fascination. The fascination, I believe, result from what Edinger has called the state of ego-self identity, when the ego is merged, identified with and inflated by the processes and forces of the self. Synchronicity, therefore, makes such persons feel particularly powerful, in control and singled out. In the more conscious and integrated individual synchronicity is experienced not as fascination but as education. It is received as an interpretation , which is the way Jung regarded the answers of the *I Ching*.

I wonder if causality and synchronicity could not be understood as two opposed but complementary methods of viewing life and events. Both are true, both are correct, just as both corpuscular and the wave theory of light are correct. But each covers a different sector of all the facts and each subserves a different function; each answers a different question. While explanations in terms of causality explain to us the world outside us and the regularity of the occurrences in it, explanations in terms of synchronicity lead us into our own inner world and confront us with ourselves. Causal explanations of an event serve to reduce the tension and numinosity of this event as a single and unique fact. Without access to the de-tensing question "why", one is forced to ask the awesome question: "what does this mean?" For the Western person, at least, the "why" question leads into the land of the familiar, the known and the commonplace and there he finds himself in a safe and reassuring landscape.

Causality and synchronicity, just like mind and matter, or physical reality and historical reality, may be two aspects of a totality. With the help of the principle of complementarity we may guess at this totality. The principle of complementarity makes us aware of our human, our intellectual limitations: it informs us that we can only attend to one aspect of a complex pattern at a time. It informs us that the answers we get depend, to some extent, upon the questions we have asked.

Both synchronicity and the concept of historical reality – if I may indulge in a final piece of speculation – emphasise the fusion of subject and object, of knower and known. This brings them very close, I think, to the idea of non-duality, which is basic to Zen philosophy, and which the students of Zen try to experience.

> When we are no longer identified with the idea of ourselves, the entire relationship between subject and object, knower and known, undergoes a sudden and revolutionary change. It becomes a real relationship, a mutuality, in which the subject creates the object just as much as the object creates the subject ... the individual on the one hand, and the world on the other are simply the abstract limits of a concrete reality which is 'between them'.

This is a passage from Alan Watts writing about Zen.[12]

> The Western scientist – physicist and psychologist – have thus arrived at a point to which the oriental philosopher attained through speculation and meditation. But I feel that a special contribution is made and a new dimension is added, if one goes along the Western road, if one follows the Western, the scientific method. For the acknowledgement of the principle of causality and of physical reality – which is in fact the acknowledgement of the reality of concepts – seems to me to be an acknowledgement of psychic reality. It is the acknowledgement that the human mind needs concepts, so as to bring order to the welter of sense data and experience; it is the acknowledgement that ordinary experience is possible only when the opposites have differentiated inside the psyche. Only through oppositeness and contrast can we exper-

ience the world. In a recent article Zuzuki remarks that when we wish to say that no words are needed, more words are needed to prove it. The Western scientist, I think, is less aggrieved, and does more justice than does the Zen philosopher, to this fact, this 'reality', this, as Zuzuki calls it, "contradiction or fatality". Causality versus synchronicity, historical reality versus physical reality, these opposites help us towards an awareness of the essential dialectics of all events and processes; the concept of complementarity on the other hand points to the underlying unity – which some may succeed in experiencing in those rare moments that Zen calls 'satori'.

I believe that in writing this paper I have, at least for myself, discovered a few bridges. Causal thinking and synchronistic thinking have always seemed to me to be mutually exclusive. I have therefore had to keep them in separate and water-tight compartments. That was limiting and uncomfortable. I have not been able to destroy the separateness of the compartments, but they seem to me now to be less water-tight. Though opposed, I can now think of them as complementary, I feel less uncomfortable ... And yet, there lurks a suspicion: is it the magic of naming which has made the mysterious appear less mysterious and so has created the illusion that I now understand?

NOTES

1. Reprinted from *Harvest* magazine, August 1962.
2. Jung, C.G. (1951) *Foreword to the I Ching*, London, Routledge and Kegan Paul.
3. Jung, C.G. (1960) *Collected Works*, Vol.8. London, Routledge and Kegan Paul.
4. Margenau, H. (1961) *Open Vistas*, New Haven, Yale University Press.
5. Russell, B. (1946) *A History of Western Philosophy*. London, George Allen &. Unwin.
6. de Broglie, L. (1955) *Physics and Microphysics*. Hutchinson, London.
7. Johann von Neumann (1932) *Mathematische Grundlagen der Quantenmechanik*, Berlin.
8. Henry Bergson.
9. Fordham, M. (1957) *New Developments in Analytical Psychology*. London. Routledge and Kegan Paul.
10. Balint, M. (1955) *Notes on Parapsychology and Parapsychological Healing*. Int. J. of Psychoanalysis, 36, 1.
11. Williams, Mary, (1961) *The Poltergeistman*.
12. Watts, Alan (1957) *The Way of Zen*. London, Thames & Hudson.

Physics and Psyche[1]

by Claude Curling

CLAUDE CURLING is a physicist, who was until recently subdean of the Faculty of Natural Science, King's College, London University. He is a member of the Teilhard Centre for the Future of Man.

I would like to try to share with you some of the excitement of developments in the new physics. Although this lecture stands by itself it is also the third of a series of four which have been concerned with the relationships between the new physics, mysticism, analytical psychology and alchemy. If you were to place mysticism, depth psychology, physics and mathematics at four poles then my major contention is that these meet at the union between inner space and outer space which is also the region of contact between the Self and the *unus mundus*. This Marie-Louise von Franz called a variation of our concept of the collective unconscious,[2] so that everything on earth has its archetypal model in the *unus mundus*.[3] The idea of the *unus mundus* is very old, but was introduced into alchemy by Gerhard Dorn in the 16th century. He himself was interested in what we would now call psychosomatic illness, and psychosomatic chemistry; he saw in his alchemy that the human psyche could recognise outer things directly by looking at inner things,[4] though he felt the *unus mundus* to be the endpoint of the alchemical quest only attained after death.[5]

Most remarkably, the mathematical physicists after eight decades of this century exploring the new physics — the physics of the very small which is called quantum physics, and the physics of the very large which is called relativity physics — have arrived at the notion of superspace, a mathematical space of infinite dimensions which seems to me to be identical with the *unus mundus*. What is studied in physics and psychology are both part of the moving geometry, the dancing forms, of superspace. Every existence exists in superspace, it is a space of spaces,[6] containing a real and potential multiplicity of universes;[7] compare this with Jung's description of the *unus mundus* as "the potential world outside time" and "the underlying unity" on which the multiplicity of the empirical world rests. Jung quotes from Abul Qasim on the *prima materia:*—

there does not exist (any conceivable aspect of any possible universe) that is not present there[8].

Secondly, compare J. A. Wheeler's comment on superspace:—

there is no such thing as time in superspace. Time is effaced[9]

with the timeless character of the *unus mundus*, described in *Aurora Consurgens;* finally compare the alchemical quest with the mathematician Paul Davies' description:—

The route to superspace is a hard one to tread, each step requiring the abandonment of some cherished notions or the acceptance of an unfamiliar concept.[10]

I had thought to accompany this paper with a table comparing the properties of superspace and the *unus mundus*, but I now intend to leave that for another time. But I have given you a map, (Fig. 1) which I must say immediately is a misleading map, which tries to represent the relationship of the things about which I am speaking. What I intend to do is to talk a little about the new physics, then about synchronicity, say a few words about archetypes, and finish with some further consideration of superspace and the *unus mundus*.

I know of few non-technical accounts of the new physics; but you should read the *Dancing Wu Li Masters* and then *Other Worlds*, and then for dessert digest the *Scientific American* article *The Quantum Theory and Reality*, and the paper from the *New Scientist* in March of this year called *Ghostly interactions in physics*. All this is very recent, and in fact, the correspondence in the May, 1980 *Scientific American* between Weisskopf and D'Espagnat is also important. I cannot recommend earlier physics books unless you are interested in the historical roots of the new physics. These go back beyond the four papers that Einstein published in 1905 which were themselves instrumental in the recognition that to study the very small or to study the very large: very large velocities, very large masses, very large times, we need new theories — the theories of quantum physics and relativity physics. In the second decade of this century Einstein developed the general theory of relativity; in the third decade quantum physics began to flower, and since then continuous development has led to a culmination in this decade, the ninth decade of the century, in which there appears to be happening a most remarkable revolution of unprecedented profundity[11] involving our ideas about ourselves, about mind and matter, and about the nature of reality, and of space and time.

This revolution seems to me to be inadequately described as a paradigm-shift. It is quite literally a revolution of the wheel of science that is plunging into the depths ideas such as dualism, mechanism, reductionism, and separability, which have dominated the scientific world-view for three centuries. What is emerging in compensation is more difficult to see but certainly there are ideas that have been neglected or forgotten, ideas that belong to ancient wisdom, alchemical ideas — these are all beginning to resurface. I have described this as the mid-life crisis in science when after three centuries it is discovered that consciousness, and the inner, the inferior and the non-dominant can no longer be ignored, but are clamouring to be integrated into a new unity, so that both our physics and our psychology need to become at once transpersonal and transcosmic.

Jung was of course in touch with the beginnings of these developments. He used to dine with Einstein and incorporated some ideas of the relativity of space and time into his concept of the psyche.[12] Later he collaborated with Pauli and hence had an understanding of the developments of both the physics of the very large and the physics of the very small. The new physics, which in some parts is very new, is vulnerable and open, and it is of great importance that while physicists are trying to free physics from its classical origins, and at the same time some analytical psychologists are following Jung's injunction to try to free psychology from its clinical origins, we do not spoil the fun by attempts to annex the territory of each other's discipline. It would not surprise me at all to discover that the exploration of the collective unconscious is relevant to physics, or to come to see that the edges of physics could provide suitable models for the behaviour of archetypes. Let me explain what I mean by examples.

A friend of mine on a visit to Zürich made some notes of a dissertation by V. G. Carlson, with the title *Black Holes: elements of the collective unconscious in astro-physics*. In this dissertation for the Institute, Carlson had the help of Dr. A. Mindell. The dissertation was inspired by Professor John Taylor's book on black holes; it makes some useful points, for example that Einstein's search for a unified field theory was connected with the *unus mundus*, thus

> eroding any idea that there is something we call the collective
> unconscious residing somewhere in our heads or bodies

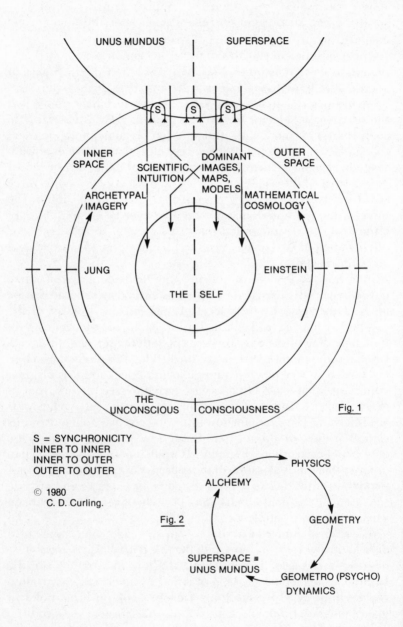

UNUS MUNDUS   SUPERSPACE

INNER   SCIENTIFIC   DOMINANT   OUTER
SPACE   INTUITION   IMAGES,   SPACE
                            MAPS,
                            MODELS

ARCHETYPAL   MATHEMATICAL
IMAGERY   COSMOLOGY

JUNG   EINSTEIN

THE   SELF

THE   CONSCIOUSNESS   Fig. 1
UNCONSCIOUS

S = SYNCHRONICITY
INNER TO INNER
INNER TO OUTER
OUTER TO OUTER

© 1980
   C. D. Curling.

Fig. 2

                                              PHYSICS
              ALCHEMY

                                                 GEOMETRY

              SUPERSPACE ≡
              UNUS MUNDUS   GEOMETRO (PSYCHO)
                                 DYNAMICS

and that *is* a useful point to make; but in general the dissertation is marred by the annexation for psychology of the physicist's discipline, e.g.

the event horizon (around a black hole) is the physicist's rediscovery of the incest barrier; the name black hole is pregnant with feminine associations, gravity is a 'mysterious presence' analogous to death etc., etc.

This does not seem to be very useful; it is of course a strong temptation to make a fairly obvious identification that I find hard to resist when Paul Davies[13] speaks of there being in space "holes with teeth". In general it would seem perhaps better to see the insights of the psychologist and the discoveries of the physicists as each coming from a common transcosmic source.

More useful is the approach of Marie-Louise von Franz in her book *Number and Time*[14] which is about the unification of physics and psychology. I was startled when I discovered that she too saw the physicist and the psychologist facing the *undus mundus* together. She saw them standing back to back; I would see them side-by-side, but my feeling about this work of scholarship is that it was a terrible shame she could not include the concept of superspace within it. She did her best with what the physicists were saying in 1965, and her book provides a magnificent commentary on matters relevant to the present position in the new physics.

She would be delighted with the recent discovery of an acausal connecting principle in physics, which John Bell showed in 1964 should follow as a prediction of quantum mechanics. The experimental evidence gathered since shows under certain specific experimental conditions there is an acausal connection between two separated events, so that what happens at one place affects what happens at another, probably instantaneously and certainly without progression through a chain of causal events. This constitutes as close a demonstration of synchronicity as physicists are likely to achieve. Jung was mainly concerned with synchronicity as an acausal connecting principle which linked the inner events associated with an intensely constellated archetype with outer events, the linkage often accompanied by conscious or unconscious emotion. I believe sychronicity should be allowed to cover meaningful coincidences whether inner to inner, inner to outer, or outer to outer. On my map I have indicated the way in which I believe the *unus mundus* manifests itself,[15] as Jung pointed out, in these three kinds of synchronistic events. I do not believe too much should be made of the physicist's demonstration of this acausal connection. Its importance is perhaps that it allows people to believe in synchronicity and explore it further in an experimental setting. This result, now well confirmed by a series of experiments, is disastrous for the naïve view of reality held by many scientists.

I would now like to say a little about archetypes starting with a quotation from Jung written as a preface to *Women's Mysteries*[16] by M. E. Harding, published originally in 1955. I quote from Jung's preface:—

> Of course (the archetype) is not meant to denote an inherited idea, but rather an inherited mode of psychic functioning corresponding to that inborn way according to which the chick emerges from the egg . . . In other words it is a pattern of behaviour.
>
> This aspect of the archetype is the biological one — it is the concern of scientific psychology.
>
> But the picture changes at once when looked at from the inside, that is from within the realm of the subjective psyche; there the archetype presents itself as numinous, that is, it appears as an experience of fundamental importance.

Jung is here distinguishing between the inner and outer aspects of the archetype. Looked at from inside, Jung saw the nature of the archetype with a clarity and insight that seems to grow in stature in his later writings. But the biological aspect of the archetype, the outer aspect of the archetype expressed as an inherited mode of psychic functioning, a pattern of instinctual behaviour, or a tendency, seems to me less easy to accept and reveals Jung as a child of his time. In fact I do not believe there is anything directly biological or inherited, or genetic, about the archetypes.

The reasons for Jung stressing the biological aspect of the archetype, a view which he maintained in his letters into the late 1950's seems to be associated with his split with Freud. Sulloway[17] in his book called *Freud, Biologist of the Mind* deals with that period and shows that both Freud and Jung sought the support of the science of biology for their psychological views. This becomes clear in the passage[18] on the phylogeny of the libido, and the suggestion that Jung made "a phylogenetic assumption to subordinate infantile determinants in favour of inborn descriptions or archetypes".[19] Although Jung tried physical and chemical models in his work there was in the physics of his day no place in which to situate the archetypes and he chose to use a biological model which subjected the archetypes to temporal process and put their origin deep in the past.

There may be a parallel here between Einstein and Jung. Einstein's general theory of relativity produced an equation which required the universe to be dynamic; but at the time it was generally thought the universe was static and Einstein therefore added a constant to the equation to allow a static solution; Einstein was wrong, as he later frankly admitted, and the equation was right, and we now know the universe to be dynamic, to be subject to the large-scale motion of expansion, that produces the red shift associated with the recession of the galaxies.

With both Einstein and Jung the dominant images of their day conditioned the models they chose. Jung chose a temporal model rather than a spatial one; Einstein a static model instead of a dynamic one. Nowadays the same space — superspace — that is the arena for the moving geometry of general relativity is also the space of spaces, the *unus mundus* from which the archetypes move in their numinosity towards the realm of the subjective psyche. The archetypes are, therefore, like the collective unconscious, not to be located in the brain as a kind of inherited mode or pattern of behaviour. They are external types in the *unus mundus*, and this is to re-emphasize the Platonic ideas from which they are derived. The relation between the structure of superspace and the universe of outer space is the same as the relation between the archetypes as they are formed in the *unus mundus* and the universes of inner space.

In a paper entitled *Archetypal theory after Jung*, Goldenberg[20] has suggested that thinking about archetypes has moved through three generations, and in the third generation, as represented by Hillman[21] and Christou[22], it is precisely this inner numinous character of the archetype which has been stressed, and of course Jung's later works bears strong testimony to the influence of this inner nature of the archetype. This I now believe can be placed within the scientific context of the new physics. The archetypes are part of the transcosmic dance that is at once mystical, psychological, mathematical and physical.

To see the archetypes within a mathematical space of infinite dimensions strongly suggests the need to develop a mathematical context for archetypes in which to fit the well-known propensity of archetypes to form clusters and to be mutually contaminating. It may be that there are still scientific statements to be made about the nature of the archetypes.[23]

Some attempt has been made by I. M. Blanco[24] to treat the unconscious mathematically and to explore the problems of talking of and thinking about multidimensional spaces in his book called *The*

Unconscious as Infinite Sets (an essay in bio-logic), and he tried to face the difficulty of handling a multidimensional order of reality with a mental system used to only three dimensions.

I should like in this last section of my paper to return to the idea of superspace and the *unus mundus*. Marie-Louise von Franz's book *Number and Time* was published first in 1970 though most of the references to physics in the text do not extend beyond 1965. In hindsight she left a challenge to physicists to find a parallel for synchronicity and the *unus mundus* within physics. Her book needed the idea of superspace. The first brief reference to superspace is in a paper by J. A. Wheeler in 1964[25]; it seems to have been an idea whose time had come.

It was about five years ago when I realised that the fringes of the new physics, the fringes of both the physics of the very small and the physics of the very large, were beginning to show characteristics of participation, multiplicity, potentiality and self-reference that showed all kinds of links with the patterns encountered in the deep unconscious in inner space. In relativity theory it seemed likely that space was shot full of holes, and this would occur at both extremes of size. Kaufmann[26] demonstrated how, at least hypothetically, journeys close to a black hole can lead to the observation of as many as seven universes at once. In quantum physics the many worlds theory[27] suggested a multiplicity of universes could exist at once, and my own experiments in exploring inner space suggested the existence of parallel time-slipped universes existing in great profusion.

For these reasons it seemed appropriate to turn the linear spectrum running from inner space through the unconscious to consciousness and outer space into a mandala in which, as the map shows, inner and outer space conjoin. And, of course, a mandala exists to help the pilgrim to move from time to eternity, and from darkness to light. In this way two predictions of Jung [28] were being fulfilled. He wrote:—

> . . . sooner or later nuclear physics and the psychology of the unconscious will draw together as both of them, independently, and from opposite directions, push forward into transcendental territory, the one with the concept of the atom, the other with that of the archetype

and also in another place:—

> microphysics is feeling its way into the unknown side of matter, just as . . . psychology is pushing forward into the unknown side of the psyche.

Their common background is as much physical as psychic, and therefore neither . . . but rather . . . in essence is transcendental.

Their common background is indeed the *unus mundus,* as Jung goes on to assert.

One way we can regard Einstein's theory is as an attempt to turn physics into geometry. Gravitation and mass are expressed as curvature of space; the idea was successful and caught on, so that there were attempts to do the same with charge, spin and other physical quantities, so just as there was mass without mass, there could be charge without charge, spin without spin, etc. The geometry was a moving geometry, a grand dance of intricate pattern known as geometrodynamics.

Wheeler and others discovered it was not possible to turn all physics into geometry; pregeometry was needed and the search for this showed that the participation of consciousness in the universe was necessary for its existence and to give it meaning, so that the "observer" far from being isolated from the surrounding world, except insofar as he opens upon it one-way windows of perception, is in a certain sense coextensive with it. This circumstance can well be conceived to boost the property of self-reference from one of a purely linguistic nature to an intrinsic attribute of the universe[29].

Hence the need for geometro(psycho)dynamics, the dance of patterned geometry in which the self participates. It also turned out that the right area for this dance of geometrodynamics is superspace, a space of infinite dimensions, which, much to the surprise of some, would not allow any representation of time within it. Thus with the identification of superspace with the *unus mundus,* an alchemical concept, the circuit from alchemy, through physics to alchemy again is complete. (Fig. 2).

You can obtain some view of what is meant by superspace by reading Davies book; each point in superspace is a complete cross section through a universe; thus what you can see of the universe at one moment, which includes all the distant stars and galaxies, all this is represented by one point; another person's view is another cross-section, another point. The entire history of the universe is represented by the points on a bent leaf, a petal, a surface in superspace. The structure of superspace produces all the phenomena of physics. Electromagnetic theory and relativity theory[30] follow from the way things are in superspace; quantum physics relates, for example, to the thickness of the petals. So there is a multitude of universes in superspace needing only the participating observer to draw them from potentiality to actuality; a universe constellates out of superspace in a way parallel to the constellation of an archetype in the psyche from the *unus mundus*. As Davies [31] says —

"Superspace is a gigantic stack of cosmic images".

Superspace just like the *unus mundus* as Jung himself wrote —

 . . . contains all the preconditions which determine the form of empirical phenomena. [32]

To see into this place where there is a nest of petals in a multidimensional space, where each petal is a complete story of a universe or a potential form of an archetype, we need to use archetypal imagination. A paper by Casey[33] on this subject shows how this goes beyond active imagination, beyond therapy and even beyond depth psychology. Archetypal imagination enables us to explore the archetypal topography of superspace or the *unus mundus*, and to —

 . . . experience the archetypal structures in their joint configurations.[34]

We gain access through active imagination to the products of superspace in inner space but to explore inner space and beyond it superspace, we need archetypal imagination and other methods, some embedded in long mystical traditions, to enable the soul to make its "odyssey through the Mediterranean multiplicity of the psychically real."[34]

As Grinnell[35] has pointed out in his book *Alchemy in a modern woman* —

 . . . we are dealing with archetypal processes going beyond therapy, which . . . tends to remain inexorably personalistic, reductive and ego-centred.

The practice of archetypal imagination needs a transpersonal transcosmic archetypal psychology — a Jungian psychology free of its clinical origins.

According to Barbara Hannah[36] the *unus mundus* —

 . . . is the foundation of everything, just as the Self is the basis of the individual and includes its past, present, and future.

Jung said: "The thought Dorn expresses by the third degree of conjunction is universal: it is the relation or identity of the personal with the suprapersonal atman, and of the individual tao with the universal tao." Western man thinks this is a mystical idea because he has no experience of any world except the outer visible world, and he cannot therefore see that the Self enters three-dimensional reality when the ego touches the potential world, the *unus mundus*.

Jung had such an experience – as we have seen and often recalled – on the Athi Plains near Nairobi when he saw:

...the world as it had always been in the state of nonbeing...There I was now, the first human being to recognise that this was the world, but who did not know that in this moment he had first really created it.

There the cosmic meaning of consciousness became overwhelmingly clear to me. 'What nature leaves imperfect, the art perfects,' say the alchemists. 'Man, I, in an invisible act of creation put the stamp of perfection on the world by giving it objective existence.'...

Jung[37] went on to say:–

Man is indispensable for the completion of creation. Human consciousness created objective existence and meaning.

Wheeler[38] has said:—

"Consciousness gives meaning to the universe"; and Davies[39] has asserted that —

. . . the existence of the human experimenter is interwoven with the fundamental features of nature and the organisation of the cosmos.

No doubt we question this:—

> Should I think the complete universe must be
> Subject to such a rag of it as me   G. Chapman.

The answer is yes; we are responsible for bringing into reality the potentialities of the *unus mundus;* but let us always remember that we too are a part of what we sustain.

It seems that Jung moved into the exploration of the *unus mundus* during his illness in 1945. The pages[40] in which he describes his visions form a kind of culmination for his studies. As Barbara Hannah reports[41] —

He said of his previous work on the book: 'All I have written is correct. I need not change a word, but I realize its full reality now'. He even told me once that his illness had been necessary, or he could never have known the full reality of the mysterium conjunctionis. In fact, it was presumably only because of his long and arduous work on the subject before, that these visions, which he described as 'the most tremendous things' that he 'ever experienced' were revealed to him.

In conclusion, it is clear we have many needs.

We need an archetypal transpersonal transcosmic psychology well rooted in the body-mind.

We need a mathematical theory of archetypes.

We need to encourage physicists and psychologists to work side-by-side on a common quest.

We need to explore the *unus mundus* by archetypal imagination and by any other proper ways.

We need to acknowledge our responsibilities to the depths within; that we are indeed open and vulnerable to the unconscious in a way not encountered before in all our evolutionary history.

There are diurnal and nocturnal regimes of archetypes and these are poles apart; the shadow exists in superspace. We may believe — I believe — that the unconscious in its depths is fundamentally good, but within we also know there exist principalities and powers, thrones and dominions. In the vision I have been attempting to hold before you, matter becomes transfigured and translucent, touched by celestial fire. In the cool language of the mathematician, Paul Davies[42]

. . . in daily life we do not experience an objective reality at all, but a sort of cocktail of internal and external perspectives.

If the effect of recent archetypal theory is radically to desubstantiate the ego [43], the effect of recent physics is radically to desubstantiate physical reality. We are left with the self face-to-face with the *unus mundus* and the surrounding mandala of inner and outer space grows shadowy in the celestial light.

Atom and archetype come together in physics and psychology but archetypal power far outshines atomic or nuclear power. Our attempts to destroy ourselves by nuclear power or any other means may yet be frustrated from within. The inner ecological crisis is at least as intense as the outer. It may be for the salvation of our world, that the ruthlessness of cosmic love will thrust into our vulnerable reality from the deep collective unconscious. That universal movement would be at once sexual and spiritual, numinous and alchemical. How, if this should happen, should we greet it? Shall we be able to welcome it with joy? Let that be our hope, for as Teilhard said:—

"Joy is the most infallible sign of the presence of God."

The divine human figure stands behind superspace, behind the *unus mundus*, holding in his hand a rose. The petals from the rose drift into the *unus mundus* and frame the nests of unformed archetypes and potential universes. And then the dance begins, creation stirs, the Self calls forth the magnificent multiplicities of reality, which "externalise themselves only in the ecstasy to which they give rise and which is inherent in them"[44]. In the measure of that dance, physics and psyche, physicists and psychologists are now partners within the exploration of the mysteries.

REFERENCES

THE NEW PHYSICS
A.   *The Dancing Wu Li Masters*, G. Zukav.   Rider-Hutchison (1979)
B.   *(AND SUPERSPACE) Other Worlds*. P. Davies.   Dent (1980)

ACAUSAL CONNECTIONS IN PHYSICS
C.   d'Espagnat, *The Quantum Theory and Reality*.
                                    Scientific American—November 1979 p.128
D.   Hiley, *Ghostly Interactions in Physics*.
                                    New Scientist—March 6th, 1980 p.746

UNUS MUNDUS
E.   *Collected Works*, C. Jung. Volume 14, etc.   Routledge
F.   *Aurora Consurgens*, T. Aquinas.   Routledge (1966)
G.   *Number and Time*, M.-L. von Franz.   Rider (1974)
H.   *Alchemical Active Imagination*, M.-L. von Franz.
                                              Spring Publ. (Zürich) (1979)

ARCHETYPAL IMAGINATION
I.   Goldenberg, *Archetypal Theory after Jung*.   Spring 1975 p.199
J.   Casey, *Towards an Archetypal Imagination*.   Spring 1974 p.1
K.   Corbin, *Mundus Imaginalis*.   Spring 1972
L.   *Spiritual body and Celestial Earth*, H. Corbin.   Princeton U.P. (1977)

SEE ALSO
     Curling, *A physicist looks at psychology*.   *Harvest* 1978 p.62
          Physics and consciousness, Vol. 4 No. 2
                    New themes for Education Conference Papers. (Dartington, 1979)
          The union of physics and psychology,
                              Mystics and Scientists III. (Wrekin Trust, 1980)

NOTES

1.   This article is a revision of the article for *Harvest* and was delivered one year later to the Guild of Pastoral Psychology under the present title.
2.   Ref. G. p. 114.
3.   Ref. G. p. 114.
4.   Ref. G. p. 109.
5.   Ref. G. p. 115.
6.   Ref. B. p. 152.
7.   De Witt in *Relativity* ed. Carmeli, Fickler, Witten. (Plenum 1970) p. 373.
8.   C. Jung C.W. Vol. *14* p. 505, p. 538; Vol. *12* p. 433.
9.   Wheeler in *Analytical methods in mathematical physics*, ed. Gilbert and Newton (Gordon and Breach 1970) p.347.
10. Ref. B. p. 78.
11. Ref. B. p. 199.
12. C. Jung, Letters Vol. 2. (Routledge 1976) p. 108.
13. Ref. B. p. 101.

14.   Ref. G. —The full title of Marie-Louise von Franz's book is *Number and Time: reflections leading towards a unification of psychology and physics.*

15.   Ref. H. p. 115.

16.   *Women's Mysteries*, M. E. Harding. (Rider 1971) p. ix.

17.   *Freud, Biologist of the Mind*, F. J. Sulloway. (Burnett 1979).

18.   F. J. Sulloway, op.cit. pp. 432-434.

19.   F. J. Sulloway, op.cit. p. 435.

20.   Ref. I.

21.   *Revisioning Psychology*, J. Hillman. (Harper and Row, N.Y. 1975).

22.   *The Logos of the Soul*, E. Christou. (Spring Publ. Zürich 1973).

23.   *Memories, Dreams, Reflections*, C. Jung. (Collins Fontana 1967) p. 248.

24.   *The Unconscious as Infinite Sets*, I. M. Blanco. (Duckworth 1975).

25.   Wheeler in *Relativity, Groups and Topology*, Grenoble Summer School, 1963. (Blackie 1964) p. 517.

26.   *Cosmic Frontiers of General Relativity*, W. J. Kaufmann. (Penguin 1979) p.214.

27.   *Many worlds Interpretation of Quantum Mechanics*, ed. B. De Witt, N. Graham. (Princeton University Press 1973).

28.   C. Jung, C.W. Vol. 9 pt. II, p. 261 and Vol. 14 p. 538.

29.   Wheeler in *Quantum Gravity*, ed. Isham, Penrose, Sciama. (Clarendon 1975) p. 591.

30.   Hojam, Kuchar, Teitelboim, Nature Physical Science *245*, 97 (1973).

31.   Ref. B. p. 108.

32.   C. Jung, C.W. Vol. *14*, paragraph 769.

33.   Ref. J.

34.   Ref. J. p. 22 and p. 28.

35.   *Alchemy in a Modern Woman*, R. Grinnell. (Spring Publ. Zürich 1973) p. 162

36.   *Jung, his Life and Work*, B. Hannah. (Putnam N.Y. 1976) p. 315.

37.   Ref. 23, p. 284.

38.   Ref. 29, p. 564.

39.   Ref. B. p. 184.

40.   Ref. 23, pp. 320-327.

41.   Ref. 36, p. 315.

42.   Ref. B. p. 108.

43.   Ref. I. p. 211.

44.   Ref. K. p. 20.

Gnosis and the Single Vision[1]

by Ean Begg

EAN BEGG M.A., is a graduate of the C.G. Jung Institute in Zürich and he is a practising analyst in London. He is a past chairman of the Analytical Psychology Club, London, and is the author of Myth and Today's Consciousness.

I owe the title of this paper to a book by Theodore Roszak called *Where the Wasteland Ends* (Faber, 1973). Continuing the analysis of the current revolution in consciousness which he began in *The Making of a Counter-Culture*, he describes two contrasting world-views and their historical backgrounds. What he calls "the single vision" is the dominant orthodoxy of contemporary Western culture. It is rationalist, mechanistic, materialist, secularist, positivist and reductionist. It has come to be accepted as the norm in all branches of the Establishment, even in the churches and among those who profess the arts and humanities in our universities. As the faith of technological man, it pervades all sections of society, an unquestioned higher generality, the intellectual wall-paper that forms the background to all our thinking. The phrase itself is culled from William Blake's letter to Thomas Butts in 1802:

> Now I a fourfold vision see,
> And a fourfold vision is given to me;
> 'Tis fourfold in my supreme delight
> And threefold in soft Beulah's light
> And twofold always. May God us keep
> From single vision and Newton's sleep.

Frequently in the course of his book, Roszak alludes rhapsodically to an alternative *Weltanschauung* which he calls the "Old Gnosis". Here are some of the things he says about it:

> . . . the higher sanity will find its proper politics when we come to realize in our very bones that we have nothing to add to the splendour of the Old Gnosis and can make no progress beyond it (p. 464). The great adventure of our age is the reclamation and

renewal of the Old Gnosis (p. 262). Many of our youth, having tasted the desolation of spirit which comes of limiting vision to the impersonal gaze of a dead man's eyes, . . . give attention once again to the Old Gnosis and defect from the dominant culture. Even among seemingly well-adjusted, middle-class adults, a subversive interest in psychedelic experimentation, non-verbal communication, sensory awareness, Gestalt therapy and contemplative disciplines begins to spread through the Growth Centers of America, threatening to erode the official reality principle (p. 222).

Now, I believe that Roszak is really on to something important here, but unfortunately he makes very little attempt to support his case by any reference to the nature of the Old Gnosis itself. The aim of my paper is to present certain ancient Gnostic ideas that may have some relevance and compensatory value for the present one-sided condition of collective consciousness. So deeply has Gnosticism been repressed in our culture that I find it is not safe, even in Jungian circles, to assume any great familiarity with the subject. I shall, therefore, give you a very brief introductory outline to what we are talking about, with apologies to those among you who know far more about it than I do, and acknowledgements to Professor Quispel of Utrecht and Louvain, to whom I owe much of my material.

"Gnosis" is defined in the *Shorter Oxford English Dictionary* as "a special knowledge of spiritual mysteries". One who possesses such knowledge is a Gnostic, and the system or principles professed by Gnostics is known as Gnosticism, though among scholars this term is now generally restricted to a heretical movement or movements within Christianity and on its fringes during the first three centuries of our era. Actually one must take the term "heresy" as applied to any doctrines in the pre-Constantinian period with a considerable grain of salt. In Hellenistic Greek, *hairesis* was applied without a specially pejorative flavour to the various philosophical schools of thought as well as to the sects of Judaism such as the Pharisees, Sadducees, Essenes, etc. There were many brands of Christianity from the beginning, and the seeds of schism are already discernible in the early Church at Jerusalem as described in the Book of Acts. By the procrustean standards of the great ecumenical councils, few if any of the earlier patristic and even apostolic writers would have passed the test of orthodoxy, since up to that time orthodoxy varied from city to city and time to time, according to the fluctuating fortunes of rival groupings. In his important work *Orthodoxy and*

Heresy in Earliest Christianity (SCM Press, 1972), only recently translated into English, Walter Bauer shows how, in all probability, Gnosticism was for longish periods the dominant form of Christianity in many of the most important centres of population in the East, especially Alexandria. Its adherents considered Gnosticism to be the true, spiritual, inner meaning of Christianity, revealed to the individual Gnostic by a private numinous experience.

It may be an academic convenience to restrict the use of the term to an obscure corner of early Church history, but Gnosticism — as one of the irreducible human attitudes — recurs in different forms throughout history, is common to all the great religions and cannot be shut up in such a box. It is not, however, my intention to approach the subject from the academic standpoint of the single vision, delving into the possible origins of Gnosticism whether in Greece, Persia, India or heterodox Judaism, nor to concern myself with the fashionable problem as to whether or not there was a pre-Christian Gnosticism. I am also reluctant to indulge overmuch in the subjective approach; but since Gnosis is rooted in personal experience, rather than in notional assent to a set of dogmatic propositions, I feel this is where I must begin. None of you who saw the film of his interview with John Freeman will forget Jung's famous "I know", when asked if he believed in God. This is the fundamental Gnostic assertion. There are many different degrees of "I know," and my own first Gnostic experience was somewhat like the awakening described in the beautiful Gnostic "Hymn of the Pearl". The narrator describes how he was sent forth into Egypt from his father's kingdom to bring back the pearl which is in the midst of the sea, hard by the loud-breathing serpent, so that he may once again put on his bright robe of glory and assume his heritage in the kingdom. He eats the food of the Egyptians and forgets the pearl for which he was sent, falling into a deep sleep. But then his parents send him a letter reminding him that he is a son of kings and recalling the purpose of his mission. The letter

> flew in the likeness of an eagle,
> the king of all birds;
> it flew and alighted beside me
> and became all speech . . .
> and according to what was traced on my heart
> were the words of my letter written.
> I remembered that I was a son of kings,
> and my free soul longed for its natural state.
> I remembered the pearl . . .

I was eighteen, on extended leave from the Army, an unthinking hedonist successfully inoculated against Christianity by a lifetime of religious observance and scripture lessons, and little given to asking questions about the meaning of life and my place in it. Then somebody gave me a book called *Vedanta for the Western World* (Marcel Rodd, New York, 1946), edited by Christopher Isherwood, with contributions by Aldous Huxley, Gerald Heard, John van Druten, Swami Prabhavananda and others. On the first page of the introduction I came across the following formulation:

> Reduced to its elements, Vedanta Philosophy consists of three propositions. First, that man's real nature is divine. Second, that the aim of human life is to realize this divine nature. Third, that all religions are essentially in agreement.

Quite suddenly I felt enlightened, and saw myself and the world in a new way. There was nothing rational about my experience; it was more as though I was remembering something I had always known through a process of Platonic reminiscence or intuition. The emotional charge of the experience is, I suspect, to be found in all cases of religious conversion, the difference, perhaps, being that I was not moved by any enthusiasm to join some organization or to convert other people, though I would have been glad to have met someone who shared my new and joyful certitude. When I look back now on a subsequent, more conventional conversion, it seems to me a diminution rather than an expansion of being, a mere falling into an opposite and a pouring of new wine into old, institutional bottles.

Professor Quispel has aptly defined Gnosticism as "the mythologization of a Self-experience'. If this is so, then one could say that religions are based on the Gnostic experience of some individual, though that experience may be interpreted in widely different ways according to the constitution and conditioning of the one who receives it. A good example of a Self-experience which developed into an organized Gnostic world religion that survived for a thousand years is to be found in Manichaeism. Its founder, Mani, describes his first encounter with his twin, or Fihrist, the angelic double who accompanies and protects him:

> And I recognized him and I understood that he is me, from whom I had been separated, and I witnessed that I am he . . . and forthwith, flying down, he revealed himself to me, that most beautiful and great mirror of mine.

Valentinus, writing in the Christian Gnostic *Gospel of Truth*, one of the treasures of the *Jung Codex*, writes in a similar vein of those who have received the revelation of Christ:

They found Him in themselves ... Joy to the man who has rediscovered himself and has awakened ... for this return, they call it metanoia.

Christ is here, the call through which man is revealed to himself.

In its struggle with Gnosticism, the Church lost much that was of value. Dogmas and creeds were formulated to keep out teachings regarded as heretical or novel, and as a result Self-experiences which failed to tally with the orthodox view fell into disfavour. Once revelation was deemed to have ceased with the death of the last apostle, there was little room within the Great Church for freelance speculative theologians and spiritual directors who followed their own interests and creative imagination, heedless of the party line. The Church honours its mystics once they are dead, but fears them living, ever mindful of its old Gnostic foe. It is a thorny problem: the Gnostic Self-experience is a high source of meaning, and to neglect or repress it is to quench the spirit of wholeness; but, on the other hand, to identify with the archetype of the Self and become either a guru or a disciple, is to fall into inflation and an equally great peril of the soul. Jung, it seems to me, held the tension admirably between these opposites, and, through his psychology, created conditions whereby people might be prepared for the assimilation of such experiences. I would like to quote to you part of a letter he wrote to a correspondent who had asked him whether he possessed any secret knowledge:

I speak only of what I know and what can be verified. I don't want to addle anybody's brains with my subjective conjectures. Beyond that I have had experiences which are, so to speak, 'ineffable'; 'secret' because they can never be told properly and because nobody can understand them (I don't know whether I have even approximately understood them myself) ... [and] 'catastrophic' because the prejudices aroused by their telling might block other people's way to a living and wondrous mystery ... Can anyone say 'credo' when he stands amidst his experience ... when he knows how superfluous belief is, when he more than just 'knows', when the experience has even pinned him to the wall? ... I don't want to seduce anyone into believing and thus take his experience from him. . . But one thing I will tell you: the exploration of the unconscious has in fact and in truth discovered the age-old, timeless way of initiation. (*Letters*, Vol. I, pp. 140-42.)

I want now to turn to another content in the collective psyche of the Church that became repressed, partly as a result of the conflict with Gnosticism. It is striking that women, who play quite a prominent role in the life of the early Church, tend to fade increasingly out of the picture, with the exception of royalty and, eventually, nuns. In many Gnostic circles, on the other hand, not only did women hold positions of influence, but the feminine principle was held in the highest esteem and even worshipped. According to *The Hypostasis of the Archons,* for example, Eve bestows spiritual life on Adam. In several other texts the feminine nature of the godhead is affirmed. In *The Gospel of the Hebrews,* Jesus is made to say: "Even now my mother the Holy Spirit took me and carried me to the great mountain Tabor." In *The Gospel of Truth,* Jesus is said to be both a mother and a father, while the Holy Spirit, who shares the symbol of the dove with heavenly Aphrodite, is described as "the breast of God". One element, central to the Gnostic myth, relates to the fall and redemption of the archetypal feminine, whether she be called Eve, Helen, Ennoia or Sophia. In the school of Simon Magus, universally execrated by patristic writers as the father of all heresy, it was taught that Ennoia, the First Thought of God and Mother of All, fell into matter and passed from body to body — Helen of Troy being one of her incarnations — suffering ever greater humiliations, until at last she was rescued from a brothel in Tyre by Simon, the Great Power of God. The Valentinian myth is more complex. In the beginning, in the invisible, ineffable heights, was the perfect Aeon, Bythos (Depth), and with him was Silence. Depth conceived the idea to send forth from himself the origin of all, and it lay like a seed in the womb of Silence. She brought forth the "only-begotten" Nous, Mind or masculine consciousness, who is like and equal to his begetter and alone comprehends the greatness of the Father. Together with him the feminine Truth was produced to complete the first tetrad. Then Mind and Truth emitted in their turn Logos (the masculine Word) and life (feminine), from whom came Man (the original man or Adam Kadmon) and Church to form the Ogdoad. Eventually a further twenty-two Aeons emanated, making a total of thirty archetypes or hypostatized divine characteristics, which, in their entirety, are known as the Pleroma, fullness or completeness, and constitute the divine realm. The last and youngest of the Aeons is the female Sophia (Wisdom). More than all the Aeons, she longed to know and beyond the author of their being. Unable to reach the Father, she went out of her mind in extreme agony and fell into outer darkness. From her sorrow, fear, despair and ignorance, the world was created, and the seas were made from her tears. In other schools, less close to mainstream Catholicism (Valentinus was once a candidate for the Papacy), the erring feminine principle gives birth to the demiurge, who, ignorant of the true source of being, believes himself the one God and creates the visible world. He is often identified with the God of the Old Testament.

It is not difficult to see in these projections onto the archetypal cosmos similarities with Jung's view of individual psychic processes. The solution for this condition of fallenness, disintegration and unconsciousness, for Jung as for the Gnostics, is reintegration and, ultimately, conjunction of the opposites. It is probably in this light that we should see the Gnostic fascination with androgyny. As an idea it is already present in the Eastern Mediterranean in earlier Hellenistic times in such hermaphroditic Great Mother figures as Agdistis and bearded Aphrodite. Philo the Jew writes in first century pre-Christian Alexandria of Sophia as "the virginal daughter of God, whose nature is male". But it is, I believe, the Gnostics who first present a psychology and theology of androgyny. Jesus, the Holy Spirit and the high female goddess Barbelo are all shown as possessing the qualities of both sexes, as, in some systems, are the major Aeons of the Ogdoad. In the *Gospel of Thomas*, Jesus lays down for his disciples the following conditions for entry into the Kingdom of Heaven:

> When you make the two one, and when you make the inner as the outer . . . and the above as the below, and when you make the male and the female into a single being so that the male shall not be male and the female not be female . . . then shall you enter.

This mysterious saying has resonances both in the Gnostics' sex-life and in the eschatological myth that inspired them. Many Gnostics, the Valentinians for example, had a positive attitude towards sex so long as it was seen within the total context of life's meaning. for materialists, or those on the way of devotional faith, it could be a hindrance on the path, leading into greater unconsciousness, but for spiritual man who meditated on the emanation of the syzygies, or archetypal couples, during intercourse, it could be an aid to integration. The danger is to seek one's soul, one's lost other half, in another, rather than seeing in sexual union the symbolic enactment of an inner process. The climax of this process is to be found in the ultimate *coniunctio*. At the death of the individual Gnostic, the soul, through the enlightenment of Gnosis and through labour, is transformed into a vehicle for the spirit, a fiery chariot to convey it into the state of consciousness known as the Ogdoad, the halfway house of archetypal images. There the soul becomes a wedding garment, and the spirit a partaker in the bliss of the pre-nuptial feast while awaiting the consummation of the world and the redemption of all spiritual particles. When all that is spiritual has been given form and perfected, and all both know one another and have become like one another, then, laying aside their soul garments, the pure essences are led by their (masculine) individual angels into the bridal chamber in the train of Sophia and her bridegroom, Christ. *Mysterium coniunctionis.*

Closely linked to the problem of the feminine principle and the necessity for its suppression, in the mind of many of the old orthodox theologians at least, is the problem of evil. A fundamentalist interpretation of the Fall relates it inexorably to the Devil, Eve and lust. Here, too, Gnosticism tends to turn the established attitude on its head. If Yahweh is the blind, foolish, ignorant, tyrannical demiurge, then those who thwart his will, like the Serpent, Eve and Cain, can no longer be seen in a negative light. They are, on the contrary, fighting on the side of evolving consciousness against the downward gravity pull of determinism and enslaving necessity. So, whatever unimaginable primeval error is responsible for man's miserable state of alienation, the solution presupposes Adam's transgression, a stepping-across into the dark world of matter, led by the inner light of gnosis which has been gained through eating the fruit of the tree of knowledge of good and evil. *Felix culpa*, indeed.

Just as the typical Gnostic is more interested in experiencing the Self than in theologizing about the unknown God, more concerned with the inner meaning of the union of the opposites than with codifying sexual norms, so for him the chief moral problem is one of ignorance, failing to understand the true issues involved, not of sin, taken in any legalistic sense. There is certainly a strong conviction of the duality between matter and spirit, but this need not imply that matter, the vehicle of life, is necessarily evil. Manichaean adepts would not, for example, knowingly eat, or indeed harm, any living thing, being reluctant even to tread down a blade of grass. To the Carpocratians, the body and its related instincts were the means whereby the Gnostic could win the experiences that, rightly understood, were the pearl for which he had been sent. It must, nevertheless, be admitted that the most characteristic Gnostic attitude is what Unamuno calls the "tragic sense of life". The body is a tomb, and the world a corpse. The true meaning is what underlies appearances, but only the Gnostic is aware of this and has any chance of escaping from the illusory realm in which we are imprisoned. Aware of his origin in the ideal world, he longs to return to it, never feeling quite at home on earth, but rather a pilgrim and stranger.

Such an attitude tends to rise to the surface in the interregnum between two cultural periods, at times of political and religious change, when the old myths and collective values cease to give meaning. In one of the earliest works of literature known, *The Dialogue of a World-Weary Man with his Soul,* which dates from Egypt in about 2200 BC, at the end of the Old Kingdom, the writer is already full of *fin de siècle* hopelessness at the way things are going, and feels suicide is the only solution. Twenty-four hundred years on, in the great age of Gnosticism, such a viewpoint was endemic. Under the Pax Romana there was relative security and prosperity, along with an uneasy feeling that the old gods had departed. Pan was dead, the oracles had ceased and a cultivated pious priest like Plutarch could write in a highly demythologizing vein of the myths he professed. Epictetus did not speak only for Stoics when he said, "Caesar can give peace from war, but not from sorrow." State religion had little to offer in the way of spiritual nourishment or consolation for the needs of the individual. Gnosticism throve in the soil of political and religious disillusionment. For the Jews, three disastrous wars against Rome had brought an end to nationalist aspirations and quenched the fires of apocalyptic Messianism. For Christians, the apostolic age had passed, and there was still no sign of Christ's second coming. The Greeks had lost an empire and failed to find a role, save that of tutor to the Roman master. The Romans themselves had realized the limits of their power — there was always another enemy beyond the Euphrates, the Rhine, the Danube or the Dniestr, and there seemed to be no cure for inflation. even the *dolce vita* became something of a bore, and corruption in high places had made people cynical about politics. On the other hand, there was a boom in astrology and magic, and thanks to the splendid system of communications throughout the Empire, exotic and esoteric oriental cults proliferated. Staid citizens became accustomed to the sight of weird-looking devotees in long flowing robes, make-up and unusual hair-styles, and muttered about what people got up to in these new temples.

Two millennia on, and we seem to have reached the same stage on the spiral. God is dead. We have social security along with a high suicide rate and much madness. The consensus has broken down, except for the general agreement that things are likely to get worse, as we stagger from future shock to future shock into the post-Christian, post-capitalist, post-Freudian, post-industrial age of zero and declining growth. To some, the myth of the golden age in the form of Marxism still give hope and meaning, especially in countries where the various forms of communism have not yet been tried. Not surprisingly, contemporary forms of Gnosticism are flourishing. In Jung's view, theosophy and anthroposophy were typically Gnostic systems, and they are merely the best known and oldest established of a multitude of groups that have come first into existence during the past century to satisfy the growing thirst for meaning, certitude and individual transcendency, as traditional church religion declines. In my view, the interest among a wide public in Jung's psychology is due less to the contribution it has made to scientific knowledge than to its Gnostic appeal as a way of individuation.

Times of crisis and breakdown, for societies as for individuals, may also be times of Laingian "break-through". The foundations are shaken, the defences shattered, and out of the ruins a new and more comprehensive adaptation and synthesis may be achieved. Neurosis is pain, but in it lies our hope for growth in being. In the agony, old repressed elements from the distant past rise to the surface and demand to be integrated. This is what has happened today as official Christianity and the principle of scientific orthodoxy face the renewed challenge of the romantic, Gnostic, individualist world-view. Gnosticism is the ancient foe of Western, Christian culture and has always run parallel to it as its dark brother, an underground counter-culture. Now it is coming in out of the cold, but not without considerable resistance. There is, for example, the extraordinary delay that always seems to attend the translation of Gnostic texts. When G. R. S. Mead brought out his edition of the *Pistis Sophia* in 1896, it was the first time an original Coptic Gnostic text became available to the English-speaking public, though the *Codex Askew,* which contained it, had been available to scholars since 1774. The other text known to the nineteenth century, in the *Codex Bruce,* had to wait a hundred and twenty years for translation. In Mead's famous *Fragments of a Faith Forgotten*, the first popular introduction to Gnosticism, he had to rely almost entirely on quotations from the polemical anti-Gnostic writings of the Church Fathers. When M. R. James produced his *Apocryphal New Testament* in 1924, which until recently was the standard text, he says blandly: "The first class of books which I have found it impossible to include is that of the Gnostic Apocrypha." He hopes this is "for sufficient reasons", but he fails to give any. The *Codex Berolinensis,* containing the important *Apocryphon of John* and bought by the Berlin Library in 1896, was not published until Till's translation of 1955. Caches of Manichaean documents were discovered at Turfan in Chinese

Turkestan in 1904-5, and in Egypt in 1933, which throw much light on the later development of Gnosticism. Neither of these has, as far as I know, yet been fully edited and published in English.

The greatest event in the history of Gnostic scholarship was the discovery — accidental, like that of the Dead Sea Scrolls — of a whole Gnostic library of fifty-four original texts at Nag Hammadi in Egypt, on the site of the former Chenoboskion, the first Christian monastic community founded by Pachomius (290-346). Most of these works date from the golden age of Gnosticism and are of the highest literary, historical, religious and psychological value. Thirty years later we at last have the full Robinson edition of these works (published by Brill, Leyden, 1977), which reveal much about the state of Christianity in Egypt in the dark century and a half of silence which preceded the emergence of Clement of Alexandria and the Catechetical School. Fortunately, one codex was smuggled out of Egypt and, after being offered unsuccessfully to the Bollingen Foundation, was acquired by Professor Quispel for the Jung Institute in 1952 with the help of Mr George Page. The *Jung Codex,* as it was henceforth known, contained five works: *The Apocryphon of James,* in which simple Christain formulations go hand in hand with Gnostic interpretation; *The Gospel of Truth; The Treatise on the Resurrection* (or *Epistle of Rheginos); The Treatise on the Three Natures;* and *The Prayers of the Apostles.* Two other important early Gnostic works have also appeared, *The Apocryphon of John,* already mentioned, with its magnificent exposition of the total transcendence of God, and the creation and fate of the world, and *The Gospel of Thomas,* which may possibly contained some authentic sayings of Jesus not contained in the canonical Gospels. These works have been published in English, but Gnostic writings have a habit of going quickly out of print, so you will be lucky to find most of them, except in the large *New Testament Apocrypha* edited by Hennecke and Schneemelcher. One other gem that has mysteriously come to light is a biography of Mani from a tomb in Oxyrhynchus, the smallest book from antiquity, only 4½ by 3½ cm, containing 192 pages that tell the unknown story of Mani's birth and upbringing in the Jewish-Christian sect of the Elchasaites.

As a result of all these discoveries, Gnosticism is now something of an academic growth industry, and no longer a quiet, scholarly backwater for specialists in Coptic, Syriac, Aramaic and other obscure languages from the past. Many of these scholars have been card-carrying   Christians,   defensively   unsympathetic   and uncomprehending towards the texts they were studying. "Gnostic" for many of them existed only in the pejorative mode along with such allied concepts as syncretistic, eclectic, heretical, hellenistic, allegorical, docetist, mystical, adoptionist, dualist, etc. Thus translations sometimes seem wilfully obtuse, as when *Metropator*, an epithet for Barbelo, the feminine counterpart of God, is rendered — quite correctly — "maternal grandfather", when a sympathetic understanding of the Gnostic penchant for archetypal androgygny might have suggested "mother-father" as an alternative. The single vision has, however, not had things all its own way in the struggle with recrudescent Gnosis. Gnosticism's greatest success was, perhaps, to have enlisted the support of C. G. Jung. Already, he tells us, during the period of his collaboration with Freud, fired by an interest in ancient myths, he "worked through the Gnostic writers", ending in a state of perplexity and total confusion. During the strange period of his encounter with the unconscious, his inner teacher and companion was personified in the Gnostic figure of Philemon. Jung came to divine the existence of a golden chain, linking earth with heaven on the vertical axis, and the beginnings of philosophical alchemy and Gnosticism with Goethe and Nietzsche on the horizontal. "In 1916", he relates, "I felt an urge to give shape to something. I was compelled from within, as it were, to formulate and express what might have been said by Philemon." And not only from within. The air was "filled with ghostly figures", which other members of the household saw. "The front-door bell began ringing frantically" without any apparent human agency. At last the house became crammed with spirits, who cried out in chorus, "We have come back from Jerusalem where we found not what we sought." At this Jung took up his pen to write the *Septem Sermones ad Mortuos*, at which "the whole ghostly assemblage evaporated." (*Memories, Dreams, Reflections*, Fontana edition, pp. 214ff.) In three evenings the work was completed, an extraordinary book quite unlike anything else that Jung published, redolent of the spirit of Gnosticism. he attributes it to Basilides, one of the greatest of all Gnostic teachers, "in Alexandria where the East toucheth the West". Considering how little was available at the time in the way of original Gnostic texts, it is remarkable how true it is, not only to the atmosphere but to the content of Alexandrian Gnosis, to which it could still serve as a useful introduction. There is, however, one significant innovation.

God and devil are distinguished by the qualities fullness and emptiness, generation and destruction. EFFECTIVENESS is common to both. Effectiveness joineth them. Effectiveness, therefore, standeth above both; is a god above god . . . This is a god whom ye know not, for mankind forgot it. We name it by its name ABRAXAS.

Hermann Hesse picked up and popularized this idea in his book *Demian*, in which he give a disguised account of his own Jungian analysis. To him Abraxas was the name of a godhead "who symbolizes the reconciliation of the godly and satanic . . . both God and Devil." As far as I have been able to ascertain from the competent authorities, Abraxas is a power invoked in Hellenistic magic, though the similarly named Abrasax, also known as Saclas or Sacloun, is used in Gnostic systems to denote the foolish demiurge. There is apparently no concept in Gnosticism of a god beyond good and evil and hence the origin of good and evil. This does not, in my opinion, deprive the notion of validity, but, on the contrary, endows it with a special significance and importance for our time.

Jung's serious study of the Gnostic writers, he tells us, continued from 1918 to 1926, "for they too had been confronted with the primal world of the unconscious and had dealt with its contents, with images that were obviously contaminated with the world of instinct. . . . But the Gnostics were too remote for me to establish any link with them in regard to the questions that were confronting me." The historical link with Gnosticism, the bridge between the Gnostic past and the future as represented by the modern psychology of the unconscious he found in alchemy, defined by one authority as the yoga of Gnosticism. What Jung would have made of the wealth of Gnostic literature that is now becoming available provides fascinating food for speculation. We know that he saw in Freud's psychology the "classical Gnostic motifs of sexuality and the wicked paternal authority." The motif of the Gnostic Yahweh and creator-god reappeared in the Freudian myth of the primal father and the gloomy super-ego deriving from that father. "What was missing was that other essential aspect of Gnosticism: the primordial image of the spirit as another, higher god who gave to mankind the krater (mixing vessel), the vessel of spiritual transformation. The krater is a feminine principle which could find no place in Freud's patriarchal world." (MDR, pp. 226f)

I hope I have said enough to convey the impression that Gnosticism is a relevant and important subject to ponder at the present time, particularly for those concerned to further the promulgation and development of Jung's ideas. It is a daunting and complicated subject whose protean nature has been further exaggerated and complicated by scholarly researches, which have tended to obscure the essential underlying unity of the Gnostic myth. Creation, whether on the scale of the macrocosm or the microcosm, implies a falling away from unity, spirit, eternity, into multiplicity, materialism and time. Man's tragedy is that, like the prodigal son, forgetful of his true home, he is reduced to the slavery of unconsciousness in Egypt, eating husks (the externals of life) with the pigs. Gnosticism is about the return journey, once he has come to himself, a light on the path and a means to surmount the spiritual obstacles that block it, a growth in understanding that is at the same time an adventure in depth. The basic Gnostic virtues are a sense of wonder, an appreciation of the ambiguity involved in man's being-in-the-world, a hunger for meaning and perseverance in seeking it. A crucial question for today, it seems to me, is whether Gnosticism ever formed part of that broad spectrum of practice and belief that we call Christianity, and, if so, whether it can be reintegrated. The contemporary Church has, after all, assimilated some strange bed-fellows, thanks to the realization that there was no pure form of Christianity that existed *ab initio*, which we can call orthodox. I wish to conclude with some words of Dr H. D. Betz which sum up a position widely held by New Testament scholars at the present time:

> In the beginning there existed merely the "heretical" Jew, Jesus of Nazareth. Which of the different interpretations of Jesus are to be called authentically Christian? And what are the criteria for making that decision? This seems to me the cardinal problem of New Testament studies today.

Jung and Marx:
Alchemy, Christianity, and the Work against Nature[1]

by David Holt

DAVID HOLT is a graduate of the C.G. Jung Institute in Zürich. He is a member of the Analytical Psychology Club, London. He practises in Oxford.

I

I have announced this lecture under the title Jung and Marx: alchemy, Christianity, and the work against nature. As what I have to say is rather strange, I think it will help us all if I start by explaining how these various ideas will be related to each other.

The central idea, round which the others are organised, is of the work against nature. I want to try to say something about the work against nature in which we all share. What I mean by this work will, I hope, emerge as my argument develops. It will emerge through my use of two words which are familiar but not easy to define: creator and virgin.

I shall not try to define what I mean by creator and virgin. I shall limit myself to try to describe a *space* between creator and virgin, for it is in this space that I believe the work against nature is being done. And it is in order to describe this space that I am bringing together the names of Jung and Marx.

To describe a space physically needs two movements of the imagination, one which expands and one which contracts: the two movements which Jung called extraversion and introversion. I shall be using the work of Marx to stimulate the extraverted movement of the imagination, and the work of Jung to stimulate the introverted.

Between the two, I hope we will become aware of the need for work of a very special kind. I shall be using some reflections on alchemy and on Christianity to try to illuminate the nature of this work. I want to use alchemy, as Jung interpreted it in terms of psyche, as the way into a questioning of what Christianity has done to the relation between man and nature. In asking this question I hope to convey some sense of what I mean by creator and virgin.

So my argument will develop in five stages. First, I want to introduce Jung's interest in alchemy. Then I shall give a brief exposition of one aspect of Marx's thought. This introduces the idea of man as involved in nature's coming-to-self-consciousness. I shall then define my own attitude to this idea of Marx's, as a transition to the other main line of my argument: what Christianity has done to man and nature. I shall conclude by saying the little that I can say about the work being done between creator and virgin.

II

Jung's work on alchemy is in the fullest sense of the word surprising. Some of you will be familiar with it. To others it may be unknown. So let me start by reading you three extracts from his autobiography, in which he describes how alchemy became one of the main interests of the last thirty years of his life.

I had very soon seen that analytical psychology coincided in a most curious way with alchemy. The experiences of the alchemists were, in a sense, my experiences, and their world was my world. This was, of course, a momentous discovery: I had stumbled upon the historical counterpart of my psychology of the unconscious. The possibility of a comparison with alchemy, and the uninterrupted intellectual chain back to Gnosticism, gave substance to my psychology.[2]

Since my aim was to demonstrate the full extent to which my psychology corresponded to alchemy — or vice-versa — I wanted to discover, side by side with the religious questions, what special problems of psychotherapy were treated in the work of the alchemists. The main problem of medical psychotherapy is the *transference*. . . I was able to demonstrate that alchemy, too, had something that corresponded to the transference, namely the concept of the *coniunctio*. . .[3]

This investigation was rounded out by the *Mysterium Coniunctionis,* in which I once again took up the problem of the transference, but primarily followed my original intention of representing the whole range of alchemy as a kind of psychology of alchemy, or as an alchemical basis for depth psychology. In *Mysterium Coniunctionis* my psychology was at last given its place in reality and established upon its historic foundations.[4]

Now what Jung is saying here is really very odd indeed. It is so extraordinary that we may easily slide over it without feeling the surprise which we should. One of my aims is to try to convey something of that sense of surprise.

What is this "psychology of alchemy" which Jung has left behind him? My thesis is that it belongs in the world of extraversion as well as of introversion, and that its extraverted mode is expressed in the intercourse between man and nature which we call economics. I want to try to establish some links between psychology and economics, in the belief that Jung's psychology of alchemy contains resources of imagination, humour and will, which could help us deal with the economic problems of today and tomorrow. But to make this link between psychology, alchemy and economics, we need "space" of an unusual kind.

Before I go on to define this space, I want to emphasise the provenance of the ideas I shall be expressing. They derive primarily from a series of my own dreams. The earliest in the series which I remember dates from 1948, when I was 22. The most recent was six years ago. The reading and thinking that lie behind these ideas originates in the need to understand dreams. What this says about the relevance of my argument for you, depends on what you make of your own dreaming. But I am sure that what I am saying will mislead unless its provenance in dreams is borne in mind.

III

Marx's vision, or analysis, of man's intercourse with nature will be familiar to many of us. But for all its familiarity, it remains difficult. For the very brief exposition which I want to try here, I shall take as my way into his thought his analysis of the changing nature of money.

Up to about the year 1400 the economic life of Europe was essentially agricultural, concerned with the same kind of problems which we now associate with the so-called "third world". There were exceptions which in retrospect can seem very significant. But taken as a whole, economic activity constituted a closed circle between man and nature, with nothing left over. Between 1400 and 1700 this closed circle broke open and began spiralling, both "out" and "in", to include within the economic process a wider and ever increasing number of commodities and desires. From 1700 onwards this spiral became more like an explosion, until today we have a situation in which on the one hand the whole system can be kept going only by the creation of new needs out of luxuries that were themselves unheard of a generation earlier, while on the other hand it is becoming more and more widely accepted that this stimulation of new needs is destroying an essential balance within the natural environment.

Within the closed system that prevailed — with significant exceptions — up to about 1400, money was essentially the medium of exchange, something to facilitate the barter of the market place. It served to lubricate a process of exchange whose driving energy was the natural cycle of agricultural seasons, supplemented by the skills and muscular energy of man. Since 1700, although it retains its old function of lubricating the economic system, money has *also* become the fuel which fires the engine which drives the whole system along. It is this change in the nature of money that Karl Marx described as the emergence of capitalism.

Marx is the prophet of this split in our experience of money. He lived and wrote at a time when the first industrial revolution had already transformed conditions of life in Britain, France, Germany and the Netherlands, and was reaching out to alter the face of our planet more radically — in relation to the passage of time — than in any previous revolution in the history of man. Marx insisted that something unprecedented was happening, and that the split in our experience of money, of which the power of capital was the outward and visible manifestation, was only one aspect of a much more pervasive and radical alteration in the whole balance between man and nature.

This unprecedented shift of balance between man and nature is today widely discussed in terms of ecology, in terms of relationship between man and his environment. It is therefore perhaps easier for us today to understand Marx if we listen to what he has to say with the contemporary arguments of ecologists in mind.

Marx was deeply impressed by the way in which this split between money as means of exchange, and money as self-generating capital, seemed at the same time both to make possible and also to justify the technological exploitation of the planet on which the industrial societies of Western Europe had embarked. He argued that the result of this interpenetration of the monetary and technological revolutions was altering the very quality of human life. All previous history had been that of men living in a world that was *given*. But now men were learning what it was to live in a world that was to an ever-increasing degree made *by* man, rather than given *to* man, in a world whose conditions were determined not by the gifts of nature, but by the manufactures of man. Marx's political economics studied the effects of this revolution on the social relations between human beings, but he emphasised again and again that to understand what was happening to personal development within this new technological and capitalist society, man must be aware of what is happening to the much more fundamental relation between the creativity of man and the material world of which man is part.

It is here that Marx touches the central idea with which I am concerned in placing his work alongside Jung's psychology of alchemy. He is defining a split, what he called an "alienation", of a new kind: an alienation of man from nature, where nature is to be thought of both as man's own nature and also as the natural world in which man makes his living. The peculiar quality of this alienation emerges from his description of how money has succeeded in breaking the circle of man's intercourse with nature.

Money has its origin in the market place where we go to exchange what we have but don't need, for what we need but don't have. Money is the medium which facilitates this exchange, but in so doing it converts the immaterial process of exchange into a thing which can itself be exchanged for other things. It is as if when things are exchanged in the market place a new power is born, a power that breaks out of the circle of man's intercourse with nature. This power has no existence in nature, yet manages to establish itself in its own right as existing over and against both man and nature.

Marx believed that with the coming of the industrial revolution, and of the concurrent financial revolution that made money out of credit, this break in the circle of man's intercourse with nature became absolute, so that the circle fell apart into a polarisation. On the one hand, we see the emergence of capital as an apparently autonomous power, able to breed out of itself with no sense of obligation to the material exchange in which it had its origin. On the other hand, we see the emergence of wage labour, which is bought and sold in the market place like any other thing, and thus valued never for itself but always for something other than itself.

But Marx did not stop at this economic analysis. He gave it another dimension altogether. He argued that with this differentiation between capital and labour a truth becomes conscious that has never been conscious before. He argues that in the consciousness of wage labour as it confronts the power of capital, nature, which in itself is virgin, becomes aware for the first time what it means to be used for a purpose outside itself.

IV

I want to stop there in my exposition of Marx's vision of the world he saw around him rather more than a hundred years ago. In selecting this one way into his comprehensive and detailed economic analysis, I am inevitably being unfair to his scholarship. But it is this seminal idea of nature coming, through man, to a new self-consciousness, which I want to place alongside Jung's psychology of alchemy. So let me repeat once again the formulation at which we have arrived: the thesis that in the consciousness of wage labour as it confronts capital, nature, which in itself is virgin, becomes aware for the first time what it means to be used for a purpose outside itself.

I believe that this is the idea which gives Marxism as we know it today, a hundred years after the death of its founder, its dynamism and fascination. I believe it to be true that a new consciousness of what it means for nature to be used for a purpose outside itself is now lodged within man. And I believe that if we, as the one world which we are become, are to solve the economic problems confronting us, it is essential that we all play our part in trying to understand what this new consciousness means for our way of life.

But this belief does not make me a Marxist. It is not only that all my training and material interests make me conservative, with both a small and a large 'c'. Marx, it seems to me, gave to this essentially true insight a twist which has thrown it disastrously off-centre. He introduced into his economic analysis messianic expectations of which he was unconscious and he located this messianism in a new chosen people, the people he called the proletariat.

If we are to assimilate Marx's recognition of the new "humanisation of society" into the great conservative and radical traditions of our society, we must learn to understand these messianic expectations. We have to ask how the Judaeo-Christian messianism which informs the whole body of Marxism affects our economic condition. And to do this I believe we must concern ourselves with man's masochism and sadism when face to face with "that which in itself is virgin".

How does Marx's vision relate to the long and confused history of Judaeo-Christian messianic psychology? I think most students of the history of ideas would agree that the answer lies in the philosophy of Hegel, and in the way Marx used and altered this philosophy. Certainly it was in Hegel's work that I found my first bridge from Marx to Jung, twenty-five years ago.

Jung has written of Hegel's philosophy:

> The victory of Hegel over Kant dealt the gravest blow to reason and to the further development of the German and, ultimately, of the European mind, all the more dangerous as Hegel was a psychologist in disguise who projected great truths out of the subjective sphere into a cosmos he himself had created.[5]

I think much of Jung's psychology can be read as a translation of

Hegel's philosophy into the experiences of ordinary men and women. In particular, I think this is true of Jung's interest as a psychologist in the ways in which the modern psyche questions what is to become of the Christian revelation. Hegel's philosophy has often been interpreted as an extension of Christian theology. A recent study by Hans Küng, for instance, has the title: *God becoming man: an introduction to Hegel's theological thought as prolegomena to a future christology.* Though he makes no mention of Jung, Hans Küng develops ideas which are familiar to readers of Jung's essays on the psychological significance of the Trinity and the transformation symbolism of the Mass. These, and other, close connections between Jung's psychology and Hegel's philosophy will be much studied in the years to come.

One result of such study will be to place Marx's Hegelian heritage in a wider and — dare we say it? — more feminine context. Within this feminine world we can find the resources of imagination, humour and will with which to assimilate the masochism and sadism which Marx has done so much to stimulate in the modern psyche.

Marx's rejection of Hegel's idealism, and his conversion of that idealism into his own historical materialism, can be understood in terms of a future christology if we are so minded. But mediaeval alchemy foretold the work of both Hegel and Marx within a tradition which kept alive the memory of what christology had done to nature. Within this tradition we have descriptions of the spontaneous response of the human psyche to the "alienation" described by Hegel and Marx. If we study Marx against this background we will, I believe, be better equipped to analyse how his messianic expectations can be related to our present economic predicament as nature begins to reassert her right to be what she is in herself.

V

Students of the history of ideas present alchemy either as a woefully unscientific precursor to modern chemistry, or as a more or less bogus attempt to find sudden wealth through the artificial production of gold, or as an esoteric, religious tradition that reached its culmination in Goethe's *Faust*. Jung recognises all three of these interpretations as partially valid. Yet for him alchemy has to do with something more than any combination of these three traditions. The history of alchemy records how the human psyche has assumed, over centuries of trial and error, a peculiar obligation in respect to matter: the obligation to reconcile matter to the fact of Christianity.

This is an extraordinary idea. It is so strange that on first encounter with it even sympathetic readers of Jung feel uneasy and prefer to avoid looking at it too closely. But for those who return to it and learn gradually to pay attention it proves itself unexpectedly effective. We find that we can read in the history of alchemy how Christianity has damaged matter, and how the human psyche moves spontaneously to make good that damage.

This assessment of the place of alchemy in the history of ideas can be summarised from two points of view: firstly, by contrasting the alchemical work with the Christian work of redemption; and secondly, by the hypothesis of a triangular relationship between alchemy, Christianity and modern technology.

The contrast between the alchemical work and the Christian atonement pervades all Jung's writing on alchemy. Two quotations must serve as illustrations. For those who know Jung's work, they will be familiar. For those who do not, taken thus out of context, they will sound very strange.

Comparing the alchemical transformation of matter with the Christian Mass, he writes:

By pronouncing the consecrating words that bring about the transformation, the priest redeems the bread and wine from their elemental imperfection as created things. This idea is unchristian — it is alchemical. Whereas Catholicism emphasises the effectual presence of Christ, alchemy is interested in the fate and manifest redemption of the substances, for in them the divine soul lies captive and awaits the redemption that is granted to it at the moment of release. The captive soul then appears in the form of the "Son of God". For the alchemist, the one primarily in need of redemption is not man, but the deity who is lost and sleeping in matter . . . Since it is not man but matter that must be redeemed the spirit that manifests itself in the transformation is not the Son of Man but . . . the *filius macrocosmi*. Therefore, what comes out of the transformation is not Christ, but an ineffable material being named the "stone" . . . [6]

The second quotation is from an essay on the sixteenth century physician and natural philosopher Paracelsus. In this, the different attitudes of alchemist and Christian to the transformation of matter are related to the question of man's place in nature at the dawn of our modern scientific era.

Whereas in Christ God himself became man, the *filius-philoso-phorum* was extracted from matter by human art and, by means of the *opus*, made into a new light-bringer. In the former case the miracle of man's salvation is accomplished by God; in the latter, the salvation or transfiguration of the universe is brought about by the mind of man — "*Deo concedente*", as the authors never fail to add. In the one case man confesses "I under God", in the other he asserts "God under me". Man takes the place of the Creator. Medieval alchemy prepared the way for the greatest intervention in the divine world order that man has ever attempted: alchemy was the dawn of the scientific age, when the daemon of the scientific spirit compelled the forces of nature to serve man to an extent that had never been known before . . . Here we find the true roots, the preparatory processes deep in the psyche, which unleashed the forces at work in the world today. Science and technology have indeed conquered the world, but whether the psyche has gained anything is another matter.[7]

On the one hand, we have the experience of man's salvation as accomplished by God. On the other, the transfiguration of the universe is brought about by the mind of man. Does the contrast, indeed the conflict, between these two works of redemption have anything to say about the dilemmas of our contemporary technology?

I believe it has. I believe Jung's studies in alchemy provide us with a crucial link in the history of ideas. It is a link between science, technology, and economics on the one hand, and the Christian doctrine of incarnation on the other, and it is organised round the Christian failure to understand what Christian faith has done to the relationship between man and matter.

The best way to present this hypothesis of a triangular relationship between alchemy, Christianity and modern technology is to pose a familiar question from the history of science: why did the questioning of nature characteristic of the Greek intellect of the 4th century B.C. stop short of the experimental method which developed in the 16th and 17th centuries A.D.?

Various answers have been given to this question. One answer — or perhaps we should say one set of answers — derives from the fact of Christianity: from the fact that over many centuries people believed this particular faith and practised these particular rites which we call Christian. It is argued that the decisive change in man's relation to matter between, say, Aristotle and Newton, was the conversion of Europe to the belief

(1) that the creator of all Being had become man;
(2) that when this man died, he had not remained dead, but had resurrected, and

(3) that following this resurrection, his flesh and blood could, by appropriate rites, be transformed into bread and wine which mankind could eat and drink.

According to this argument, the result of this conversion was a fundamental shift in the distribution of creative power within the universe. Something got into man which had not been there before. Over many centuries of disciplined intellectual effort the Christian mind trained itself in asking questions which were inconceivable to the classical Greeks. These questions had to do with the dual nature of Christ as both God and man; with the nature of his mother who was both virgin and yet also in the fullest sense mother of a man; with how three can be one and one three and what this implies for the relation between person and substance; and, perhaps most crucial of all, with the nature of the change that took place in bread and wine in the eucharist. Gradually, imperceptibly, questioning like this separated mind and matter in a way they had not been previously separated. A space opened up between mind and matter which was altogether and absolutely new in the history of mankind. Mind was seized of the very special "objectivity" which separates creator and creature.

It was this qualitatively new objectivity which made possible the scientific revolution of the sixteenth and seventeenth centuries. A thousand years of intricate and passionate reflection on the mysteries of Christian faith and practice had separated mind from its original participation in nature. Within the space made by this separation man had room to experiment, and to sustain his experimenting, in a way that had never before been possible. He learned to enjoy putting nature to the torture.

This view of the origin of modern science is of course not universally accepted. This is not the occasion to take the argument further. What I want to do is put it forward as an hypothesis, and draw attention to one consequence which would follow if this hypothesis were to be proved.

So let us assume that the objectivity of modern natural science, the "space" which separates the mind of both the experimental and the applied scientist from the matter on which they work, derives from reflection on the central doctrines of Christianity. If this were true, what would it mean for those of us — and that means now almost everybody in the world — who live off the technological fruits of natural science?

It would mean that we are all, Christian and non-Christian alike, living off a reflective act of which we are unconscious. But the reason for this unconsciousness would vary between those who think of themselves as Christian and those who think of themselves as non-Christian.

For the overwhelming non-Christian world which has now taken possession of natural science it would mean that we are living off reflection on something which in varying ways we deny, or even despise or abhor. It would mean that if the act of which we are unconscious should insist on becoming conscious we would have to admit to a contradiction running through all our intercourse with matter: a contradiction by which we allow ourselves to enjoy the fruits of a distinctively Christian separation between mind and matter, while refusing any obligation to the Christian work of atonement.

For Christians, it would mean that we are the guardians of a secret which we dare not acknowledge. Because if Christianity has fathered and mothered the scientific revolution of the last three hundred years it has conspicuously failed to retain the faith of its own offspring which has, moreover, succeeded in doing what Christianity wanted to do but failed to do: converting the world. So if this secret of which we are unconscious should presently insist on becoming conscious it would mean for Christians that we would have to acknowledge that our faith has secreted out of its central moments of reflection a power greater than itself.

Now, always assuming that our thesis of the Christian origin of modern science is true, we have here a situation whose danger every dynamic psychologist will recognise. There is an unconscious secret which is shared by two contrasting attitudes. But although it is shared, its structure and dynamism is different in relation to each of the two conscious attitudes. The danger is that when the need to repress an unconscious content is shared with another person, but the reasons for this need differ, then fear of what is unconscious converts into fear of the other person. One kind of fear then feeds on another in preventing us from even beginning to question the presence of such a secret. The failure of the other person to admit to its existence confirms me in the righteousness of my own denial, and simultaneously makes the other person the bearer of the guilt of my denial.

This kind of situation is familiar in family life! But in relation to the damage which Christianity has done to matter, it is a situation with which our whole world is now having to familiarise itself.

Can the non-Christian heirs to Christian technology accept that Christianity guards the secret of their power over nature? And can the Christian guardians — both living and dead — accept that there is, and always has been, a dimension to their faith which only non-Christians can understand?

It is here, I believe, that Jung's psychology of alchemy will prove relevant for our future. For Jung has rediscovered a world within which we can analyse what nature endured in those long centuries of evolving Christian consciousness which gave birth to the experimental sciences of the last three hundred years. In this rediscovery, he has given us the 'content' of that secret which is now insisting on becoming conscious, a secret for which neither Christianity nor technology can find room: the secret of what it means for nature, which in itself is virgin, to be used for a purpose outside itself.

What can be said about the content of this secret?

VI

The alchemical *opus* has its beginning in filth and dirt, and its end in gold. The beginning and the end are one. But between beginning and end, both separating and also linking them, is the work, the work against nature. What is the secret of this work that 'conjugates' filth and gold? It is a secret to which both economist and ecologist would like to have the key. But the key is costly: costly of *spirit*. And that is not the kind of payment which our contemporary economic theory comprehends.

Alchemy studies the intercourse between man and matter at a level which we have forgotten, though it was still accessible up to about the eighteenth century, that is to say up to the technological and economic revolution whose first fruits were witnessed by Marx. This intercourse is of a kind that seemed grossly material to the Christian consciousness of its day, but which nevertheless presupposes that matter is *ensouled*. The materialism of alchemy was never of that kind which exalts the life of the intellect over against the deadness of matter. For the alchemist, matter is alive, and the intercourse of man with matter was not that of the experimental scientist who puts nature to the torture, but of the worker who mixes his labour with the stuff which is essential to existence. This quality in the work of the alchemist is reminiscent of the language of Marx.

But for the alchemist, unlike Marx, this mixing of labour with matter involved something which he was willing to call spirit. In his analysis of what went on between himself and matter he was prepared to recognise the presence of an agent that was neither 'I' nor 'it', an agent necessary to the intercourse between I and it, which nevertheless eluded all attempts to grasp it in terms of I and it. Through the presence of this agent he came to describe a work which modern materialism rejects as grotesque, as absolutely repugnant to common sense.

At the risk of serious over-simplification, we can distinguish four levels in this work. At the first, we are asked to accept that matter is not dead, but alive. Then we are asked to credit that this aliveness of matter is like the intercourse between male and female. At a yet deeper level, alchemy then confronts us with something even more awkward to our understanding: the life of matter is not only compounded of a dialectic like human sexuality, but this dialectic wants to convert an unintentional *incest* into the celebration of a deliberate *marriage.*And finally, we are asked to believe that in making this conversion from incest into marriage, matter has need of a personal, human intervention.

Has this kind of hocus-pocus anything whatsoever to do with the economic problems of our world? If it has, I think the link is to be found in the word sacrifice.

Economic theory, and particularly economic argument, recognises the need for sacrifice to be made. But there is no relation between our economic and our psychological experiences of sacrifice. What we understand by sacrifice is something much weaker, much less effective and integrated, than in other cultures. We don't really believe that the sacrifices we are asked to make will work *on* the material world. Instead we suspect that they will in some way be used against us by some agent or power which we cannot define but are quite able to project onto each other.

This split between our economic and psychological experience of sacrifice is the central problem to which I am addressing myself here. I believe it originates in our failure to remember the particular sacrifice which sustains our technological culture, a sacrifice which is made between creator and virgin. Alchemy is the necessary link between psychology and economics because it remembers this sacrifice.

It remembers it on two levels: first as pre- and non-Christian; secondly, as radically altered by the fact of Christianity.

Outside Christianity, alchemy reminds us that our bodies cannot take matter for granted. The alchemist realises that matter exists by virtue of a work in which our bodies share, and that our enjoyment of matter — what economists call wealth — depends on our attitude to that work. If we are afraid of that work, then our enjoyment of matter remains enclosed within an incestuous circle which collapses the essential distinction between maker and made. But if we can learn to enter into that work, to do it knowingly, then our enjoyment of matter opens into the deliberate celebration of the difference between maker and made: a celebration which we can think of as analogous to human marriage.

But the advent of Christianity introduces a new twist into the relation between body and matter. The faith that the *maker* of all that is has deliberately chosen to be part of what is *made*, and that the particular part chosen was the body of man, secretes as it were into the relationship between man and the rest of nature a new potentiality: the potentiality that man could appropriate to himself the unique, and terrible, "objectivity" of the maker in the face of that which is made. This potentiality Christianity further encouraged by ordaining that mankind should, first, eat and drink the flesh and blood of the maker, and then use mind to reflect on what this ingestion did to the relation between person and substance.

That was the new situation in which the post-Christian alchemist found himself. On the underside of the long centuries during which the faithful celebrated the sacrifice of the eucharist, a new question was arising between man and matter. If the Christian were free to appropriate to himself the "objectivity" of the maker in the face of that which is made, would he also take on himself the corresponding obligation: the obligation to remember the "understanding" between creator and virgin on which all making depends?

Jung argues that the alchemists of the late middle ages and renaissance were trying to keep this memory alive, but that the science and technology of the last three hundred years have not only suppressed it, but fed on that suppression. This suppression gives to the relationship between modern man and nature its special quality of masochism. Jung's psychology of alchemy offers us an opportunity to analyse this masochism, to undo the suppression at its root, to begin the work of remembering so that we can build again on an understanding of which Christianity and its offspring have made us forgetful.

As an example, we can think of the urgent need to relate our sexuality to our food supply. At the recent world food conference in Rome, we heard the pope agree with the representatives of state Marxism in arguing that the need to control the level of population was being exaggerated by those who already enjoy technological wealth as a new kind of warfare against those who do not. For those of us who are persuaded of the real dangers of the population explosion, it seems as if catholic and communist hierarchies share a common interest in hunger. There is no area of world argument in which we have more need of cross-fertilisation between psychology and economics if we are to be saved from the self destructive cycle of sado-masochism.

Alchemy describes the economics of sexuality and hunger in a way which the Christianity and Marxism we heard speak at Rome do not understand. It is an economy which depends on using our enjoyment of sex to discriminate between two kinds of hunger. On the one hand, there is hunger which can be satisfied within a biological cycle of production and consumption. On the other, there is hunger which can only be satisfied by the very special kind of "making" which goes on between creator and virgin, a making which precedes the very possibility of production and consumption. The alchemical work hinges on the distinction between these two kinds of hunger.

We must incorporate this distinction into our economic theory and practice. But if the psychology of alchemy is to be trusted, this will require a change of which both Christian and Marxist hierarchies seem to be deeply afraid. Economics will have to bring an altogether new kind of gravity to the study of what goes on between male and female. The business which men and women have with one another must become a primary centre around which we organise our understanding of wealth and its enjoyment. Instead of being a peripheral interest, the exchanges between male and female must be allowed to find their true weight at the very centre of the economic process, and from that centre to generate the metaphors and models we need to balance the economy between man and nature.

Such a shift in the centre of economic gravity would not save us from controversy and the need for difficult and painful choices. On the contrary, it would open up new areas for argument and persuasion. But it would enable us better to define the choices that matter if we are to balance sexuality and food within our technological civilisation. So let me conclude with an example of such choice, the example with which all I have said so far has been concerned: the choice as to who sacrifices what to whom when creator and virgin come face to face.

On the one hand, we have the Christian experience of Mary's "be it unto me according to thy word", which opening the way for the maker into the body of the made. Eighteen hundred years later the new breed of experimental scientists and colonisers assumed the

same acquiescence in the body of the material world which they
believed themselves entitled to explore. We have lived on the fruits
of that assumption. We are beginning to realize the debt that may
have to be paid should that assumption be called into question.

The alchemists could not make that assumption. They
remembered a different scene, a scene which is becoming familiar to
us once again as the third world insists on making its presence felt.
The scene is described in a text which Jung quotes in his essay on
the visions of Zosimos.

'Isis the Prophetess to her son Horus: My child, you should go
forth to battle against faithless Typhon for the sake of your
father's kingdom, while I retire to Egypt's city of the sacred art,
where I sojourned for a while. According to the circumstances of
the time and the necessary consequences of the movement of the
spheres, it came to pass that a certain one among the angels,
dwelling in the first firmament, watched me from above and
wished to have intercourse with me. Quickly he determined to
bring this about. I did not yield, as I wished to inquire into the
preparation of the gold and silver. But when I demanded it of
him, he told me he was not permitted to speak of it, on account of
the supreme importance of the mysteries: but on the following
day an angel, Amnael, greater than he, would come, and he could
give me the solution to the problem. He also spoke of the sign of
this angel — he bore it on his head and would show me a small,
unpitched vessel filled with a translucent water. He would tell me
the truth. On the following day, as the sun was crossing the
midpoint of its course, Amnael appeared, who was greater than
the first angel, and, seized with the same desire, he did not
hesitate, but hastened to where I was. But I was no less
determined to inquire into the matter.'[8]

And Jung goes on to comment that she did not yield, and the
angel revealed the secret.

There is a world of difference between the responses of Mary and
of Isis. If psychology and economics are to join in providing the
resources our technological civilisation needs, we must make room
for this world. Between these two understandings of how creator
and virgin can behave toward one another we have the human space
within which we can explore our choices as to who sacrifices what to
whom. This is the space we need if we are to respond freely to the
economic predicament of mankind as nature — 'our' nature, yet not
ours — begins to reassert her right to be as she is in herself. And it is
in this space, so I believe, that Jung's psychology of alchemy will
prove itself.

NOTES

1. Public lecture given at the Royal Society of Medicine, London, on 21st November, 1974, under the auspices of the Analytical Psychology Club, London.
2. C.G. Jung. *Memories Dreams Reflections*, Vintage Books, New York, 1963, p. 205.
3. *Ibid.* p. 212-213.
4. *Ibid* p. 221.
5. C.G. Jung. *Collected Works*, Vol. 8, p. 169, published by Routledge & Kegan Paul, London, 1960.
6. C.G. Jung. *Collected Works*, Vol. 12, para. 420, published by Routledge & Kegan Paul, London, 1953.
7. C.G. Jung. *Collected Works*, Vol. 13, para. 163, published by Routledge & Kegan Paul, London, 1967.
8. *Ibid* para. 99.

The Inner Journey of the Poet[1]

by Kathleen Raine

KATHLEEN RAINE, poet and scholar, has lectured at Eranos and in the United States, and has received many prizes and awards in Britain, France and America. She is the author of Blake and Tradition, Blake and Antiquity, William Blake *(World of Art Series, Thames and Hudson),* Thomas Taylor the Platonist, *some dozen volumes of poems and three volumes of autobiography. A number of her books have been translated into French and other languages. Her latest publications include collected poems and papers entitled* The Inner Journey of the Poet *and* The Human Face of God. *She is a founder editor of the review* Temenos. *A collection of papers on W.B. Yeats entitled* Yeats the Initiate *is in preparation.*

Of all those great contemporaries in whose times I have lived, C.G. Jung is one of the two, or perhaps three, minds to whom I am most indebted.

Nevertheless I am not a Jungian. In two senses this is so. First, of course, I am not a trained psychologist, and although I have read most of Jung's published writings with pleasure and profit I have never attempted to master his terms in the exact sense required by professional rigour. In the second place I suspect – though with Jung one can never be sure for he is himself often deliberately ambiguous, that in some important matters I would not share his point of view. What, for example, in *Answer to Job,* does he mean by the "God-image"? Does he mean that "God" is a psychic image, amongst others? Or does he mean that man bears in his psyche the image of God? Since I unambiguously adhere to the traditional teaching that man is made in the image of God, it may be that here I part company with many Jungians, and even perhaps with Jung himself; and probably in other contexts where metaphysical quest-ions are involved; though Jung disclaims metaphysics and a poet would always be wise to do so.

The Inner Journey is certainly a theme poets and psychologists have in common; one might almost say that journey has, one way or another, been the theme of most of the imaginative poetry of mankind. And since there is not one of us who must not sooner or later set out upon that journey we may expect to learn from the poets some of the stages on the way all must travel. For, as Blake wrote, "these States Exist now. Man Passes on, States remain for Ever; he passes thro' them like a traveller who may as well suppose that the places he has passed thro' exist no more, as a Man may suppose that the States he has passed thro' Exist no more." (Ed Keynes, p. 606.)

In the middle of the road of life Dante, supreme poet of Christendom, came to himself (*mi ritrovai* – literally "found myself again") to discover that he had lost his way and was in the middle of a dark forest. How he came to be there he did not know because, as he tells us, he was "full of sleep" when he missed his way. The great *Commedia* is an allegory; and yet the opening scene has upon us the impact of a dream we might ourselves have dreamed. Dante's fear, when he finds himself entangled in natural life, in "the forests of affliction", the "forests of the night" as Blake was later to call that place, communicates itself to us because the symbol evokes in us a resonance at a far deeper level than mere allegory. There Blake met his Tyger; and Dante too met a beast, "burning bright"; not a Tyger but a fierce creature at once leopard, lion and wolf. He allegorises the beast; and yet the encounter has the quality of some dream or vision in which forest and beast alike arise from the unconscious mind which creates such encounters for us. The encounter was, in any case, the determining moment of his inner life, the starting point of his own interior journey.

As the poet fled, bewildered by the forest and terrified by the beast, there came towards him one of those figures we meet on the road of life at the moment of need, sometimes in dreams, sometimes in the person of a human being: the poet Virgil, an Italian like himself who, more than twelve hundred years before, had made (in the person of the hero of his epic poem, Aeneas) his own descent into Hades. Virgil is said to signify, in Dante's poem, human wisdom and tradition, and on one level this may well be so; yet seen in terms of the psyche and its symbolic figures, Virgil is recognisable as the archetype Jung has described as "the wise old man" who counsels many a dreamer, or whose knowledge we project onto some teacher or master.

Virgil becomes Dante's protector and companion and guide; and the two poets, Virgil the shade, and Dante the living man, set out upon an inward journey into "an eternal place", the same that Aeneas had entered, guided by the Sibyl of Nemi. For those who have so "found themselves" there can be no going back; the beast, when once we have discovered it in ourselves, forbids return; we must flee, literally, for our lives in the hope of escaping the monster we have discovered within. But the first stage of the journey takes us, not to Paradise as we might hope, or at all events to some better and safer place or state, but into the hells. To the ancient world those shadowy regions of alienation were thought of as external to ourselves; regions not of memory or of fantasy but the real habitations of discarnate spirits both human and non-human. So the descent into Hades is presented by Virgil, whose Aeneas there met the discarnate spirits of many he had known in life: his father, happy in the Elysian fields; Dido, whom he had deserted, who turned away in silence, still unforgiving. Virgil's Hades is in its turn based upon the still more primitive account given in the *Odyssey* of Ulysses' visit to a temple in a dim northern land (which some have thought to be Stonehenge) there to consult the spirit of the wise Nestor, who in life had advised the Greek heroes, on how he should get home to Ithaca. There he met his former companions – Ajax, and Achilles, still striding in his wrath, bitterly said that it were better to be the meanest labourer on earth than a hero among the dead. We are in a world of primitive necromancy, the kind of consultation with the ancestors to be met with in all primitive tribes. If the journey is inwards those who make it are not aware that this is so.

I must say here that I hold it, on the evidence, as probable that in our inner journey we do encounter such discarnate beings as Homer, Virgil and Dante describe; our own dead, and whatever spirits besides may inhabit the unexplored regions on which our consciousness impinges. Here again I may well hold a view Jung himself may not have shared; yet he was at one time a psychical researcher and in his *Septem Sermones ad Mortuos* he is nearer to Virgil (whom he so often quotes) than to Freud.

Dante's inward journey stands midway between the ancient and the modern world. In his hells, his heavens and his purgatories he did indeed meet, like Aeneas and like Odysseus, many he had known in life, besides persons who had lived in former times. But the *Commedia* is also something else: it is an exploration of the psyche, of the inner worlds and states of the poet himself. And the "lost traveller's dream under the hill" – as Blake was later to describe that journey through the hells – begins with a descent into the depths. I believe that every pilgrimage must begin in the same way: if Freud did nothing else, at least he made us aware that these regions are in each of us, and that the only way out is through, the way that Dante took into the dark regions of human souls.

His journey follows a descending course through ever-narrowing circles, each representing some one of the sins that deform the soul;

and there, in each of the states, the poet is moved, now with pity, now with horror, to find persons he had known on earth. But each successive hell is at the same time a recognition of what lies within himself. In his encounter with the adulterous lovers, Paolo and Francesca, he is so moved with pity that he faints; for had he not loved Beatrice to that extreme by which he knew that he might have become like them; aware only of one another? T.S. Eliot has, in *Little Gidding*, recaptured Dante's dismay at another meeting, with his old teacher Brunetto Latini, in the "What, are you here?" of his own encounter with the "familiar compound ghost" of his literary masters. The empathy that so shook Dante to the heart is surely an identification of ourselves with the state of another soul; we discover ourselves in them, and them in ourselves. For the hells through which Dante moved are not places but states, all of them recognisable to every one of us.

At the bottom of the abyss, that narrows and narrows to those self-enclosed ice-bound prisons in which the souls have lost all freedom, the poet comes to the throne of Satan. I have never undergone analysis (otherwise than through poetry and the other arts, which is after all the more ancient and normal way of self-exploration) but I understand that at an early stage of self-discovery the patient may expect an encounter with the figure Jung calls the Shadow. This figure may appear in our dreams as a sinister, repulsive *alter ego* whom we are as loath to recognise in ourselves as was Shakespeare's Prospero to accept Caliban; and yet to the monster of his isle Prospero said at last, "This thing of darkness I acknowledge mine." Perhaps Dante's meeting with the beast in the forest was his first glimpse of the Shadow, as a protean, theriomorphic form, like some dream-monster who may inspire terror without obliging us to recognise in so alien a shape an aspect of ourselves. But just as in a series of dreams the same archetype may present itself in a series of guises, Dante was to meet the Shadow again, in more terrible and inescapable form. He confronts Satan, the ruler of evil who has his throne within each of us in the most hidden and remote depth of those regions of evil we in vain deny.

The limit of the descent into Hell is the point of total inertia, the centre to which everything falls. The narrowing circles whose terraces the poet, led by Virgil, has all the while been traversing, lead to this place where no further freedom is possible. As in Poe's story of the pit and the pendulum, Hell narrows and narrows until the point is reached at which the final terror is inescapable. Here Satan is enthroned, the hidden ruler of all the hells; Jung's Shadow, encountered inescapably at the heart of the soul's labyrinth. Dante can see no way of escape, but the confrontation with the principle of evil face to face proves, on the contrary, to be the point of reversal. The journey has been, hitherto, always a descent into darker and worse places, the claustrophobia closing in until Hell's ruler is encountered and identified as the Shadow. William Blake has called Satan, the Selfhood or ego, which in each of us perverts our acts to selfish ends. Now that the ruler of the hells has been seen and identified, Virgil half leads, half carries the horrified Dante through a narrow passage under Satan's throne, below the hairy thighs of the half-animal half-human figure of the Devil. What takes place is a kind of rebirth through "a round opening"; and like the new-born Dante can now for the first time see the sky and the stars. And there is literally – and how dramatically – a change of point of view: Satan on his towering throne is now seen reversed beneath the traveller's feet; his power is gone. He is no longer the ruler and the centre of the psyche. What has taken place Jung has described as the re-integration of the personality when we find the Self - the "other" mind within us – and not, as we had hitherto supposed, the ego, to be the ruler and centre of the soul.

Dante's journey surely meets the experience of many whose first steps in self-knowledge have been the discovery of the hells within: under the volcano; the waste land. Blake was surely thinking of Dante when he wrote of

The son of morn in weary night's decline,
The lost traveller's dream under the hill.

Dante at the beginning of his spiritual adventure had no idea of even the existence of these hells; and so it is in perhaps every interior journey. Those of you who have read Bunyan's *Pilgrim's Progress* will remember that his journey to the Celestial City also began in the City of Destruction. But the Pilgrim had lived for many presumably contented years in that city before he recognised that familiar neighbourhood for what it was, and set out to flee from it, leaving his own family and the friends and neighbours of a lifetime. Bunyan's City of Destruction; Dante's City of Dis whose domes glow in a red sky, so like a modern city; Milton's Pandemonium, adorned with all the skills and arts of architecture and technology; or those terrible false paradises of Aldous Huxley's Brave New World where nobody is allowed to suffer or to desire anything better than perfect adaptation to existing conditions – all these are adorned with all the amenities of civilised living. None of the poets has ever suggested that Hell is a place of pitchforks and boiling tar.

Dante, emerging through the opening at the bottom of Hell, the extreme limit of his own inner darkness, finds a new orientation. Whereas in the hells he has been enclosed within the caverned world of his own subjectivity, he now emerges into the greater universe and beholds the heavens and the stars above him. In Hell, native inertia had facilitated the poet's descent; but from this point he will have to climb. Did Dante here think of the line of Virgil Jung so often quotes, "Easy is the descent into Avernus, but the reascent – *hoc opus, hic labor est*"? And yet the poet undertakes the climb gladly, for he knows, now, where his journey is leading him. Once there is a goal, and that goal is seen, there can be no going back. The wise teaching of the Church is that none who has entered Purgatory can thereafter return again to Hell, the closed world with no outlet, no greater context to give meaning and orientation to our life. In the hells the poet had witnessed and experienced each of the human energies misdirected in the service of the satanic ego; in the purgatories, whose states he must now traverse on his ascending spiral path, each of these energies will be set right, and the poet freed, one by one, from those faults we all share. In the heavens beyond, opening in widening circles, each of the seven energies or functions of the soul which in the hells had found a distorted expression as the "seven deadly sins", will be seen in their aspect of seven cardinal virtues; for they are the same energies now operating in obedience to the divine order.

Dante's re-orientation involves a new way of seeing even the hells; for now he understands that what had seemed an endless descent had all the time in reality been the first stage of the upward climb towards Paradise: while he had thought he was descending he was in truth already spiralling upwards towards the point of transformation of consciousness. Had he not emerged through that dimensionless point of reversal, to see the stars overhead and the light of dawn rising over the sea, he would never have made this discovery; for the hells are states of, precisely, absence of this light of hope, and ignorance of the whole of which even they form a part. While we are in hell it seems that there is no way out; we are there, as it seems, eternally. Only as we emerge do we see evil in its true proportion. And once we have set foot on the Mountain of Purgatory we are free from those inner prisons, the self-enclosed world of the ego cut off from God, and already aware of belonging to a greater whole.

At the summit of the mountain is the earthly paradise: the state of unfallen man. Thus far Virgil has led him – wisdom, or reason, or whatever may be symbolised by that figure of the "wise old man". But in order to enter the heavens, the worlds of the blessed spirits who behold God, wisdom does not suffice; and it is here that Beatrice comes to meet him; and it is she, the embodiment of love – of heavenly love, the love of the soul – who must lead him into those higher worlds or states that knowledge alone cannot enter. Jung's figure of the *anima,* the soul-figure, is said to be ambiguous, at once desirable and cruel, angel and temptress, beyond good and evil. We may find the shadow of Beatrice in Francesca blown by the winds of passion; but Beatrice is the soul-image purified and transfigured by the transforming experience through which the poet has passed. But when the poet invites us to gaze with him into the great cosmic mandala of the mystic rose of the heavens of which Eliot wrote

> When the tongues of flame are infolded
>
> Into the crowned knot of fire
>
> And the fire and the rose are one

he leads us beyond the range of experience to which most of us have attained; yet he enables us to glimpse the goal to which we are even now travelling. In the poet's supreme vision of the multitudes of the heavenly spirits, even Beatrice herself becomes one among the numberless blessed souls who draw their life from God.

Dante's *Commedia* may serve to remind us that, whereas our present knowledge of the inner world is uncertain and fitful, there are old maps of that country. But at the end of a civilisation whose concern has been almost exclusively the exploration of nature and physical space, we have all but forgotten what country it is the old maps are describing. Materialists imagine that because the hells are not to be found among the rocks, or the angels where the astronauts fly, that these are unreal; but not outer, but inner space promises to be the theme of a new age; and the old maps may prove useful again.

There is at this time a complete withdrawal of the old projection of the hells and the heavens into an external elsewhere; a recognition that all the old supernatural population is to be found in ourselves. A recent volume of poems by Thomas Blackburn reflects, in many fine and deeply self-searching poems, this change of standpoint; like this on the Scandinavian demon Grendel, another shadow-figure:

> After the marsh was drained and its vast monsters
>
> Had gasped their lives out in the well-rinsed air,
>
> Our city corporation cleaned the fosse up
>
> And charged us sixpence to see Grendel's lair.
>
> We thought that with the great Panjandarum banished
>
> An era of sweet dreams was sure to start;

But gracious no, only his cave has vanished;
Don't look now, but he's walking in your heart.

Perhaps we meet Dante again not full-circle, but on a higher turn of the spiral of development. Dante suffered from the dualism of mediaeval Christianity which makes redemption from the hells eternally impossible. Blake was perhaps the first Christian poet (or prophet, as he called himself, for he held the poets to be the prophets of the modern world) to challenge this dualism, and to say that though all the hells remain as eternal possibilities, and although those within them may see no way of escape, none is eternally binding on those who enter them. They are part of the one universe in which we travel. "Distinguish between the man and his present state," Blake said. His belief that none need remain eternally in hell is more Buddhist than Christian. Yet this same belief is surely implicit – though not explicit – in Dante's poem; for he himself made the journey to be reborn through that narrow opening; thereby showing that there is a way.

Dante's journey is of course everyone's journey; but the poet is the explorer, the opener of the way, who ventures, in a state of inspiration, into regions of consciousness which in most of us remain dark and unexplored. The honour in which poets and prophets were formerly held was in virtue of this "inspiration" from the "other" mind which to us is unconscious, but which according to the old maps is the habitation of the all-knowing and never-sleeping gods. That I think is an important difference between the old maps and the new: according to tradition it is we who are unconscious, receiving our knowledge from the omni-present eternal mind that knows all things, Jung's "collective unconscious" is perhaps that country sighted from afar and its coastline drawn with the kind of distortion new continents ever show in early maps of an unexplored region.

Poetry nowadays is thought of as being suitable for children, who are encouraged to write it (seldom to read it) because children do not yet know that God is dead and the soul no longer immortal. We still allow children to see the world, as primitive people do, as being alive and full of meaning. For adults, "art" (again as an activity, seldom as a serious study of great works) is thought of as "therapeutic", like making mud-pies. The objectification of neuroses seems to have moved from the psychiatrist's consulting-room to the art-schools and from the art-schools to the galleries, and from the galleries to the national collections. This form of self-expression may be helpful to the patient, who might at the same time recover more completely through a serious study of the art of poets and societies who possessed knowledge in regions where we are ignorant and imperceptive. But of what use are such psychological waste-products to anyone else? Knowledge can be learned but what can be learned from ignorance?

The current view that one piece of self-expression is as good as another would of course be true were it not for the archetype. It is not for self-expression that we look in great art, or only as the universal is communicated through the individual mind, whose stamp and style is given to the work. But in great imaginative art the collective archetype is the informing principle. The great Gothic cathedrals are works of mathematical harmony of which the unknown architects seem rather the discoverers than the inventors. They bear the signature not of any individual mind but of the cosmos itself. So it is with diatonic music whose scale Pythagoras discovered rather than invented. From this mind also comes the inspiration of the poet. Dante's poem holds before us images of an inner world all share; of an eternal order, not of time or place, which is the measure of our humanity; the pattern, the scale (using the word in its musical sense) to which we are attuned. In those works of art which are true to the archetype we discover our own laws, our own inner order. We speak of "beauty" because "the beautiful" is what is true to the archetype and true to the cosmic order that upholds the world. What we call beauty brings us back to the archetype, harmonises us with ourselves and indeed with others since it is by virtue of this inner order that we are alike. Without such works human society must suffer the kind of moral and spiritual sickness so prevalent at the present time. The necessary food of the spirit is missing; and instead of healing us and restoring us to our humanity much modern art and music is (whether deliberately or in ignorance) Satanic, destructive in an almost physical sense, dislocating the psyche, as discord will bring down a building. The housing in which people live, the music to which the populace listens, the visual images presented to us by a commercial society, are calculated to destroy rather than to harmonise the soul. There are of course exceptions in every art, but all too few, and these against the spirit of the established values of the time.

Plato taught that all knowledge comes from memory – recollection; but not memory of our own experience of a few years of mortal life. Plato's memory is a cosmic memory; not memory as the behaviourists would define it, something gathered from the experience of the senses, but instead a memory from which we are, from the confined nature of bodily perception, shut off. This universal mind has been known by many names: it is the Logos of the Platonists and of Christian theology; the prophetic spirit of Israel; the soul of the world, the Hindu Self, Blake's Divine Humanity, the human archetype. Jung borrowed his term – the Self – from India; although whether the Jungian Self – the true centre of the psyche found when we abandon the notion of the centrality of the ego – is the same in all respects as the Self of Vedanta, or that concept an exact equivalent of the Platonic Logos or the *anima mundi*, is a question I am not qualified to answer. The poet is concerned, like the psychologist, not with metaphysics but with living experience, and inspiration has always been known to the poets and traditionally associated with the very idea of poetry. Have we not all the sense of some memory lost, or just out of reach? By common consent, within any traditional society, the poet is "inspired" by the Muse, the Holy Spirit, the Instructors – that is to say from the "other" mind. To those who believe with the behaviourists that all knowledge comes through the senses, what meaning have Wordworth's lines,

> Our birth is but a sleep and a forgetting,
> The soul that rises with us, our life's star,
> Hath had elsewhere its setting,
>   And cometh from afar
> Not in entire forgetfulness...

For the behaviourists (as for the eighteenth-century philosopher Locke), the new-born come trailing no clouds of glory, bring with them no memories. But for the Platonic tradition, which makes not matter but mind its starting point, Wordworth's lines are not figuratively but literally true; they are after all but a paraphrase of the teaching of Plotinus. And for those who hold, in whatever terms, this belief, poetry and the other arts are the chief and, indeed, the normal means by which we relate ourselves to the timeless. Blake wrote of poetry, painting and music as man's three ways of "conversing with Paradise"; which is only another way of saying the same thing.

The Platonic philosophers held that we, in our natural state, are "asleep". Our relationship with the timeless is expressed in a number of myths of sleep and waking, remembering and forgetting. A similar view is taken by Jungian psychology, but with an important difference. Whereas the Greeks held that the "other" mind is wakeful and conscious, is the omniscient mind of the immortal gods, and the mortal condition a "sleep" and a "forgetting", the terms of modern psychology are at best ambiguous. The very term "unconscious", though descriptive of our empirical situation in our relation to the "other" mind, is misleading because it suggests that conscious knowledge is in some respects more perfect; that the knowledge of the unconscious is in some sort of rudimentary state, merely potential. This is not the teaching of the ancients, nor that of the Indian philosophers, nor of the Christian theologians who taught the omniscience of God and the relative ignorance of man. As against Locke and the behaviourists and, I suppose, the Freudian psychologists who hold all knowledge to come through the senses, all Platonists believe that knowledge comes through recollection — anamnesis — which means, literally, "unforgetting".

Plato attributes our forgetfulness to the limitations of a physical body. The myth in the tenth book of the *Republic* to which Wordsworth's lines finally refer tells how the souls about to enter generation "descend", like shooting stars, and then must cross a desert between the two worlds or states. They come to a river — the river Lethe, or forgetfulness. This river is interpreted by the late Platonists as ever-flowing matter, of which water is the universal symbol. The souls are thirsty for matter's sleepy draught, and some drink deeply so that their oblivion of their former state is almost complete. Others drink less deeply, and arrive on earth "not in entire forgetfulness". All the Greek myths relating to knowledge and inspiration assume that we may in certain circumstances recover our lost knowledge of the universal mind. There are, according to Plato, three kinds of souls who are rememberers: the philosophers, who have knowledge – and for Plato philosophy was, above all, metaphysical; the lovers, who through their devotion to beauty come to knowledge of the "beautiful itself"; and the "musical souls", who are the artists. It is the function and the task of these to create in this world "copies" of the eternal originals, or archetypes "laid up in heaven", in stone or metal or music or dance or words, according to their skills. These copies will awaken in those who behold them — even if only momentarily — recollection of the eternal order of which all are part, and attunement to that order.

The poet's "muse" is more than a literary covention: it is the experience of every creative person that inspiration comes from beyond our knowledge. According to Plato there are nine muses, each giving guidance in some one particular art. The poet is said to have the gift, when inspired (though not at other times), of flying to the Garden of Muses where he gathers, as bees gather honey, the sweetness of his song.

I think every poet knows what is meant by the muse or daimon

who seems to give us knowledge we do not normally possess. Plato
wrote of the Daimon of Socrates. The God of Israel "spake by the
prophets". Shakespeare's Ariel is the very essence of the spirit who
flies free but who will serve the poet-magician who knows how to
control his inspirer. Milton invoked the "Heavenly Muse" and so did
Blake, with a difference: Blake was a modern man and knew that the
muse is within; paraphrasing Milton, he summons the "Muses who
inspire the Poet's song" in a manner at once homely and sublime.

> . . . Come into my hand,
> By your mild power descending down the Nerves of my
> right arm,
> From out the Portals of my brain where by your ministry
> The Eternal Great Humanity Divine planted his Paradise.

The Divine Humanity is Blake's term for the Logos or Self. Yeats
had his "instructors", Robert Graves his White Goddess. Often the
figure of the muse is projected, as Dante projected his Beatrice or
Bloch his "beautiful lady", onto some human figure. Many still hold
the old belief, inherited by Christendom from the Greeks, of the
holy guardian angel who accompanies each of us throughout life.
To speak for myself I cannot remember a time when I was not aware
of the companioning presence of my own daimon. I never thought
of this inner companion as an angel, for this daimon spoke always of
freedom and delight and beauty, never of such restrictive matters as
religion dealt in. But if the daimon is not moral, neither is it
immoral; carnal desires, or indeed any other self-interested
thoughts, served only to drive away this delicate companion. Of the
twin demi-gods Castor and Pollux it is said that one is incarnate, one
in the other world or state; and I wonder if this myth does not
describe precisely the relationship we each have with the daimon
or guardian angel? Poets, in any case (Dante and Yeats were both
born in the sign of Gemini), seems to be more than normally aware
of the relationship with the "other" mind. Of course there are many
levels: as the aspiration, so the inspiration. Porphyry tells that the
Delphic Oracle revealed that Plotinus was inspired by God himself,
the universal spirit.

I attempted in a poem to express the relationship with the
diamon:

> Long ago I thought you young, bright daimon,
> Whisperer in my ear
> Of springs of water, leaves and songs of birds
> By all time younger
> Than I, who from the day of my conception

... the painter, the mosaic worker, the worker in gold and silver, the illuminator of sacred books, were almost impersonal, almost perhaps without consciousness of individual design, absorbed in their subject matter and that the vision of a whole people. They could copy out of old gospel books those pictures that seemed as sacred as the text, and yet weave all into a vast design, the work of many that seemed the work of one, that made building, picture, pattern, metalwork of rail and lamp, seem but a single image; and this vision, this proclamation of their invisible master, had the Greek nobility ...

The "invisible master" is the Logos, the archetype so inadequately described in the phrase the "collective unconscious"; the inner order which is in truth the author of all "inspired" art.

In his poem *Sailing to Byzantium* Yeats summarises his own philosophy of inspiration. He begins by evoking generated life in all its beauty; but he turns away from nature because all in nature is flux and impermanence – in the words of another poet, "birth, copulation, and death". The poet must rather seek "monuments of unageing intellect", Plato's timeless world of the archetypes. The body ages – "an aged man is but a paltry thing" – but the soul is unageing. It does not belong to nature. Yet the soul can only discover its own native country from those works which are themselves expressions of the inner order:

> Nor is there singing-school but studying
> Monuments of its own magnificence;
> And therefore I have sailed the seas and come
> To the holy city of Byzantium.

He calls the icons from the walls to be his teachers; and we must here remember that the icon – a Greek conception – is not conceived or intended as a copy of nature, but as an expression of the spiritual essence of the archetype being it depicts. Therefore the icon itself is in a sense "sacred" and can teach, or impart knowledge of some state of being:

> O Sages standing in God's holy fire
> As in the gold mosaic of a wall,
> Come from the holy fire, pern in a gyre
> And be the singing-masters of my soul.
> Consume heart away, sick with desire
> And fastened to a dying animal
> It knows not what it is; and gather me
> Into the artifice of eternity.

The last stanza of the poem describes, literally, the glory, the hammered gold and mosaic, of Constantine's city; the golden tree with artificial singing birds sent by the Caliph to the Emperor, which might be literally able to "keep a drowsy emperor awake". But that golden artifice of song might equally serve, on another level of meaning, as a symbol of the poet's art that can keep the drowsy soul from sinking into forgetfulness. Yeats meant us, perhaps, to be reminded of Hans Anderson's story of the dying emperor and the nightingale who restored him to life and drove away his terrors by her song. And does the golden bough carry also an allusion – for it is by means of such allusion that poets work – to one of Yeats' "sacred books", Frazer's *The Golden Bough*, that great treasury of myth and symbol? But the bird is also the type of Plato's "musical soul" who sings on earth the music of eternity. Therefore the poet, "once out of nature", aspires to be the voice of the soul and to speak from a knowledge not to be learned on earth of the timeless order of the things of the Kingdom of Heaven, which is, as all know, "within"; treasures which are, as the Gospel says, "both new and old",

> ... such form as Grecian goldsmiths make
> From hammered gold and gold enamelling
> To keep a drowsy Emperor awake,
> Or sit upon a golden bough and sing
> To lords and ladies of Byzantium,
> Of what is past, or passing, or to come.

NOTES

1.   Public lecture given at the Royal Society of Medicine, London, on 19th March, 1976 under the auspices of the Analytical Psychology Club, London.

Current Coventure Titles

Art as Healing* *by Edward Adamson*   0 904575 24 1
The remedial value of creative self-expression, with over 100 colour illustrations by people in Adamson's care.

The Heart Attack Recovery Book *by Elizabeth Wilde McCormick*
                                                                            0 904575 37 3
A look at the emotional and practical problems encountered during rehabilitation, for patients and their families.

The Baby Massage Book* *by Tina Heinl*   0 904575 15 2
"A gentle, helpful and reassuring book." *Illustrated.*

The New Male–Female Relationship* *by Herb Goldberg*
                                                                            0 904575 39 X
An immensely encouraging blueprint for a new kind of sexual relationship.

The Challenge of Fate by *Thorwald Dethlefsen*   0 904575 35 7
How life around us reflects our inner nature.

The Unknown Spirit by *Jean Charon*   0 904575 18 7
French physicist Jean Charon explains how "physics has discovered spirit".

The Opening Eye by *Frank McGillion*   0 904575 03 9
The pineal gland and our link with cosmological phenomena.

Relating: An astrological guide to living with others on a small planet* by *Liz Greene*   0 904575 28 4

Looking at Astrology* by *Liz Greene*   0 904576 86 8
A sound introduction to astrology for children. *Illustrated.*

Myth and Today's Consciousness by *Ean Begg*   0 904575 30 6
The mythological expression of forces behind the acceptable face of consciousness.

Germanic Mythology by *Margrit Burri*   0 904575 36 5
The world of myth which belongs to our pre-Roman, pre-Christian, psychic origins.

The Inner World of Childhood* by *Frances G. Wickes*
    0 904576 64 7
The fruits of Frances Wickes' practical experience in child psychology.

The Inner World of Choice* by *Frances G. Wickes*   0 904576 66 3
A reprinting of the classic by Jung's longstanding friend and colleague.

Dynamics of the Self by *Gerhard Adler*   0 904576 92 2
Essays on the themes of the psyche, the self and individuation.

In the Wake of Jung ed. *Molly Tuby*   0 904575 23 3
Articles mostly by working analysts, illustrating the practical application and development of many of Jung's ideas.

In the Wake of Reich ed. *David Boadella*   0 904576 58 2
A collection of important papers by colleagues and students of Reich, including Ola Raknes, Gerda Boyesen and A.S. Neill.

The Symbolic and the Real* by *Ira Progoff*   0 904576 63 9
A programme for personal growth.

Mirror to the Light by *Lewis Thompson, ed. Richard Lannoy*
    0 904575 19 5
"Poetic aphorisms of great density and beauty" – Lawrence Durrell.

Prospero's Island: the secret alchemy at the heart of "The Tempest" by *Noel Cobb.*   0 904575 26 8
Illustrated.

A Vision of the Aquarian Age* by *Sir George Trevelyan*
    0 904576 52 3
A new spiritual worldview for an age stifled by materialistic values.

A Tent in Which to Pass a Summer Night *by Belle Valerie Gaunt and Sir George Trevelyan*   0 904576 35 3
An anthology of poetry and prose concerning reincarnation and the soul.

Magic Casements *by Sir George Trevelyan*   0 904576 91 4
The use of poetry in the expanding of consciousness.

The Psychology of Nuclear Conflict *ed. Ian Fenton*
                                                             0 904575 35 7
Insights and views which become a phenomenology of the subjects for professional and general readers.

The Work of Creation *by Frank Avray Wilson*   0 904575 33 0
The aesthetics of art and science to show a wholistic and human-centred creation.

Withymead *by Anthony Stevens*   0 904575 32 2
A Jungian community for the healing arts.

The Grail Legend *by Emma Jung and M.L. von Franz* 0 904575 31 4

Available from Element Books Ltd., Longmead, Shaftesbury, Dorset SP7 8PL. Telephone Shaftesbury (0747) 51339.

*Coventure edition not available in the United States.